THE LIBRARY

OF

BIBLICAL STUDIES

Edited by

Harry M. Orlinsky

INTERPRETING
THE PROPHETIC TRADITION

INTERPRETING
THE PROPHETIC TRADITION

THE GOLDENSON LECTURES
1955-1966

INTRODUCTION BY

HARRY M. ORLINSKY

THE HEBREW UNION COLLEGE PRESS / CINN.
KTAV PUBLISHING HOUSE, INC. / NEW YORK
1969

Manufactured in the United States of America
Library of Congress Catalog Card Number: 68-58444

TABLE OF CONTENTS

INTRODUCTION

It was a happy act on the part of Congregation Emanu-El
of the City of New York to establish the Samuel H. Goldenson Lectures. The congregational minutes dealing with the
matter (graciously made available to me by Dr. Nathan A.
Perilman) read as follows:

> Dr. Goldenson's desire was that in commemoration of
> his Fiftieth Anniversary of graduation from the Hebrew
> Union College and his ordination as a Rabbi, there be
> established a Samuel H. Goldenson Lectureship at the
> Hebrew Union College; that this Lecture each year
> should be on some aspect of Prophetic Judaism; that the
> Lecture should be delivered by some outstanding schol-
> ar; that the Lecture should be printed and disseminated
> among the Rabbinate and lay leaders of our movement.
> It was further the desire of Dr. Goldenson that the Lec-
> tureship in his honor be given at the Hebrew Union
> College in Cincinnati where students will be able to
> attend. Dr. Julius Mark added the suggestion that copies
> should go to the members of our Congregation.

Over half of the Lectures in this series are meaningful to
the biblical scholar as well as to the student of theology and

to the learned layman, and the problems that they dealt with continue to confront us today. Thus Dr. Blank's paper undertook to analyse the basis of the prophet's authority; after all, he was not the owner of a shrine, or a member of a guild, or the apprentice to a master from whom he acquired a diploma, as it were. Why should the Israelites listen to *him?* Whence *his* authority?

Dr. Silberman took as his theme the manner in which various medieval and modern Jewish philosophers interpreted biblical prophecy and revelation. "The question," in the words of the lecturer, "cannot be avoided: what do we mean when we speak of prophets and prophecy? Is it at all possible to give these words any substance within our contemporary universe of discourse? . . ."

Dr. Albright, unlike the first lecturer, found the beginnings of the prophetic movement in Samuel. "Our contention that Samuel was the first great religious reformer after Moses," he asserted, "and that he rejected—or diminished— the spiritual role of priests and Levites at the same time that he turned to ecstatic prophets and local sanctuaries to replace the Shilonic system is actually not hard to defend."

The purpose of Dr. Hyatt's Lecture was "to try to determine the grounds on which the prophets objected to the worship of their age, and to ask why they criticized it," and in this attempt he found that "There were five factors in the popular worship of their time against which the pre-exile prophets protested in the name of their God."

In the Lecture of 1964, the writer advanced the opinion that the concept of a Suffering Servant—one who acted "as a substitute for the guilty who deserved punishment because this servant, while himself innocent of sin, bore their punishment for them"—was originally foreign not only to Isaiah 53 but to the whole Hebrew Bible. Indeed, "The element of vicariousness was completely unknown . . . until after the death of Jesus and in consequence of it."

Father de Vaux traced the history and status of Jerusalem from the time that Israel emerged as an entity until the prophets turned the city into "the city of Yahweh, and under this religious aspect . . . given preferably the name of Zion. Such had been the name of the Jebusite acropolis of the city conquered by David . . . The prophets, like the Psalms, have resumed this archaic name to designate the City of Yahweh . . . The last step was to make Jerusalem the center of the earth. It is already prepared by Ezekiel . . ."

Other papers were directed more to the implications of the prophetic writings for our own time and problems. Thus Dr. Agus sketched the figure of the prophet as he emerges in modern Hebrew literature. From a broader perspective, Dr. Bamberger traced the image of the prophet as it was conceived from the days of the Second Jewish Commonwealth through the Talmudic and Middle Ages to the present, and he closes with a statement on what his own conception of the prophet is.

The pertinence of other essays is apparent from their titles: "The Prophets: Our Concurrence and Our Present" (Dr. Abraham Cronbach), "The Voice of Prophecy in the Satellite Age" (Rabbi Edgar F. Magnin), "The STONE which the Modern Builders Rejected" (Rabbi Levi A. Olan), and "Prophetic Religion in an Age of Revolution" (Rabbi Leon I. Feuer).

Two things in this collection stand out for the writer. Firstly, these papers should generally be treated as but introductions to the themes they dealt with. Thus Dr. Blank went on to publish a volume on *Jeremiah: Man and Prophet* (Hebrew Union College Press, 1961), and the writer elaborated on his theme in *The So-Called "Servant of the Lord" and "Suffering Servant" in Second Isaiah* (vol. XIV of *Supplements to Vetus Testamentum*, Brill, 1967).

Secondly, these essays serve admirably to stimulate the reader, be he scholar or rabbi-clergyman or learned layman, to further study: has the last word really been said on the source of the prophet's authority, or on the beginnings of the prophetic movement, or on the attitude of the prophets toward Israelite worship, or on the Servant of the Lord and the concept of vicariousness in the Hebrew Bible and the New Testament, or on the role that Jerusalem played in Israel's history and prophetic thinking? And so on.

In this light, *Interpreting the Prophetic Tradition* may be sent forth in full knowledge that all who read it will be instructed and stimulated by what the Goldenson Lecturers have had to say. And would that more such Lectureships be launched in other institutions, and not only in Bible but also in Rabbinic Literature, Jewish History, Jewish Philosophy, Medieval and Modern Hebrew Literature, Liturgy, Sociology, and the like.

HARRY M. ORLINSKY
Professor of Bible,
Hebrew Union College—
Jewish Institute of Religion
New York City

Erev Rosh Hashanah 5729
September 1968

"OF A TRUTH
THE LORD HATH SENT ME"

AN INQUIRY INTO THE SOURCE
OF THE PROPHET'S AUTHORITY

Sheldon H. Blank, *Professor of Bible*
Hebrew Union College–Jewish Institute of Religion

THE GOLDENSON LECTURE OF 1955

I AM truly most grateful—grateful to Temple Emanu-El for establishing the Dr. Samuel H. Goldenson Lectureship; grateful to you, Mr. President, for inviting me to offer under its auspices this year the first of the projected annual lectures on the thought of the prophets; grateful to Dr. Goldenson for being what he is, a man whose religion is the religion of those prophets. I would wish that from year to year the value and the significance and the relevance of these lectures might grow, that they might thus become a worthy tribute to a worthy son of this Hebrew Union College.

There is a kind of link between us. Both of us—at different times, to be sure—were students of Moses Buttenwieser, and we share a reverence for his memory. Of him, Dr. Goldenson has written:

> "No man on the Faculty meant more to me . . . I became close to him from the very first year at College . . . For two years I lived at his home at Mt. Auburn and during many summers we had adjacent cottages in Southampton, Ontario . . . I think I saw everyone of his books in manuscript and he and I had many, many discussions on current problems from the standpoint of prophetic insight and teaching" (quoted from a personal letter).

These feelings were, of course, mutual. There was no student in whom Moses Buttenwieser took greater pride, none

3

for whom he had more affection. And, indeed, Samuel Goldenson is a disciple to swell the heart of any teacher. His life is dedicated to prophetic ideals; and it is with an eminent sense of fitness that Temple Emanu-El, establishing a lectureship in his honor, designated prophetic thought the subject.

It is also fitting that the first of the lectures honoring Dr. Goldenson should center upon that one among the prophets for whom his revered teacher's enthusiasm was boundless, the prophet Jeremiah. Furthermore, in view of our search in a liberal seminary for the sources of religious authority, one in particular of the many facets of Jeremiah's varied life and thought, namely: his own attempt to discover and proclaim the source of his authority, holds for us both lasting and topical interest. Studying his problem over again, and following his quest, we would be inquiring into his religious experience and his personal religion—a task indeed worth undertaking.

But, first, before embarking on the study, a word to students past and present. I wonder whether students know (I think they do) the role they play in the life of a teacher. I want to express my own indebtedness. What I have to say here this evening was written in the classroom—it took form amidst the open give and take of the classroom. The student's comments spoken and unspoken, his questions, arguments, objections and suggestions, the stare, the puzzled frown, the perceptive, or even the confused answer in an examination, the nod, the compliment, even the too ready adoption of a new idea—all these are stimuli to a teacher's growth. They are the warnings and the guideposts on the way to deeper insights, clearer definitions. Dead classes are stupefying; they are fortunately rare on our campus, where almost any student, if coaxed (and some without coaxing), would be ready to change places with the teacher. Yes, I think my friends on the Faculty will agree with me that in the classroom, in the very process of communication, as a part of the serious, difficult business of communication, we achieve our own greatest growth. We owe thanks to all students, past and present, who make us go on thinking.

ND now, the problem: How convince the unwilling? Even to the sympathetic, it is hard enough to demonstrate the truth of any proposition; how much more difficult to convince the unwilling! And the prophets' contemporaries were unwilling, and the prophets had their problems. The bitter fact that nobody listened to them—that nobody that was anybody listened—was the common denominator in their experience (Jer. 6.10,17). Whether spoken to arouse the complacent or to comfort the despairing, their words appeared equally futile. Not only the first Isaiah whose metallic tones struck fear (6.9f.) but even the gentle, rhapsodic Isaiah of the Exile had to complain of a people of unseeing eyes and ears that did not hear (43.8; 42.19). Ezekiel's sarcastic comment betrays that prophet's bitterness; God told him, he says: "To them you are only as one who sings ditties with a pleasant voice skillfully; they hear your words, yes, but do nothing whatever" (33.32). The first Isaiah sensed the cause of their deafness: the deaf, he had said, were not able to hear simply because they preferred not to hear (28.12; 30.9,15). Man's ability to shut out the unpleasant—not to see, not to hear—may be a biological necessity, but it is the prophet's Sambatyon. He stands thwarted on the hither shore. And none had a greater sense of frustration than Jeremiah.

Despite the tradition that he was a priest, we will neither call Jeremiah a "cult prophet" nor suggest that what he said carried weight simply by virtue of any office or any title of his. On the contrary, he enjoyed no respect which he had not earned, no authority beyond what he could win for himself. His was a kind of nightmarish nakedness: he had no framed diplomas, no transcripts of academic records, no recourse to colleagues in a conference. By nothing extrinsic could he command belief.

But he must be heard! Since the fate of his people depended upon his success with them and, specifically, his ability to make them see that he brought them an urgent message from their God, and since there was so little time, his mission had a grim earnestness and his argument was no collegiate debate, no matching of wits for empty honors.

To be sure, an argument is a deceptive course, in which it is often hard to determine whom one is trying to convince, one's opponent or oneself. No doubt, at times, Jeremiah, like all who argue, was battling his own uncertainties, and what he achieved in the process was not so much the favorable verdict of the market place (which was never his in his lifetime) as it was fortitude and a moral courage which enabled him to proclaim the word, regardless of the adverse opinion of others. He came out of the controversy stronger than when he went in, for it was in fact "a controversy for the sake of Heaven."

Jeremiah's supreme attempt to assure his people that God had sent him, and his own quest for certainty, they are not really two things but one. The others ask him how he knows and, agonized, he seems to ask himself in turn, How, indeed, do I know?

Jeremiah wrestled persistently with the twofold problem. His book is not alone the record of his concern to convince the eyebrow lifters that, though the form was the form of Jeremiah, the voice was the voice of God, but, especially in the confessions and elegies, the record also of his own seeking.

He did not prepare a legal brief, did not muster his arguments: "one, two, three, four a, four b." And yet, on page after page, his book reflects the ongoing controversy, and his reasoning emerges. The questions his opponents raised (which were at the same time his own questions) ; the doubts the unworried merchant expressed, and the tolerant minister, the prosperous farmer, and the well-paid prophet (which were at the same time his own doubts) led him through mental anguish and the stress of conflicting emotions, not to a reasoned answer, but to the stuff from which at this great distance we can, with some assurance, distill his answer—the answer which he, the prophet Jeremiah, managed to live with, however well or ill it satisfied his scoffing generation. His book contains matter for the whole variety of his arguments. Isolate and sift the material, translate it into such terms as we use, and then arrange it—it makes a strong case.

That is to say: It makes a strong case in the framework of religious experience. Reasoning is possible only among persons who start with the same assumptions. Suppose we would discuss the question: What does God want of man? Obviously we can discuss it only with persons who speak the language of the question. (Can two talk together, except they be agreed?) And so it is if we ask: Did Jeremiah truly speak the word of God? Only we can discuss it who speak the language of our question. It is fortunate that this is our language here; otherwise what follows would be meaningless. As it is, in the framework of religious experience, Jeremiah's case, as we can reconstruct it, carries conviction.

And this is his case, restated, rephrased, and set forth in the form of six propositions:

I

The argument which was, and is still, no doubt, the most convincing to the greatest number is the argument based upon fulfilled predictions, the proposition that a prophet can be accepted as authentic when what he prophesies comes to pass. But to Jeremiah the pragmatic test was probably the least satisfying of his several criteria.

We know that in those days prophets gave "signs" to prove their authenticity. These were their credentials. In a stratum of the Exodus narrative, which is probably later than the Second Isaiah and shows his influence, the true and highly reputed prophet Moses performs successful signs before Pharaoh to validate his message (see my "Studies in Deutero-Isaiah," *HUCA*, *XV*, p. 46, n. 88). In a law in Deuteronomy the possibility is envisaged that, as a test of Israel's devotion, even an heretical prophet may propose a sign and the sign come true (Deut. 13.2f.). To convince a king, the legendary Isaiah said that the shadow on a sundial would move backwards—and it did move ten steps backwards (Isa. 38.7f.).

And it would be false to say that even Jeremiah was contemptous of facts and laid no store by successful predictions. Once, in prison, he had a premonition that a cousin would come to him and offer him the chance to purchase a certain field. When, the next day, his cousin comes to the prison on that same errand, Jeremiah himself sees in the act the will of God—because it happened as, in advance, he knew it would happen (Jer. 32.6-8).

On another occasion, when he has an opening, he says: I told you so. Zedekiah the king has sent for him, fetched him from prison to learn God's word. And why? Because, of all the prophets, Jeremiah was the one who had said the Babylonians would come, and they had come. Jeremiah is human; he does not resist the temptation or fail to point the moral: "Where now are your prophets who said: The king of Babylon will not attack you or this land?" (37.19). He gloats here, even as on yet another occasion he challenges: "As for the prophet that predicts peace, when that prophet's expectation is realized, it will be known that God truly sent him" (28.9; cf. 17.15; 44.28; Ezek. 13.6b). By the light that is in him, Jeremiah foresees the disappointment which all such prophets must experience, whereas he, predicting war, will triumph. There is little to dis tinguish his challenge here in anticipation from his I-told-you-so in retrospect. He is not averse to the proof of fulfillment—only that this proof comes for him too tragically late. It is grim satisfaction to be proved right by an occurrence which frantically you strove to prevent. Thus Jeremiah had little enthusiasm for the argument based on fulfilled predictions—though he made use of it, too, needing all the support he could muster. Nevertheless, what men might call "success" seemed to him a prop too frail to buttress his conviction.

II

Apparently for Jeremiah his strongest argument is no argument at all but a simple affirmation. His only plea before the court when, charged with the capital offense of heresy, he fights for his life is a simple affirmation. This argument amounts to an affidavit—just this and nothing more, a bare statement in court:

> "It is the Lord who sent me to prophesy to this house and to this city all the words which you have heard ... I am in your hands; do to me as seems good and proper to you. Only, know that if you kill me you incur the guilt of spilling innocent blood ... for, of a truth, the Lord hath sent me to you to speak in your hearing all these words" (26.12-15).

No careless statement this; considering the circumstances, we suspect that the prophet had no stronger argument in his arsenal than this certain knowledge that he spoke for God. I am impressed anew whenever I read this simple statement: "It is the Lord who sent me . . . Of a truth the Lord hath sent me." What more can a man say?

If chapter twenty-six is an "affidavit," chapter one is the nearest thing to a "diploma." "God told me, Say not: I am a lad; for wherever I send you you shall go, and whatever I command you you shall speak . . . Then God put forth his hand and touched my mouth. And God said to me, Behold! I have put my words in your mouth" (1.7,9). It is like a diploma, yet not a diploma; it bears no one's seal or signature but his own: "God said to me," "God told me" (cf., also 15.16,19).

This passage is one of several descriptions of his experience with God. According to these, Jeremiah's conviction was not the conclusion of a syllogism but the result of a religious experience—his Sinai. He has "stood in God's private council" (23.22), been admitted to intimacy with God, shared and mirrored his moods, divine indignation, divine disappointment:

"My heart breaks, I shudder all over;
    I am as one drunk, overcome with wine,
    Because of the Lord, yea, the words of his holiness."
"I am filled with divine indignation,
    Exhausted with holding it in" (23.9; 6.11).

Not in public utterances alone, but in prayer as well, he speaks in this manner:

"Because of your overpowering hand I sat alone,
    Because you had filled me with gloom" (15.17).
Withal, Jeremiah very much remains Jeremiah. What he describes is not a mystical union but a sharing: Jeremiah sharing with God.

This is his second and strongest argument: his reference to the immediacy of his experience, his solemn assurance, his deposition that, sharing God's mood, he truly and faithfully speaks God's word.

III

His quest for the source of his message next involves the elimination of possible sources other than God. His voice, he says—and this is his third proposition—is not the *vox populi;* Jeremiah speaks indeed the unpopular word. He leaves all cliches to the plagiarizers, to the dealers in used oracles of whom God says: "They contrive to make my people forget my name with their dreams which they repeat one to another" (23.27) and "Therefore, lo! I am against the prophets . . . who pilfer my words a man from his fellow. Lo! I am against the prophets who appropriate phrases and oracularly boast 'Behold, an oracle!' " (23.30f.)

Jeremiah pointedly dissociates himself from the popular prophets. He has not borrowed his words as they have done, nor does he echo the rumblings of the crowd. Indeed, so much at odds with common belief is his own word that he passes for a madman (*meshugga,* 29.26). He stands "the test of ridicule"—yet is discredited.

Of this he complains to God, the very cause of his grief:

"Thou, O God, has enthralled me
        and I am enthralled . . ."
(this is Buttenwieser's perceptive translation) . . .

"I have become a constant target for laughter:
        every one mocketh me . . .
The word of God but serveth to bring upon me insult
        and derision without end" (20.7f.).
On another occasion, in a similar context, gently he reproaches his God:

"Know that for your sake I have borne disgrace" (15.15)
He mentions the taunt which he hears on all sides:

"Lo! they say to me:
'Where is this word of God? Let it come to pass!' "
(17.15).

The implications of the record must be clear: the source of Jeremiah's word is obviously not the crowd. His voice is not the *vox populi*. What is it then but the *vox dei*?

IV

Or does another presumptive source suggest itself? Could he be deceived; could it be his own voice that he mistakes for the voice of God? His repudiation of this alternative is his fourth argument. For two reasons he must rule out the possibility that the words he speaks are his, not God's:

a) They are not his words because no one would be such a fool as to invite the disasters which his speech entails. What has it got him, this speaking for God? Curses (15.10) and a flogging (37.15), another flogging and exposure in stocks (20.2), taunts (15.15; 17.15; 20.7f.) and accusations (26.11; 37.13; 38.4), arrest and imprisonment (37.15; 38.6), the plight of a fugitive (36.5), of a pariah (16.5,8; 15.17), a life of loneliness (16.2).

To speak of "disinterest" would be to understate the case. To the question: *cui bono?* he could reply: Certainly I have no profit from my labors. Quite the contrary; the message I bring is my ruin.

This is an argument which, if Plato may be trusted, Socrates also used a couple of centuries later in his futile attempt to prove that God had sent him:

"That I am given to you by God is proved by this:— that if I had been like other men, I should not have neglected all my own concerns . . . and have been doing yours . . . And had I gained anything, or if my exhortations had been paid, there would have been some sense in that; but now . . . not even the impudence of my accusers dares to say that I have ever exacted or sought pay of anyone; they have no witness of that. And I have a witness of the truth of what I say; my poverty is a sufficient witness" (from Jowett's translation of Plato's *Apology*).

Like Jeremiah, Socrates asked in whose interest, then, he spoke; certainly not in his own. From his condition, each con-cluded that it was not he but God who set his dolorous way.

b) Jeremiah for another reason must repudiate the impli-cation that his words are his own invention. He would say quite different things were he to obey his own impulse. His speech is not, indeed, automatic; nevertheless it is beyond his power to refrain from speech. He is possessed with a sense of inevitability:

> "If I say, I will not remember him
> Or speak any more in his name,
> Then there is in me, as it were, a raging fire
> Pent in my bones;
> I weary myself to contain it—
> But in vain" (20.9; cf. v. 7 and 11; also 6.11).

Similar again is Socrates' claim and similar his desperate inability to evoke belief. This is how he puts it:

> "Some one will say: Yes, Socrates, but can you not hold your tongue . . . ? Now I have great difficulty in making you understand my answer to this. For if I tell you that this would be a disobedience to a divine command . . . you will not believe that I am serious; and if I say again that the greatest good of man is to converse about virtue . . . and that the life which is unexamined is not worth living—that you are still less likely to believe. And yet what I say is true, although a thing of which it is hard for me to per-suade you" (from the *Apology*).

Two men claimed they had to speak: the one lost his case and drank the hemlock; by some magic, the other escaped.

Yet, sad is Jeremiah's plight: he has to speak; and when

he does, he only says the wrong things, for in very fact he
loves this people.

> "Would my head were water," he laments,
> "And my eyes a spring of tears,
>   That I might weep by day and night,
>   For the slain of the daughter of my people!" (8.23).

And again:

> "If you will not hearken
>   My soul must cry in secret
>   For the arrogance, and weep,
>   And my eye shed tears
>   When God's flock is taken captive"
> (13.17; cf. 10.19).

Is it conceivable that he could wish down judgment on the
people whom he loves with such tender affection? Quite the
contrary! When he is Jeremiah and not God's agent, he inter-
cedes for them with God. When he is speaking not for God
but to God in prayer, he prays for them. Though forbidden:

> "Pray not for good for this people!" (14.11),

And

> "Pray you not for this people,
>   Nor take up any cry or entreaty,
>   Nor intercede with me,
>   For I will not hear you" (7.16) —

though twice forbidden, he yet dares to pray and in one of his
"confessions" he admits his insubordination:

> "Is good to be rewarded with evil?" he asks.
> "Remember how I have waited on you,
>   To speak good on their behalf,
>   To avert your anger from them" (18.20).

He speaks of it twice:

> "Indeed I interceded with you in a time of calamity,
>   And in a time of disaster on behalf of the enemy"
> (15.11b; cf. Isa. 1.21,24).

And it is on record that once the king and once the people sought him out to pray for them (21.2; 42.2), which they would hardly have done had their errand seemed implausible.

There is one passage in which the prophet appears to recognize the ambiguity of his position. Here, again in the context of a "confession," he says:

"I have neither sought to escape serving you
Nor desired the grievous day" (17.16).

Serving God he has announced, but being Jeremiah he has not desired, "the grievous day."

And this is the fourth of his proofs. Even as his voice was not the voice of the crowd, so it was not the wish child of his own heart, being the contrary of his wish for his people.

He admits no further alternatives; it must then be the voice of God.

V

The fifth and the sixth of his propositions may be paired. Together they differ somewhat from the others, being based on the content of the message. He seems to be shifting ground now and putting it this way: If you do not choose to believe me, and refuse to accept my life as a proof; if you will not let me say: "It is true because it is God's word," then let me say: "It is God's word because it is true."

As concerns the content of his message, he denies, first of all, that it is heresy, and aligns himself with predecessors tried and true. He commends the ancient, tested ways:

"Stand by the ways and observe,
And inquire of the ancient paths
Which way is the good way, and follow it,
And find your security" (6.16).

(He may have repeated this thought in 18.15, but the text is in disorder and the meaning uncertain.) Jeremiah agrees: God spoke to the fathers when he brought them from Egypt—it is only that a false, a formalistic tradition has arisen concerning what he then said (7.22f.).

Rejecting the current slogans, Jeremiah yet espouses no new heresy; he represents a tradition. It is the others who are out of step. In the present situation, it is the prophets of peace who have left the road—those prophets who "too lightly heal the hurt of the daughter of my people, crying 'Peace!' though peace is lacking" (8.11; cf. 4.10; 14.13; 23.17). Jeremiah regards himself as one of a succession of prophets "from of old" who "prophesied to many lands and great kingdoms of war and disaster and disease" (28.8). No newfangled notion, no heresy his; he stands with those prophets squarely facing reality, grim though it be.

From what he says, from its normative character, one may know that of a truth God sent him.

VI

And his final argument is similar. What Jeremiah says for God is ethical and rational and thus comports with the nature of God; it is what such a God as he knows must naturally say. The words are the words of a just and constant God, whose purpose expressed by his prophet is to turn his people, through knowledge of him, into ways of righteousness. "Of this one may boast," says God through Jeremiah, "that he understands and knows me, as one who acts on earth with constancy, justice, and righteousness and that these are what I desire" (9.23; cf. 5.28f.; 7.5f.; 22.3). "Knowing" God he elsewhere equates with doing justice and righteousness, judging the case of the poor and needy (22.15f.).

In *The Prophets of Israel*, Moses Buttenwieser, speaking of Amos and Micah, Isaiah, Jeremiah, referred to "the great basic truths or principles of which they were cognizant through their moral consciousness, and which, constituting their revelation from God, formed the centre and essence of their prophecy" (p. 152). Pointing to such "basic truths," the substance of his knowledge of God, Jeremiah can say: By these I know, by this you may know: "of a truth the Lord hath sent me."

In Jerusalem Jeremiah has seen adulterous, lying prophets strengthening the hands of malefactors (23.14). But God has not sent them, he says. Had they "stood in God's council," they would be exhorting the people in words designed not to confirm them in wickedness but to divert them from their evil way (23.21f.).

Unlike them, Jeremiah is a prophet who has enjoyed the intimacy of God, and as proof now speaks a fitting word—"a faithful messenger" to him who sent him. His words bear the imprint of their author.

Once the prophet even seems to say: He is no parochial, regional God whom I represent; universalize my words and they will stand the test. They are the words of a God transcending people and land, who says:

"Am I a God nearby and not a God far off?
... Do I not fill the heaven and the earth?" (23.23f.)

So Jeremiah rests his case with the prima-facie evidence of the message itself as the final test of its authenticity and his own veracity.

He has made a good case. He has probably reached a satisfying conclusion, laid a foundation on which to build a life. The knowledge of God is inscribed on Jeremiah's heart.

Related perhaps to this answer which he found is the vision of the end of days that goes by the name of the "new covenant." There is, to be sure, some legitimate doubt, though this vision appears in his book, that the prophet Jeremiah is its author. But whether it is his own or not, it seems to be an implication of Jeremiah's quest for certainty. He (or another), reflecting upon his experience, the source of his authority, the source of his certainty, reached out beyond the personal to the universal, made general the particular experience, and so attained to that imposing vision. It is such certainty as his that, in the end of days, each will have, when *torah* is written on every man's heart, when a man must teach his neighbor no longer saying "Know the Lord," for each will know him, small and great (31.31-34). Jeremiah's quest quite naturally led to this ultimate in messianic expectation.

THE analysis which, properly speaking, was the goal of our study is complete. We have read the record of a man's quest for certainty; we have explored the grounds for his "Thus saith the Lord." On this score there is no more to say. But it would be well before leaving the matter to briefly note two thoughts for our times.

The first is this: that the case which Jeremiah makes for the authority of his words is very much the same as the case for the authority of Scripture as a whole. For us, at least, who regard the Bible as a record of the religious experiences of great men, and of Jeremiah as not the least among them, that prophet's defense of his "inspiration" serves at the same time as a defense of the inspiration of Scripture. Jeremiah was not the only one to defend his calling. Amos, when challenged, asked simply: "When a lion has roared who can but fear? If the Lord God has spoken who can but prophesy?" (3.8); and he claimed: "God took me from behind the flock and said to me: Go, prophesy to my people Israel" (7.15). And there were others like Amos but none with such clarity as Jeremiah. And the most leave us quite in the dark. We wonder what proofs better than Jeremiah adduced, those nameless ones called "J" or "D" or "P", could have offered to support their claim that of a truth the Lord sent them, or what any writer—the author of Job, of Proverbs, of Psalm 73, or the nineteenth chapter of Leviticus (they were people, whether or not we know their names)—what else any of them experienced that lent their words authority and themselves conviction. Jeremiah, the articulate prophet, must speak to us for them all.

And lastly now: as rabbis or as candidates for the Reform rabbinate, we ourselves pose a comparable problem. Though we are neither prophets nor prophets' disciples, like Jeremiah we too seek conviction, if not indeed authority. Where are we to find certainty, and what virtue do our words possess that men should lend them credence?

Or, not as rabbis, but simply as Reform Jews, we sometimes wonder: with no dogmatic tests, no catechism, not being told what we must believe, what *do* we believe? What are our own convictions, and what their source, and what their authority, not now for others, but for ourselves? "How am I to know?" we ask, and lo! we are involved in the prophet's quest.

I suppose this final thought is not so much a thought as a question. Can we fight through our doubts, each for himself as our liberal religious orientation demands—a way more difficult than orthodoxy—and by what experience can we find our sure knowledge of God? And by what means can those of us, who may be called to leadership, find the heart to say: Of a truth the Lord hath sent me?

THE PROPHETS:
OUR CONCURRENCE
AND OUR DISSENT

Abraham Cronbach
Professor Emeritus of Jewish Social Studies
Hebrew Union College–Jewish Institute of Religion

THE GOLDENSON LECTURE OF 1956

TOWARD THE PROPHETS ALL OF US HARBOR
feelings of profound reverence. We cite the prophets to substantiate some of our most cherished convictions. To the prophets might well be applied that which Carlyle says of Dante and of Shakespeare: "It is impiety to meddle with them . . . They dwell apart in a kind of royal solitude."[1]

Yet the fact remains that the prophets lived many hundreds of years ago, and between six and seven thousand miles away. The culture in which they breathed and moved was inconceivably different from ours. Inevitably we of today will hold ideas which conflict with some of the prophetic ideas. For that reason I give to this evening's talk the title: "The Prophets: Our Concurrence and our Dissent." I shall divide the subject into three parts:

1. Prophetic ideas to which we subscribe
2. Prophetic ideas to which we do not subscribe
3. Prophetic ideas to which we subscribe in part and which we reject in part.

I. *Prophetic Ideas to Which We Subscribe*

One need not be a pacifist in order to be captivated by that sentence in the Book of Zechariah: "Not by might, nor by power, but by My spirit, saith the Lord of Hosts."[2] Those

23

words are inscribed on one of the windows of this chapel. At least in theory, all of us concede that "Not by might, nor by power, but by My spirit, saith the Lord of Hosts."

The same applies to other passages in that same Book of Zechariah, passages such as these:

> Show mercy and compassion every man to his brother; and oppress not the widow, nor the fatherless, the stranger, nor the poor . . . Speak ye every man the truth with his neighbour; execute the judgment of truth and peace in your gates; and let none of you devise evil in your hearts against his neighbour; and love no false oath.[3]

With thoughts such as these none of us are at variance.

It is likewise with this passage from Amos:

> Are ye not as the children of the Ethiopians unto Me,
> O children of Israel? saith the Lord.
> Have I not brought up Israel out of the land of Egypt,
> And the Philistines from Caphtor,
> And Aram from Kir?[4]

The Ethiopians were the colored people of those days. In the environment of Amos there may have been those who affirmed white supremacy. Amos makes short shrift of white supremacy. According to Amos, God is color-blind. In the sight of God, white and black, Hebrew and Ethiopian are alike. The Philistines mentioned by Amos were Israel's ancient foes. Between the Philistines and Israel, the wars were many and bloody. Similarly the Arameans. Numerous and gory were the conflicts between Israel and Aram. Amos singles out precisely these inveterate foes of Israel in order to convey that, among the nations, God plays no favorites. In the sight of God, Israel and Israel's enemies are alike.

God has no part in mankind's petty squabbles. God stands above the battle.

That, at least, is what Amos appears to mean. Of course, no matter what a prophet may appear to mean, some Bible scholar may caution us that the prophet does not mean what he seems to mean but that he means something else. Still, as regards what Amos seems to mean, we of this gathering are undoubtedly of one mind with the prophet.

In these days of psychoanalysis, how readily can we appreciate the words of Jeremiah!

> The heart is deceitful above all things,
> And it is exceeding weak—who can know it?[5]

And when Jeremiah bursts forth into the supplication,

> Heal me, O Lord, and I shall be healed;
> Save me, and I shall be saved;[6]

how aptly are the prophet's words suited to our own devotional needs!

II. *Prophetic Ideas to Which We Do Not Subscribe*

One could continue much longer instancing prophetic thoughts with which we are in accord. But there are some prophetic thoughts with which we are not in accord.

A. DIVINE RETRIBUTION

One of these is the prophetic doctrine of divine punishment. All of the prophets believed in divine punishment. All of them preached divine punishment. The prophets arraign

Israel, as well as other nations, for their sins; and vivid and harrowing are their depictions of the impending doom. The prophets run the entire gamut of horrors—famine, pestilence, defeat, massacre, exile, devastation, ruination, desolation, extermination. Wherever there is a calamity, the prophets interpret that calamity as the punishment for someone's wrongdoing.

There may be, in this gathering, some who believe in divine punishment. But some of us do not thus believe. Some of us have seen too much of life. Too often have we noticed that no one, virtuous or wicked, is immune to misfortune, and that no one, virtuous or wicked, is inaccessible to good fortune. Jewish tradition itself fosters some skepticism on this point. The Talmud contains a passage which states bluntly that, at least on earth, meritorious deeds fail of their due reward.[7] And, much earlier than the Talmud, the Book of Job vigorously and candidly questions whether boons await the righteous and penalties the wicked. "The prosperity of the wicked" is the bitter concern of the seventy-third Psalm. One of the prophets himself queries:

> Wherefore doth the way of the wicked prosper?
> Wherefore are all they secure that deal very
>   treacherously?[8]

Perhaps you sympathize with this strain of Jewish skepticism. If you do, you are not of one mind with the prophets.

In our own land and age, human conduct has been subjected to scientific inquiry. There have been scientific attempts to transmute unacceptable behavior into acceptable behavior. Those scientific procedures involve change of environment, change of training, sometimes medical care, sometimes psychiatric care—at the very worst, detention.

Severity plays, in these approaches, little if any rôle. Some people, in fact, maintain that punishment makes people not morally better but morally worse.

Strange to say, the futility of punishment is perceived by the prophets themselves. The prophets comment on that futility. They complain about that futility. Thus Isaiah deplores:

> The people turneth not unto Him that smiteth them,
> Neither do they seek the Lord of hosts.[9]

Jeremiah laments:

> O Lord . . . Thou hast stricken them, but they were
>   not affected;
> Thou hast consumed them, but they have refused
>   to receive correction.[10]

Hosea bewails:

> Strangers have devoured his strength . . .
> But they have not returned unto the Lord their God.[11]

The same vexation crops up repeatedly in the discourses of Amos.[12] One would imagine that, discerning the futility of punishment, the prophets would abandon the belief in the desirability of punishment. But the prophets do not draw that inference. In this gathering there may be those that do draw that inference. If you do, you are again out of line with the prophets.

Punishment may not serve the purpose of improving people morally. But it does serve a purpose. That purpose is retaliation. Retaliation is deeply engrained in all organic life, so deeply engrained that, when we profess to punish people in order to improve them morally or in order to protect society, we are stating not our real reasons but our rationalizations, that is to say, our spurious reasons, our make-believe reasons, our pretexts; when our real motive is that of getting even. In the prophets, that linkage between punishment and retaliation is not entirely obscured. This is to be noted particularly, though not exclusively, in Jeremiah. With his predictions of punishment, Jeremiah mingles supplications for revenge. "Let them be ashamed that persecute me . . ." he beseeches,

> Let them be dismayed . . .
> Bring upon them the day of evil,
> And destroy them with double destruction . . .
> Let me see Thy vengeance on them.[13]

We will not find fault with Jeremiah for his vindictiveness. The provocation he suffered was stupendous. There is not one of us but would, even under less provocation, prove no less vindictive. Still, we cannot but recall those words in Leviticus: "Thou shalt not take vengeance nor bear any grudge."[14] Perhaps you have been fascinated by those words. If you have, you are out of accord with any prophet or with anyone else who seeks retaliation.

B. DENUNCIATION

The prophets not only predict punishment. They also inflict punishment. They fulminate. They denounce. And denunciation can be punishment of a severe kind. Regarding denunciation we might raise some questions. We might ask: Can one be denunciatory and, at the same time, just? Does not most denunciation, perhaps all denunciation, rest upon

ignorance of the facts? When we know the facts of a situation, are we likely to denounce? Think of the times when
you yourself have been denounced. Was your denouncer
aware of the circumstances which caused you to act as you
did? Could your denouncer have denounced you had he
or she known those circumstances? The prophets themselves
suffered denunciation. From what they underwent they
might have learnt how unfair denunciation can be. But the
prophets did not learn that lesson.

The fifteenth Psalm, listing the traits of the ideal person,
specifies, among other things, that "he taketh not up a re-
proach against his neighbour."[15] If you agree with the
fifteenth Psalm, you do not agree with the prophets.

The Talmud teaches: "Judge not thy fellow man until
thou art come into his place."[16] The Talmud also teaches:
"When judging another, give due weight to that person's
better qualities."[17] One passage in the Talmud goes so far as
to declare that the accuser is guiltier than the accused.[18] If
you agree with these Talmudic precepts, you do not agree
with the prophets.

Spinoza pointed out that we are never exasperated at an
act of human conduct whereof we have traced the causes.
A French proverb runs: "To comprehend all is to pardon
all." A well-known American sociologist once wrote: "In
truth, the consciously flagrantly wicked man is, and perhaps
always has been, for the most part, a fiction of denunciation."[19] If you agree with Spinoza or with that French proverb or with that American sociologist, you do not agree
with the prophets.

Besides, we must remember that different people embrace
different conceptions of right and wrong. What one person
or group pronounces right, another person or group pro-

nounces wrong, and vice versa. The result is that, when we denounce people, we are more than likely to be denouncing those people for doing what they themselves sincerely and conscientiously believe to be right, and the omission of which they sincerely and conscientiously believe to be wrong. If you are aware of this, you are again outside the thinking of the prophets.

Did the prophets accomplish any good with their denunciations? That question we must leave to the scholars. In our own generation it has been said that some needed social reforms have been delayed by the acerbity of their proponents. One would imagine that, to advance one's cause, one would have to win friends for one's cause. But excoriation does not win friends. Excoriation creates enemies. The prophets were protagonists of social justice. They were the tribunes of the underprivileged. For that, we admire them. In that, we should follow them. But the prophets assumed that they could aid the underprivileged by castigating the privileged. Were they correct in that supposition? What if the most effective way in which to aid the underprivileged would be to gain for them the friendship of the privileged? A number of centuries after the era of the prophets, some Jewish teachers contended that changing a foe into a friend is the highest form of heroism. If you agree with that appraisal, you do not agree with the prophets.

Finally, denunciation is something negative. It is nonconstructive. It sets forth what ought *not* to be. It fails to expound what *ought* to be. Impressive, in this regard, is the contrast between the prophets and the Pentateuch. The Pentateuch is likewise a friend of the underprivileged. But the Pentateuch offers constructive proposals. The Pentateuch ordains that whatsoever grows in the corners of a field[20] or whatsoever grows spontaneously during the fallow period every seven years should not be harvested but should be left for the needy;[21] that whatever produce is dropped or forgotten at the harvest should be left for the needy.[22] Every seven years was to bring a cancellation of debts[23] and, every seven years, was to occur the liberation of slaves;[24] and the manumitted slave was to receive, at liberation, an allowance of generous proportions.[25] The wages of a hired worker had to be paid before the end of the day on which the work was performed.[26] These are but a few of the Pentateuch's constructive measures. If you favor constructiveness, you will prefer not the prophets but the Law.

C. ANTI-RITUALISM

There are yet other particulars in which our outlook does not coincide with that of the prophets. One of them concerns the prophetic attitude toward religious ritual. Not all of the prophets are anti-ritualistic. Ezekiel welds a host of rituals into an extensive system. Haggai, Zechariah, and Malachi urge the preservation and the improvement of ritual.[27] But there are prophets who vehemently oppose ritual. Thus Amos quotes God as saying:

> I hate, I despise your feasts,
> And I will take no delight in your solemn assemblies.
> Yea, though ye offer me burnt-offerings and your
>   meal-offerings, I will not accept them;
> Neither will I regard the peace-offerings of your fat
>   beasts.
> Take thou away from Me the noise of thy songs;
> And let Me not hear the melody of thy psalteries.

But let justice well up as waters,
And righteousness as a mighty stream.[28]

Of like tenor is Isaiah:

To what purpose is the multitude of your sacrifices
    unto Me?
Saith the Lord;
I am full of the burnt-offerings of rams,
And the fat of fed beasts;
And I delight not in the blood
Of bullocks, or of lambs, or of he-goats.
When ye come to appear before Me,
Who hath required this at your hand?
Cease to trample my courts, to bring oblations.[29]
A vain offering is incense, it is an abomination
    unto Me.
New moon and sabbath, the holding of convocations
I cannot endure . . . Iniquity (goes with) solemn
    assembly!
Your new moons and your appointed seasons
My soul hateth;
They are a burden unto Me;
I am weary to bear them.
And when ye spread forth your hands,
I will hide Mine eyes from you;
Yea, when ye make many prayers,
I will not hear . . .
Wash you, make you clean,
Put away the evil of your doings
From before Mine eyes.
Cease to do evil;
Learn to do well;
Seek justice, relieve the oppressed,
Judge the fatherless, plead for the widow.[30]

Amos and Isaiah, as well as Jeremiah, unequivocally combat the belief that the rituals were divinely ordained.[31]

The best known of the anti-ritualistic passages is the one in the collection named after the prophet Micah:

> Wherewith shall I come before the Lord,
> And bow myself before God on high?
> Shall I come before Him with burnt-offerings,
> With calves of a year old?
> Will the Lord be pleased with thousands of rams,
> With ten thousands of rivers of oil? . . .
> It hath been told thee, O man, what is good,
> And what the Lord doth require of thee:
> Only to do justly, and to love mercy, and to
>   walk humbly with thy God.[32]

One of the prophets assails the practice of fasting. The name of this prophet is not known, but his utterance is to be found in the collection called "The Book of Isaiah." The prophet quotes God as admonishing:

> Is such the fast that I have chosen?
> The day for a man to afflict his soul?
> Is it to bow down his head as a bulrush,
> And to spread sackcloth and ashes under him?
> Wilt thou call this a fast,
> And an acceptable day to the Lord?
> Is not this the fast that I have chosen?
> To loose the fetters of wickedness,
> To undo the bands of the yoke,
> And to let the oppressed go free . . . ?
> Is it not to deal thy bread to the hungry,
> And that thou bring the poor that are cast out to
>   thy house?
> When thou seest the naked, that thou cover him,
> And that thou hide not thyself from thine own flesh?[33]

With such anti-ritualism none of us stands in harmony.
By some, in this gathering, certain rituals are favored. By
some of us certain rituals are observed. Surely none of us
joins Amos in his antipathy to sacred music or Isaiah in his
opposition to prayer. Some of us fast on the Day of Atonement, and are thus in disagreement with the prophet by
whom fasting is deprecated. And even those of us who do
not favor the rituals and do not recommend the rituals, even
we dissent from those extreme attitudes. While we ourselves
may not enjoy the rituals, we at least respect the people who
are attached to the rituals. Among those people may be our
own parents or some of our dearest friends. Though we do
not care for the rituals, we do not berate the rituals; we do
not objurgate the rituals. Even the most radical among us
are not on the side of the prophets.

Nowadays we often hear and read that the observance of
rituals will improve people morally. This is the diametrical
opposite of what is affirmed in some of the prophetic passages. Thus, Amos exclaims:

> Come to Beth-el, and transgress,
> To Gilgal, and multiply transgression.[34]

Beth-el and Gilgal were, in those days, the holy shrines.
Suppose that someone were to arise in this audience and
shout: "Attending synagogue will make of you more of a
rascal than you are already. Participating in a religious
service will make of you a bigger scoundrel than you are
already." If someone in this audience were to harangue in
that way, we would silence him. We might even eject him.
Yet, precisely that was what Amos meant when he called
forth:

> Come to Beth-el, and transgress,
> To Gilgal, and multiply transgression.

Similarly Hosea:

> Ephraim hath multiplied altars to sin,
> Yea, altars have been unto him to sin.[35]

We have just noticed how, with "solemn assembly," Isaiah brackets "iniquity." Identical is the thought of the unnamed prophet who attacks the custom of fasting. That prophet quotes God as saying:

> Behold, ye fast for strife and contention,
> And to smite with the fist of wickedness.[36]

In other words, the more the fasting, the more the villainy! At least that seems to be the sense of the prophet's rebuke.

None of us in this gathering holds such opinions. Even those of us who deny that, by the observance of ritual, people's morals are improved, also deny that, by such observance, people's morals are impaired. We surmise that rituals make people neither better nor worse. But that is not the viewpoint of the passages just cited.

D. PROGNOSTICATION

A final occasion for divergence between the prophets and ourselves centers in the claim of the prophets that they possessed supernatural powers of prognostication. Prognostications are taking place this very day. Astronomers prognosticate, physicians prognosticate, sociologists, statisticians, and weather forecasters prognosticate. But those prognostications rest upon a scientific basis. They emerge from certain scientific processes. The environment of the prophets knew nothing of scientific method. The predictions of the prophets were understood to be something occult, mysterious, and supernatural.

We might ask whether the prophets meant their predictions to be taken literally. Scholars point out that the prophet Hosea lived to see one of his predictions invalidated, but that he let the prediction remain. He did not withdraw it; he did not cancel it. Hosea prophesied that the Kingdom of Israel and its reigning dynasty would end on one and the same day.[37] As matter of fact, the Kingdom of Israel outlived the reigning dynasty by forty-two years. Three subsequent dynasties arose before the final collapse. Yet, Hosea did not rescind his prognostication.

Nonetheless it is likely that the prophets did mean their predictions to be taken literally. A passage in the Book of Jeremiah states that the fulfillment of a prediction is the evidence that the prophet was divinely sent. A similar statement occurs in the Book of Kings and in the Book of Deuteronomy.[38]

That prediction of Hosea was, by no means, the only prophetic prediction that was never fulfilled. Most of the prophetic predictions were never fulfilled. A well-known Bible scholar told me once that none of the prophetic predictions was ever fulfilled. To be sure, if predictions are numerous enough, some of them would, by the sheer laws of chance, be fulfilled. Besides, many of those predictions were predictions of doom, and predictions of doom are fairly sure to be fulfilled. Life abounds in doom. Sooner or later, disaster is going to strike. But, that the prophets possessed occult, mysterious, and supernatural powers of forecasting the future, we of the modern mind are strongly disinclined to believe.

Nor are these the only points of difference between the

prophets and ourselves. There are yet others.[39] But, upon those we shall not dwell. We hasten to the third division of our subject.

III. *Prophetic Ideas Accepted in Part and Rejected in Part*

When I quoted those passages that protested against the rituals, I extended the quotations to include the prophetic urgings of social justice—that social justice which the prophets proposed as a religion to substitute for the rituals. We may refuse to share the anti-ritualism. But, to the pleadings for social justice, how readily we respond!

We may not assent to the prophetic doctrine of divine punishment. But the conduct singled out for punishment— the conduct branded as evil—is also the conduct which we of today would reprobate as evil—conduct such as falsehood, treachery, oppression, exploitation.

We may disallow the prophetic predictions of the future, but the ideals encased in those predictions, how they appeal! For example, that famous passage in Jeremiah:

> Behold, the days come, saith the Lord, that I will make a new covenant with the house of Israel, and with the house of Judah; not according to the covenant that I made with their fathers in the day I took them by the hand to bring them out of the land of Egypt; forasmuch as they broke My covenant . . . saith the Lord. But this is the covenant that I will make with the house of Israel after those days . . . I will put My law in their inward parts, and in their heart will I write it.[40]

That prediction was announced more than twenty-five hundred years ago. It has not been fulfilled. It will not be fulfilled. The statement, moreover, mentions a covenant. A covenant is a contract. A Deity who enters upon a contract is an anthropomorphism not at all congenial to our modern views. The passage also refers to the Exodus from Egypt. Scholars, all over the world, are debating how much of the Exodus story is legend and how much is history. But, when the prophet quotes God as saying: "I will put My law in their inward parts, and in their heart will I write it," then we have something of unfathomable worth.

A noted American philosopher once declared that religion, in its development, exhibits a progressive inwardization. Those words of Jeremiah mark such inwardization. The British philosopher, Herbert Spencer, believed that evolution is leading to a time when every human being will spontaneously seek the welfare of all other human beings. In that ideal society, according to Spencer, there will exist no evil passions and no need for governments or for laws to curb men's evil passions. Jeremiah anticipated Herbert Spencer by fully twenty-five hundred years. Neither the prognostication of Jeremiah nor that of Herbert Spencer has been fulfilled. Nor is it likely to be fulfilled. But, as an ideal to approximate, how infinitely precious!

We venture the same comment on that radiant passage in the anthology named after the prophet Isaiah, where some prophet quotes God as saying:

> I will . . . make peace thine officers,
> And righteousness thy magistrates.[41]

This means that there will be such peace and such righteousness that officers and magistrates will be no longer needed. The passage continues:

Violence shall no more be heard in thy land,
Desolation nor destruction within thy borders;
But thou shalt call thy walls Salvation,
And thy gates Praise.

The sun shall be no more thy light by day,
Neither for brightness shall the moon give light
   unto thee;
But the Lord shall be unto thee an everlasting light,
And thy God thy glory . . .

Thy people also shall be all righteous,
They shall inherit the land forever;
The branch of My planting, the work of My hands,
Wherein I glory.[42]

This has not been fulfilled. It cannot be fulfilled. But something else has been fulfilled. Something has been fulfilled in our souls. Those shining words irradiate the idealism within us. Can anything be more glorious?

This also characterizes the oft repeated passage:

They shall beat their swords into plowshares,
And their spears into pruning-hooks;
Nation shall not lift up sword against nation,
Neither shall they learn war any more.[43]

Before that prediction is fulfilled, the human race may destroy itself by nuclear warfare. But, as an ideal for which to strive, how magnificent!

The same pertains to many another prophetic outburst:

And the work of righteousness shall be peace;
And the effect of righteousness quietness and
   confidence forever.
And my people shall abide in a peaceable habitation,
And in secure dwellings, and in quiet resting-places.[44]

Or that description of the ideal king:

> With righteousness shall he judge the poor,
> And decide with equity for the meek of the land . . .
> And righteousness shall be the girdle of his loins,
> And faithfulness the girdle of his reins.
> And the wolf shall dwell with the lamb,
> And the leopard shall lie down with the kid;
> And the calf and the young lion and the fatling
>   together;
> And a little child shall lead them.[45]

This has not been fulfilled. It cannot be fulfilled. Yes, it need not be fulfilled. Of these, as of many another prophetic passage, we can speak in the words of Robert Browning:

> The high that proved too high, the heroic for earth
>   too hard,
> The passion that left the ground to lose itself in the sky,
> Are music sent up to God by the lover and the bard;
> Enough that he heard it once: we shall hear it by
>   and by.[46]

One more illustration, and I will have finished. This comes also from the anthology named after Isaiah:

> He giveth power to the faint;
> And to him that hath no might He increaseth strength.
> Even the youths shall faint and be weary,
> And the young men shall utterly fall;
> But they that wait for the Lord shall renew their
>   strength;
> They shall mount up with wings as eagles;
> They shall run, and not be weary;
> They shall walk, and not be faint.[47]

It is not true that the devout are immune to frustration and anguish. Numberless devout people have undergone reverses and tribulation; although it may well be that devoutness will avail considerably to solve some problems of human relationships. As a prediction, that passage is unacceptable. But that passage is more than a prediction. It is a vision, a vision of a superb ideal. It is more than a vision. It is literature of exquisite beauty. And who does not agree with the poet that "A thing of beauty is a joy forever"? In that sense, many a prophetic passage is a joy everlasting.

Thus, though we may take issue with the prophets on this score or on that, the soaring idealism and the ravishing loveliness of many a prophetic utterance makes that utterance veritably an approach of the Divine unto our souls.

NOTES

[1]"The Hero as Poet."
[2]Zechariah 4.6
[3]Zechariah 7.9, 10: 8.16
[4]Amos 9.7
[5]Jeremiah 17.9
[6]Jeremiah 17.14
[7]Hullin, near end of p. 142A
[8]Jeremiah 12.1, 2
[9]Isaiah 9.12
[10]Jeremiah 5.3
[11]Hosea 7.9, 10
[12]Amos 4, 6-11
[13]Jeremiah 17.18: 20.12. See also Amos 7.16, 17
[14]Leviticus 19.18
[15]Psalm 15.3
[16]Abot II, 5
[17]Abot I, 6
[18]Baba Kama 93A, near top
[19]Charles Horton Cooley, in *American Sociological Review*, 1949, p. 103
[20]Leviticus 19:9: 23.22
[21]Exodus 23.10, 11
[22]Leviticus 19.10: Deuteronomy 24:19
[23]Deuteronomy 15.1, 2
[24]Exodus 21.2: Deuteronomy 15.12
[25]Deuteronomy 15.13, 14
[26]Leviticus 19.13
[27]Haggai 1.8, 14: 2.10ff.: Zechariah 3.1-9: 6.13: 14.20, 21: Malachi 1.7ff.
[28]Amos 5.21-24
[29]Following the emendations of Duhm
[30]Isaiah 1. 11-17
[31]Amos 5.25: Isaiah 1.12: Jeremiah 7.22, 23
[32]Micah 6.6-8
[33]Isaiah 58. 5, 6, 7
[34]Amos 4.4
[35]Hosea 8.11
[36]Isaiah 58.4
[37]Hosea 1.4
[38]Jeremiah 28.9: I Kings 22.28: Deuteronomy 18.22
[39]For example, their imperialism (Isaiah 41.15, 16: 45.14: 49.7, 23: 55.4, 5: 60.6, 7: 61.5, 6: Obadiah 1.18-20: Micah 7.12, 16, 17: Zechariah 9.10), their ridiculing of other religions (Isaiah 44.14-17: 46.6), their religious intolerance (Zechariah 14.16), not to mention their constant anthropomorphisms, including what often looks like polytheism. Condemning the worship of "the other gods," the prophets often speak of "the other gods" as if those "other gods" were actual existences.
[40]Jeremiah 31. 31-33
[41]Isaiah 60.17, following the translation of Duhm
[42]Isaiah 60. 18, 19, 21
[43]Isaiah 2.4: Micah 4.3
[44]Isaiah 32.17, 18
[45]Isaiah 11.4, 5, 6
[46]"Abt Vogler," Paragraph X
[47]Isaiah 40.29-31

THE PROPHET
IN MODERN HEBREW
LITERATURE

Rabbi Jacob B. Agus
Beth El Congregation, Baltimore, Maryland

THE GOLDENSON LECTURE OF 1957

THE PROPHET IN MODERN HEBREW LITERATURE*

JACOB B. AGUS, Baltimore

EVERY culture is the collective effort of a human society to rise above the sheer pressures of life and to attain a victory, however small, of spontaneity over routine, freedom over necessity, love over callousness, spirit over matter. While the content of the human spirit and the nature of the resisting matter undergo endless variations, the contest is usually represented in symbols and images that are concrete enough to appeal to the popular imagination. Always, the underlying impetus of any culture is visualized in the guise of a hero, who has already attained, and in the fullest measure, that which the group as a whole sets as its goal. The hero is the underlying *élan* of a society, incarnate and resplendent. In ancient societies, the hero usually belonged to the misty caverns of the past but, whether of the past or of the future, he represented at all times the consummation of the dearest hopes of his society.

The central hero-image in Jewish religious culture is the prophet. Round this image are concentrated the memories of Israel's greatness — Moses and the exodus from Egypt, the emergence of those religious ideals that made possible the return from Babylonia, and the genesis of the two daughter-faiths of Judaism, Islam and Christianity. Upon the assurance of the prophetic words, the hopes of the Messianic future rested, and the Kingdom of God was to be marked by the universal attainment of prophecy, or at least by every Jew's achieving this rank.

The Messiah too was to be a prophet (Sanhedrin 93b).[1] In addition, the great pietists during the medieval and early modern period dreamed of attaining some of the lower degrees of prophecy. And, in

---

*Goldenson Lecture of April 24, 1957.

[1] Saadia describes the Messianic age as follows: "Then prophecy will reappear in the midst of our people so that even our sons and slaves will prophesy. Thus, Joel declared: 'And it shall come to pass afterward, that I will pour out My spirit upon all flesh. And your sons and your daughters shall prophesy. Your old men shall dream, your young men shall see visions. And also upon the servants and upon the handmaids in those days will I pour out My spirit'" (Joel 3.1, 2).

It follows that when one of the children of Israel will go to a distant land and say, "I am of Israel"; people will say to him, "Tell us what the morrow will bring!" (*Emunoth VeDeoth*, chap. VIII, 6).

45

modern times, the prophet was the symbol of Jewish originality, since he articulated the deepest longings of the people in the days of their sovereignty, and he battled valiantly against the incursions of foreign influence. Creative originality is almost inevitably envisaged in the terms of the prophetic situation — the hero who disdains the clamor of the crowd and shatters the idols of the market place, listening with single-minded zeal to the "still, small voice" within his breast that is the voice of God.[2]

The central significance of the image of the prophet in the evolution of Judaism can be understood only when it is compared with the hero-images of other cultures. Without presuming to be exhaustive, we limit our survey to the Western World and call attention to the hero-image of the philosopher in Hellenism, the saint in Catholicism, the artist and the engineer of modern times.[3] To understand the similarities and dissimilarities of these hero-images, we shall do well to envisage the three coordinates of the spiritual life. These three lines of intellectual and emotional dynamism converge upon the soul of man, and all the variations in the history of human culture can be plotted in this three-dimensional space. The three coordinates are the channels leading from the soul to nature, either to the elements of nature within the human personality or physical nature generally; from the soul to human society, either a limited group of people or humanity as a whole: the avenue leading from the soul to God, either God as the transcendent Absolute or a lesser god reflecting a more primitive stage of religion. Along each of these three coordinates, the soul might be conceived as a recipient of values or as a progenitor of standards and goals — i. e. the human soul might be in an active or a passive position.

Plotted on this spatial graph, the philosopher is active or outgoing in respect of nature. He seeks to impose the logical order of mathematics upon physical nature and, within the human personality, he seeks to enthrone the reflective and free sovereignty of the soul by

[2] Yeshurun Kesheth expatiates on the modern significance of the prophetic heritage in his brilliant essay, *Shirath Hamikra* (*Devir*, Tel Aviv, 1955). He maintains that only a return to the prophetic pattern of spirituality can save mankind, for in prophecy "the love of truth is blended with the love of the good" (p. 90). Though his analytical procedure is different from the one followed in this essay, he too recognizes the phenomenon of prophecy as the epitome of Hebraic cultural creativity.

[3] The hero-image of Medieval Knighthood is a composite creation, containing two antithetical facets, deriving, the one from Christianity the other from primitive paganism, and appealing, the one to Christian culture and the other to the aggressive instincts of pre-culture man.

means of rigid training and self-discipline. He is both active and passive along the coordinates of human society — active, in that the ideal philosopher is either the ruler or the teacher of rulers; yet, also passive because the philosopher's strength consists in his ability to withdraw from the pulls and pressures of society. The coordinate of human society was in Hellenic literature at first limited to Greeks, and, within the Hellenic world, to one community or *polis*. But this limitation was overcome by the early Stoics, and the philosopher was envisaged as a citizen of the universe. In respect of the third co-ordinate, the philosopher was conceived as active, attaining knowledge of the Divine by means of active, sustained search. The philosopher was an athlete of the spirit reaching by gradual ascents the highest levels of contemplation of the Supreme Being.

The saint is active in respect to his own human nature, striving constantly to subdue it to God's service; yet, he is also passive, disbelieving in the sufficiency of his own powers and acknowledging that success in this endeavor is an act of Grace. While the classic philosopher maintained that truth was possible and the Stoic sage asserted that virtue was possible and the Epicurean master claimed that happiness was possible, the saint contended that none of these goals was attainable without the gift of Grace. The saint responds in a passive manner to the challenge of physical nature, seeking to withdraw from it, not to master it. His attitude to human society is both active and passive — active, in that he seeks to convert people to his ways of piety; also passive, in that, for the most part, he withdraws from society into a limited or nuclear City of God, whether it be the Church or the Monastery. In regard to the coordinate leading to the Absolute, the saint is totally and typically passive. And therein the burning focus of his personality is to be found. He is completely and without any reservations submissive, yielding his mind, his feelings, his moral judgment and his will to God.[4] He sees no source of values other than those which God dictates and, at his best, is completely the passive vessel of the Divine Will. At the loftiest peaks of his religious experience, the saint is a mystic, feeling himself governed from without, led about hither and thither, almost without a will of his own.[5]

[4] Instructive is the observation of the Midrash concerning the difference between Abraham and Noah (Jewish prophet and non-Jewish saint). While Abraham attained perfection of piety by his own powers, Noah needed the constant aid and support of God (Genesis Rabba, XXX. 10).

[5] Evelyn Underhill devotes a whole chapter to this stage in the life of the mystic. See her *Mysticism*.

The predominant feature of the artist is his passivity toward nature. As a craftsman, the artist is a perfect seer and hearer of the plenitude of impressions that impinge upon his consciousness. As an artist in the Western World, he does not, like a spider, spin silken threads out of his own peculiar fancy but selects, for emphasis, the aspects of nature that are particularly meaningful to the people of his time. When art is turned into a philosophy of life, human nature in all its fulness is celebrated and afforded expression. The ideal of "living according to nature" emerges into full view. The artist does not seek to reform society, and the tension within the soul of Tolstoy is an illustration of this point. In respect to the coordinate of pure being or God, the artist again is passive, allowing validity neither to man's reason nor to man's conscience, seeking to grasp the fulness of existence as a unity — i. e. he employs intuition, arriving at philosophies like those of Bergson or of Schelling.

The hero-image of the engineer is still in the making. It is active along all three coordinates. Physical nature is to be molded at will, and human nature is to be fashioned eventually according to precise specifications. The society of mankind must be run according to a unified all-embracing plan. Even God is to be treated pragmatically and employed insofar as He "works." As passivity along all three coordinates is the mark of the artist, activity is the distinguishing feature of the engineer, who is the emergent cultural hero of secular civilization.

The prophet is both active and passive along all three coordinates. He is both artist and engineer, both philosopher and saint, so that perpetual tension and dynamic restlessness is the characteristic mark of his being.

He is both active and passive in regard to the Supreme Being, submissive in his function as a messenger of the Lord but assertive in his insistence on the validity of the promptings of his conscience. The distinguishing feature of the Hebrew prophets is not their submissiveness to the ecstasies of mysticism, which was a familiar phenomenon in the ancient world, but their firm conviction that the voice of conscience somehow merged insensibly into the Divine Will. Not that conscience alone was a sufficient guide. The prophets were mystics as well as humanists, yielding alternately to the Divine command and to the ethical challenge in the unshakable conviction that the two imperatives were somehow one in the ultimate mystery of the Divine Will. Thus, the prophets could on occasion remonstrate with the Deity. They sensed the peace that passes understanding, even as does the mystic, but they did not focus attention on their feelings. The Word of God was for them a supreme Command, transcending all rational understanding, but, parodoxically enough, continuous and congruous with the voice of conscience.[6] In contradiction to Kierkegaard and his neo-orthodox followers, as well as in opposition to liberal humanism, the point in the tale of Abraham's sacrifice of Isaac was double-pronged. Abraham was to obey the Divine Command even when it seemed irrational but, in the final analysis, the Divine Will merges and coincides with the rational promptings of man's own nature. The ideal prophet is solicitous both for "the honor of the son as well as the honor of the Father" (i. e. for man as well as for God), (Machilta, Bo).

The prophet is also both active and passive in regard to human society. He is concerned with the task of bringing God's Word to the children of man, establishing the Kingdom of Heaven in time and on earth. Yet, the prophet is not a futurist, seeking to rush mankind by forced marches to the ideal goal. Unlike a revolutionary reformer, he is humble enough to wait for God's own time, and unlike a pseudo-Messianist he holds that the drama of redemption takes place within the human heart. He envisions the future as clearly as if it were within reach, yet in saintly humility he bides his time, praying for the favor of Him Who at times "hides his face" (Isa. 8.17). His message is not of the moment and not directed to one individual. The prophet assumes that all his hearers can tell the authenticity of his message, for God speaks to all men, though more clearly to prophets. Those who act as if they did not hear God's Word deliberately shut their ears. The appeal of the prophet is to a kind of "intersubjective hearing" and judging.

This twofold attitude to human society is best seen in the attitude of the prophets to the two societies in the Divine scheme — the people of Israel and humanity as a whole. Ultimately, God's Will is to prevail throughout the world, but He will achieve this consummation in His own good time. The prophets do not undertake missionary journeys among the nations, save one, Jonah, and he reluctantly. Their vision of a redeemed humanity is to be achieved neither by universal conquest, nor by the infectious enthusiasm of a world-wide preaching tour, but in quietude and resignation. However, within the community of Israel, the prophets assume an active, even aggressive role; insisting that the "vineyard of the Lord" be kept utterly

---

[6] In Cabala, where vestiges of the prophetic tradition are contained, *Din*, or the incomprehensible Divine decree, is in the highest spheres, completely absorbed in *Raḥamim*, which is the humanly experienced quality of Mercy.

free of weeds and be made immediately to produce luscious fruits. The prophetic message to the people of Israel could well be summed up in that famous motto, which could be made to serve several different philosophies of life — "to thine own self be true." In the genius of the prophets, Israel was to be true to itself in such a manner as to be for that very reason true to the universal soul of mankind. This is the deeper meaning of the prophetic conception of the Covenant.[7]

In respect to the coordinate of nature, the prophet again is both active and passive. Having grown out of the institution of "sons of the prophets," the prophet was doubtless originally a person who practised some form of ascetic self-discipline. Elijah was obviously an ascetic. Yet, in contrast to the prophets of the Baal, his preparatory exercises were predominantly prayer, earnest contemplation, and whole-souled listening to the voice of God. In later Judaism, the ideal image of the prophet involved an arduous ascent on the ladder of self-conquest. Rabbi Pinḥas ben Yair lists a series of steps leading to the gift of *Ruaḥ Haḳodesh*, and Maimonides describes *Ruaḥ Haḳodesh* as the lowest of eleven degrees of prophecy (Abodah Zara 20b, *Guide of the Perplexed*, II, 45).

At the same time, the prophets take account of the fulness of human nature. They do not advocate either celibacy or mortification of the flesh or incessant struggle against the impulses of nature, or resistance to the advance of civilization. A deep appreciation of the dignity of the human personality is embraced in the prophetic message. (Isa. 13.12, 13, the translation should be in the present, not past tense.) Jeremiah commends the Rechabites for their loyalty to their ancestral way of life, but he does not demand that the Israelites should give up city life. In all their descriptions of the future world, there abound earthly joys and the healthy fragrance of fields and forests. Their motto is "life according to God's Will," not "according to nature;" yet, they do not demand that which is against nature.

It follows that the hero-image of the prophet has affinities with the hero-images previously described. Alike to the philosopher, in the coordinates of nature and mankind, the prophet differs in respect to his attitude toward God. Alike to the saint in respect of society, he differs in respect of both God and nature. The artist and the engineer represent one-sided images of him, for they are either wholly passive or wholly active along all three coordinates, while he maintains a

---

[7] R. Ḥasdai Crescas offers a somewhat similar explanation of the failure of the prophets to organize preaching missions to the gentiles. They preach *about* other nations, not *to* them (*Or Adonai*, 2.4, 3).

dynamic, tense equilibrium and a sense of balance in all three domains of the spiritual life. Yet, the artist as poet and the engineer as social planner or reformer reflect tangential aspects of his towering personality.

In one essential respect, the prophet differs from the other hero-images. As a rule, prophecy is regarded as the peculiar gift of God to Israel. While occasional passages maintain the occurrence of prophecy among other nations, this opinion is confined to certain personalities mentioned in the Hebrew Scriptures. The predominant opinion in our sacred tradition is that only Israel is the people of prophecy. In a sense, all sons of Israel are "sons of the prophets." The Jews beheld in the image of the prophet an ideal representation of their own collective being. Thus, the ambivalence of pride and dedication that is implicit in the concept of chosenness was focused on the image of the prophet. On the one hand, the prophetic ideal reflected the noblest aspirations of the Jewish people, their dedication to the task of bearing the knowledge of God to the nations. On the other hand, the calling of the prophet lent an aura of superiority and self-worshipping adulation to Jewish consciousness. And the tension between these two polar attitudes within the heart of Israel contributed in no small measure to that peculiar awareness of isolation which is the soul of his tragic history. The vision of the prophet towered high as the mountain of Sinai with the cloud of glory resting upon it; the masses of the people saw chiefly its earthly base and stood at a distance, while only a few brave souls ventured like Moses into the cloud, up the steep slopes and toward the holy summit.

As the prophetic ideal receded into the mists of the past, Judaism entered the phase of crystallization, making do with the leadership of lesser personalities. The First Ḥasidim still preserved the pattern of prophetic piety, at least as an ideal. Along the coordinate of nature, puritan zealotry made its appearance; along the highway to mankind, the wide vistas were narrowed and high barriers were raised; along the gateway to God, submissive feeling was threatened by the frost of formalistic obedience, and the assertive spirit was curbed.

The descent from the peak of prophecy is implicit in the ideal itself. For prophecy is a momentary phenomenon. The prophet is not "transfigured" permanently, as in Buddhist or in some Christian theologies. When the lightning-like moment of the dialogue with God is over, the prophet can only seek to recall the golden moment and yearn for its recurrence. Hence, the lyrical pathos in his utterances. Also, he brings the ineffable fluid content of ecstasy into the light of his intelligence, where the protean glow of belonging to the Infinite is transformed into the firm assurance of a binding, permanent relationship, the awareness of being "covenanted" unto God. The "covenant-relationship" is the ecstasy of the dialogue-experience translated into sober terms and projected outward into the external world of time and space. By degrees, this relationship is spelled out in a series of general principles and specific laws. Thus, the prophet, descending from the summit, becomes successively: a preacher, recalling the Covenant; a sage reexamining the life of his day in the light of Divine first principles and against the background of his vision; a priest, seeking to preserve the element of mystery in the Divine encounter and to dramatize this mystery in a series of rituals; a scribe, preserving the laws, the crystallized expressions of fluid moments of inspiration, counting the letters of sacred Scriptures and transmitting the tradition to successive generations.

It follows that these hero-images of Judaism were not anti-prophetic but representations of the prophet, in his sober uninspired moments. Aaron, the priest, is the spokesman and pragmatic interpreter of Moses. Alas, at times, too pragmatic. The conflict between Amos and the high priest of Beth-el, however, is not as typical as the nearly unbroken record of collaboration between prophets and priests. In later Judaism, the high priest was vouchsafed the privilege of approaching the Shechinah once a year. And Ezra, the priest was also the scribe, par excellence. His function was to count the words and interpret the meaning of previous revelations, but he was not completely devoid of the prophetic aura. "Ezra was worthy of being the agent for the Almighty to give the Torah, but Moses preceded him" (Sanhedrin 21b). The sages of later years were frequently said to be worthy of the Shechinah's resting upon them. For prophecy was taken from the prophets and given to the wise (Baba Bathra 12a). Great rabbis were believed capable of ascending to heaven for conversations with heavenly beings (Midrash *Eleh Ezkerah*, Yellinek, 64–72). They were believed to be effective intercessors for the people, providing they possessed a "broken and humbled heart," as well as an immense store of sacred learning (Ta'anith 24a).

Still, the hero-image of the prophet was never completely forgotten, and whenever it reappeared on the horizon, a renascence of Judaism took place, We recognize the lineaments of this vision in the personality of Hillel and in the movement he led to base the Oral Law on the foundation of an implicit, inner logic and by recognition of the golden rule as its central core. We recognize the prophetic ideal in the life and thought of Philo and in the great movement of philosophical Judaism, which seeks to recapture the essential tension of true religion, in both its active and passive phases, i. e. the tension between piety and ethics, mysticism and rationalism. Fragments of this ideal are recaptured in the Essenic societies, in the circles of proto-cabalists and cabalists. And as we approach the modern age and the rebirth of Hebrew literature, we encounter once again the heroic image of the prophet on the threshold of the new era.

II

The first titanic figure of modern Hebrew literature was a prophetic personality of many and diverse talents. Rabbi Moses Ḥayyim Luzzatto shared in the ecstatic visions of the Hebrew prophets, in their sense of total identification with the life of the people, in their overwhelming sensation of the overpowering nearness of the Divine Being, in their hunger for purity of soul and the perfection of love, in their lyrical quality of poetic composition — above all, in the power to see all things with the freshness of a creative imagination. Compelled to interpret his immense gifts, psychic upheavals and volcanic imagination in terms of the complex and rigid dogmas of his day, Luzzatto believed that saints of long ago and winged seraphim conversed with him, dictating to him magnificent works of sacred lore. In the prevailing concepts of his generation, the protean events of his great and restless soul could no longer be described in the simple formula of the Biblical prophets, "thus spake the Lord." During the Talmudic and post-Talmudic period, the normative conception of God in Judaism became ever more decisively transcendent. In the official "targumim," the Word (*Memra*) or the Presence (*Shechinah*) or the Glory (*Kavod*) of God was interposed in those places where the text read God. In the Mishnah, no angels are mentioned at all, save for the quasi-angelic figure of Elijah. In the Talmud and later Midrashim, ecstatic and mystical experiences are pressed into the mold of a "revelation of Elijah." As the subterranean stream of cabalistic mysticism burst into the open in the latter half of the thirteenth century, "prophetic cabala" made its appearance in the erratic career of Abraham Abulafia. Elaborate schemes were worked out for the attainment of interviews with diverse heavenly beings, ranging from the imaginary characters of the Zohar to a class of anonymous *Maggidim*, or "revealers."

Pressed within this dogmatic context, the prophetic consciousness degenerated into a feverish catharsis of self-exaltation. In the *Maggid Mesharim* of Rabbi Joseph Karo and in the *Sefer Haḥezyonoth* of Rabbi Ḥayyim Vital, we look in vain for the stirring of a noble passion or the insights of a creative imagination. Virtually the sole

content of both books revolves round the wondrous greatness of
the two authors, describing the amazing delights that await them in
heaven.

Though Luzzatto's *Maggidim*, heavenly "revealers," conformed to
the general type, there were remarkable and fresh overtones in his
writings. The Hebrew style of his writings is chaste, simple, precise
and responsive to the logic of modern grammar. Whatever the nature
of his inspiration, the quality of his literary creations is uniformly
high. In him, the lyricism of the prophets is reborn as well as their
ethical fervor and their genius for distinguishing the kernel of piety
from its shell. His "revelations," for all their superstitious framework,
open up a new era. Themes borrowed from Italian poetry blend
naturally with ideas and symbols deriving from cabala. The love
of God takes on, in his dramas, the charm and gentleness of earthly
love. Mundane life and love are seen fresh and new, as if they were
bathed in heavenly radiance. The human personality in its yearning
for beauty and the fulness of expression, moves back into focus and
the great movement of Jewish humanism is launched.

Different aspects of Luzzatto's personality appealed to the different
builders of the Hebraic renaissance. The *Maskilim* were enthralled by
his poems and dramas, seeing in him the first author of secular literature in the new era. The Ḥasidim loved and studied his mar-
velously lucid expositions of cabalistic metaphysics and psychology.
The "lovers of Zion" expatiated on the symbolic significance of his
journey to the Holy Land, since his visions could be considered pure
and holy only if they occurred in the ancestral land of Israel. The Gaon,
Elijah of Vilna, himself a center of renewed interest in secular wisdom,
admired above all Luzzatto's ethical-pietistic classic, *Mesillath Yesharim*. He who so cruelly castigated the Ḥasidim for their exaggerated
adulation of their *Ẕaddiḳim*, is said to have declared, "had the author
of the *Path of the Righteous* been still living, I should have set out on
a pilgrimage to learn the ways of piety under his guidance" (Zinberg's
Di Geshikhte fun der Literatur bei Yidn, vol. V, p. 221). And the opinion
of this preeminent scholar coincided in this instance with the feelings
of the unlearned masses who formed societies for the study of this
little volume.

Indeed, the *Path of the Righteous* is a reflection of the prophetic
consciousness, at its best. In this volume, the vagaries of mystical
feeling are brushed aside, so that the relation of man to God might
be presented in all its chasteness and sublimity, its heaven-storming
aspiration and its earthly practicality. Truly remarkable is the absence
in this work of that dismal phantasmagoria of superstitious piety,

centering round Satan and his hordes, the "outsiders" who plot the downfall of man in this world and stoke the fires of hell in the hereafter. Suffice it to bring to mind two popular ethical-pietistic works of the same genre, *Kav Hayashar* and *Reshith Ḥochma*, to note the uniqueness of Luzzatto's work. The first work is replete with malicious devils, tales of horrible punishment for the least infraction of any ritual law and instructions regarding various devices for the overcoming of the "other side." Man was created "to observe the Torah, the laws and the commandments," and woe betides him, if he is neglectful (Chap. 1). Elijah di Vidas' work, *The Beginning of Wisdom*, commences its exposition of piety with the "gate of fear," detailing the injury done to the sinner's personality, to his higher soul and to the Shechinah by every infraction of the Law. It describes the horrors of *Ḥibbuṭ Haḳever*, the beating of the dead at the grave as well as the terrors of the various caverns of hell, adding for good measure, the fear of being reborn in this hateful world (*Reshith Ḥochmah*, First Gate, Tractate *Gehinnom*).

In contrast to this fear-born jungle of fantastic horrors, Luzzatto's world is fresh and sunny, high as the heavens and open on all sides. Hell is not even mentioned and its dark, ubiquitous minions are brushed aside. The purpose of man's life is defined not in the servile terms of blind obedience, but in the accents of happiness and fulfillment. "Man was created for the sole purpose of delighting in God and basking in the radiance of His Shechinah, for this pleasure is the greatest and most genuine of all joys in existence" (Chap. 1). To be sure, the goal of man's life is set in the hereafter, but it is a bright and beautiful vista, in which all men may share to the extent of their merit. Nor is the radiance of the Shechinah totally removed from the ordinary concerns of our mundane existence, for the Spirit of Holiness (*Ruaḥ Haḳodesh*) may be attained in our lifetime. Not only the preeminent Torah-scholars but every ordinary artisan may aspire to "direct his heart toward the goal of clinging truly unto God, till a spirit from above is poured upon him, the Name of God is bestowed upon him, even as the Lord acts toward His saints. Then he will become actually like an angel of the Lord with all his deeds even the lowliest and the most material being accepted as sacrifices and offerings" (Chap. 26).

The piety of Luzzatto is prophetic in the brightness of its spiritual horizon, in the goal of quasi-prophecy that it sets for the pious and in the powerful ethical quality of its teachings. A child of his age, he could still write "that forbidden foods introduce real uncleanliness into the heart and spirit of man so that the holiness of the Lord re-

moves itself and departs from him" (Chap. 11). Nevertheless, his
predominent emphasis is purely ethical. He reflects the spirit of the
Renaissance in his call for a principle of balance and harmony to
govern the aspirations of piety (Chap. 20). Thus, he allows that the
pious must take account of the way their deeds impress men and
women outside the fold, refraining from actions which excite ridicule
(Chap. 20). If Luzzatto's sage advice had been followed by the
Ḥasidim of Poland, the tragic battles regarding the *Kapotes* and
the *Yarmulkes* would not have been necessary. While Luzzatto did
not embrace all of mankind in his purview, he did accord some weight
to the opinions of non-Jews. To the veritable horror of his rabbinic
judges, he studied the secular and Latin cultures of his day and, in
his literary works, he strove for grace and precision of expression.
Remaining within the walls of the Law, he concentrated attention on
its spiritual kernel. And, going beyond the Law, he called for new
and creative ways of serving God, so as to articulate in original actions
the dynamic spirit of piety.

III

Luzzatto was a lonely and exotic reincarnation of the ideal image
of the prophet. But, his tragic career proved the impossibility of the
resplendent ideal for the European Jews of the middle of the eighteenth
century.

In some of the Western countries, the fresh breezes of a new
world were beginning to be felt, consigning to oblivion the mystic
muses of Cabala. In the East, Rabbi Ḥagiz, the leading persecutor
of Luzzatto, aroused widespread support with his motto, "whatever
is new is prohibited by the Torah." When the unitary stream of
European Jewish history was bifurcated into Western and Eastern
currents, the prophetic ideal was fragmentized in both areas of Jewish
settlement. And, in both East and West, the respective fragments
were sufficiently potent to win a massive popular following.

In Western Europe, a significant fragment of the prophetic vision
was recaptured in the ideals of the Haskalah. In the horizon of the
classical prophets, the Jewish people were seen against the background of mankind as a whole. God was concerned with the salvation
of Assyria and Egypt even as He strove for the redemption of Israel.
The Jewish people did not monopolize the entire horizon of the
prophets, who interpreted the Jewish task in the light of the needs
of all mankind. This synoptic vision, all but lost in the dark centuries
of persecution, was now made the central focus of Jewish interest.

In the philosophy of Mendelssohn, man is the object of Divine concern, not solely the people of Israel. The Torah, Divine though it be, is not really necessary either for the good life in this world or for salvation in the hereafter. The *Mitzvoth* were interpreted as ceremonies, binding upon the Jew, because God willed it so, but not intrinsically of significance to the rest of mankind. Furthermore, it is through the realization of all the potentialities of man's nature, especially his love of beauty and his faculty for reasoning, that God is best served.

N. H. Weisel propagated the ideals of Haskalah in pamphlet after pamphlet, calling for the acceptance of the "Torah of man" — i. e. humanistic values and goals. Yet, his humanism was profoundly religious as well as ethical and esthetic. In his campaign for a new program of education, he stresses the prophetic approach — i. e. emphasis on the spiritual core of religious life. Neither Mendelssohn nor Weisel followed the counsel of the Talmud to limit the pursuit of secular studies to the twilight hour, "which is neither day nor night" (Menaḥoth 99b). They considered philosophy, literature, and culture to be part of the "Torah of man." The *Maskilim* translated into Hebrew the apocalyptic literature, and in their schools they stressed the teaching of the Scriptures, as against the Talmud. Their followers composed moralistic tracts along with literary creations, and the greatest achievement of the German *Maskilim*, appropriately enough, was the long epic of Weisel on the life of Moses, "the Master of the prophets."

Another fragment of the heroic image of the prophet became a dynamic force among the Jews of Eastern Europe. Rabbi Israel Baal Shem Tov, virtually a contemporary of Luzzatto, rediscovered the full pathos and splendor of mystical piety, thereby launching the magnificent mass-movement of Ḥasidism. To be sure, the *Ẕaddiḳim* did not claim the rank of prophecy, but they averred that they were blessed with the wondrous gifts of the Spirit of Holiness (*Ruaḥ Ha-ḳodesh*) which Maimonides describes as the first level of prophecy.

So successful were the *Ẕaddiḳim*, in the early years of the movement, in attaining high states of mystical ecstasy that they wondered why it was so easy in their day to commune with the Shechinah, though in earlier ages it appeared difficult. The assertive aspect of prophetic piety was exemplified in the bold innovations of the Ḥasidim — chiefly, their insistence that the unlearned man could reach the highest places in heaven and their declaration that it is the soul of Divine service that matters, not its external forms. In folk-Ḥasidism, Rabbi Levi Yizḥak of Berdichev emerged as the great protagonist of the people of Israel who, in the ardor of his defense, dared to challenge the justice of God Himself, as it were.

Ḥasidism was in many ways a revival of popular prophetism. The attainment of mystical ecstasy was consciously set as the goal of all *Baalei Madregah* (those who aimed at high levels of achievement). (See description of five stages of ecstasy in *Kuntros Hahithpaaluth* of *Der Miteler Rav*.) While some Ḥasidic groups envisaged this goal in the crude terms of the ancient bands of prophetizers and modern backwoods revivalists, other groups developed exceedingly refined and subtle forms of mystical contemplation. On a less ethereal plane, they rediscovered the meaning of prayer as a Dialogue with God and the possibility of worshipping him in new and unconventional ways. Along the highway of the soul to man, they developed a new communal form, the voluntary community centering round the saint. On the plane of human nature, they combatted the ascetic tendencies of an earlier era, cultivated the arts of singing, dancing, and story-telling, and stressed the joys of fellowship and conviviality.

The *Ẓaddiḳ* of the Ḥasidim was a prophet in miniature. Some *Ẓaddiḳim* were modelled after the wonder-working early prophets, like Samuel, Elijah and Elisha, while the truly great teachers among them sought to exemplify in a small way the careers of the classical prophets. Rabbi Naḥman of Bratzlav taught that the "true *Ẓaddiḳ* of every generation was in the category of Moses-Messiah" (*Liḳḳutei Moharan* I.9; 118). Through him, the flow of Divine Grace was channelled from heaven to earth. Even so intellectual a teacher as Rav Shneur Zalman taught that the people generally derived their "sustenance" through the agency of the saints of their day (*Tanya*, chap. 2). While the *Ẓaddiḳ* was not an agent of revelation, he was himself a representation of Divine Revelation, since the non-Divine soul in his personality was completely transformed into a Divine entity. Accordingly, even "the way he put on his stockings" was Torah. In other Ḥasidic writings, the Ẓaddiḳ was exalted to such dizzying heights, as to surpass even the hero-image of the prophet. Thus, Rabbi Elimelech of Lizensk asserted that "the eyes of God are in the Zaddik, so that it is within his power to open the eyes of the Creator, blessed be He, upon Israel" (*No'am Elimelech, lech lecha*). The Ẓaddik was thus elevated to the rank of a mediator, for it is through him that not only God's Word, but His sustaining vitality is channelled (*ibid., Miketz*). No achievement is beyond his power, not even the final redemption. "The Ẓaddiḳ can bring about all things, including the advent of the Messiah" (*ibid., Shemoth*).

IV

The fragmentation of the prophetic hero-image ended in frustration and tragedy for both branches of European Jewry. In the West, preoccupation with esthetic goals and humanistic values lowered the barriers of the inner ghetto walls to the point where total assimilation became a mass-movement. The one-sided emphasis of the German Haskalah on the "Torah of man" awakened longings for immediate union with the nations of Europe so as to end the long travail of exile. For the sake of an emergent new humanity in Europe, many a Jew was willing to sacrifice the consolation and comfort of his traditional heritage. The men and women who led the way to the baptismal font in the Nineteenth Century were not always sick souls, afflicted with self-hatred (the term was not yet invented) but, in many cases, idealists who were lured by the universalistic facet of the prophetic vision. Many of them did not forsake their people with cold, calculating callousness, but they allowed their Jewish loyalties and sentiments to be sacrificed on the altar of their new faith in humanity and European culture. Men like Heine and Börne, Friedrich Stahl and Edward Gans were not vulgar materialists. Some of the best sons of our people belonged to the tribe of which Heine sang, "those who die when they love." Dazzled by the bright prospect of one humanity, they could see no purpose in Jewish survival and, as they severed their last ties with their past, they imagined that they helped fulfill the vision of the prophet.

> "Yea, at that time I will change the speech of the peoples to a pure speech, that all of them may call on the name of the Lord and serve Him with one accord" (Zeph. 3.9).

Thus, the fragment of prophetic vision in Haskalah led to its own decay and disappearance.

Similarly frustrating was the fate of that fragment of prophetism that was embodied in Ḥasidism. While the German Haskalah saw only the man in the Jew, the Ḥasidim saw only the Jew in the Jew and mighty little else in the world beside the Jew. From the sacred writings of Cabala, the Ḥasidim received the belief that only the souls of Jews were derived from God (*Shefa Tal*, chap. 1). Non-Jews possessed only sparks of the various "shells," whence too, Satan and his demonic cohorts were derived (*Liḳḳutei Amorim*, by R. Shneur Zalman, chaps. 1, 6). Operating with this fundamental principle of "psychology," the Ḥasidim allowed no room in their world either for humanity or for human values. Their religious life, for all its intensity and nobility, was therefore exceedingly narrow, benighted and utterly unworldly.

In the mists of folk-legendry enveloping the figure of the Baal Shem Tov, we can recognize occasional glimmerings of a wider horizon. Thus, we are told that, in one of his ascents to heaven, he learned that the heavenly tribunal was planning severe decrees against the Jews, because of the sins of Jewish peddlers in cheating the ignorant peasants (*Shivḥei HaBesht*, 34). There are extant, too, literary versions of folk-tales extolling the virtue of kindness to gentiles (Peretz's *If Not Higher*). But, on the whole, the Ḥasidim ruthlessly limited the horizons of their world to the concerns of Jews and things Jewish. With misplaced zeal they fought against the efforts of the Russian government to have them wear European garments. (See *Ger* by Alfasi, a history of the "Gerer" dynasty.) With the redoubled fanaticism of the hopeless and despairing, they conducted a holy war against secular education and against the intrusion of humanistic values. (See Shoul Ginsburg's *Historishe Verk*, volume one, p. 63.) Within two generations, the Ḥasidic movement lost all the creative *élan* that it ever possessed; the light of originality was quenched for want of fresh air, and the smoke of fanaticism grew ever more dense and acrid.

The moral failure of Ḥasidism to take into account the wide horizons of humanity and the hard facts of reality generated the mood of widespread rebelliousness among the literary *Maskilim* in Russia. Levinson, "the Mendelssohn of Russia," protested against the prevailing spirit of unreality, the inability of the pious masses to take stock of their opportunities in the fields of agriculture and skilled labor. So unworldly were the masses and so visionary were their leaders that it was necessary for quasi-heretics to urge the people to engage in agriculture and in physical labor.

Most of the Hebrew writers in the first part of the Nineteenth Century were satirists and protestants. And the target of their bitter criticism was the hero-image of the prophet, distorted as this image had become in the shadowy world of Ḥasidism. Isaac Erter and Joseph Pearl attacked the image of the *Ẓaddik* directly in their clever parodies. Other *Maskilim* fought the battle for humanism on the front of education, proclaiming as their motto, "Be a Jew in your tent, and a man when you go out." Publicists and novelists in their several ways, bewailed the abuse of the "prophet-people" conception.

The leading figure of Russian Haskalah assailed the image of the prophet, which he beheld in the guise of the Orthodox rabbis, who by his time had made common cause with the Ḥasidic *Ẓaddikim*. Thus,

J. L. Gordon, foremost spokesman of Haskalah, capped his career with a long poem of bitter invective against the prophet Jeremiah. In *Zidkiyahu beveth Hapekudoth*, the last King of Judah is heard lamenting,

אך מה און פעלתי? מה פשעתי?

But wherein did I err? What is my guilt?

יען לפני ירמיהו לא נכנעתי?

Because to Jeremiah I did not submit?

לפני איש רך הלב, בעל נפש נכנעת

The soft-hearted man, of soul cringing,

אשר יעץ לנו בשת, עבדות, משמעת

Who counselled shame, servitude, yielding.

ואני מאנתי עצתו לשמע,

But I refused his counsel to take,

כי אמרתי ברזל, ברזל ירע

For I said, iron should iron break. . .

— —

— — — —

עוד זאת, ברית חדשה ברא ליהודה

This, too, he a new covenant for Judah proposed,

כל עם הארץ, מקטנם עד גדולם

All the people, young and old

ילמדו דברי ספר, תורה ותעודה.

Should study bookish things and teachings.

— — —

— — —

איש ואיש יאמר לא אחרש, לא אדוש

Every man should say, I'll not plow, I'll not harvest.

כי בן ממלכת כהנים אני וגוי קדוש.

A son am I of a kingdom of priests and a holy people.

Gordon's protest against the prophetic hero-image reflected the struggle of the enlightened against the wizened Orthodoxy of both the Ḥasidim and the Mithnagdim. Weak echoes of the debate on religious reforms in the West appeared in Hebrew literature, but the predominant concern of the *Maskilim* was to make room for secular and humanistic interests within Jewish life. Their tragedy was the absence of any objective foundation for a secular culture. A prophet-people Israel could be, but not just a people. In the sixties and seventies of the last century, Russian Haskalah saw itself in the strange position of winning a battle and losing a people at one and the same time. Masses of Jewish people heeded the call of the *Maskilim* all too well, and, rebelling against the narrow horizons of Jewish life, plunged into the wide ocean of Russia, leaving behind them the new Hebraic literature as well as their ancient faith.

V

The fragmentation of the prophetic ideal into mysticism and humanism ended in tragic futility in both East and West. But, it was not long before the prophetic ideal in its fulness was rediscovered in the West, making possible a subsequent revival of prophetism in Russia.

In Germany and Austria, the rise of liberal or non-dogmatic Judaism with its two wings, the "prophetic" and the "historical" recreated the original conception of the prophet and the prophet-people. The builders of Reform Judaism recognized the error of Mendelssohn in reducing the specific area of the Jewish religion to the domain of rites and ceremonies. If what is essentially Jewish is the ballast of rituals which an advancing people steadily leaves behind it, there is no justification for Jewish existence. Judaism must be seen as a call to cooperate in building the future, not as an archaic remnant of a "Jerusalem" that once represented the Will of God.

Geiger and his associates discovered that, in terms of essential religious ideas, Judaism was far more congruent with the mature modern mind than Christianity. For in Judaism, the relation of man to God is active as well as passive, a stirring call to the daytime tasks of building the kingdom of heaven, not merely a soothing whisper for nighttime rest in the comfortable assurance of salvation. The hero-image of Judaism is the prophet, while the hero-image of Christianity wavers between the saint and the mystic, the crusader and the monk. And, if Judaism asserts its authentic message in the accents of the contemporary world, Christianity, too, is drawn away from the blandishments of its pagan components and toward a genuine prophetic faith.

Thus, the call of Reform was for a return to the prophetic faith, all along the line. Judaism was to become prophetic in stressing the inwardness of faith, in affirming the central ideals of ethical monotheism, and in preaching the essence of religion to all men. Prophetic, too, Judaism was to be in the sense of taking religion to be that which is alive within the heart of its people — hence, a willingness at all times to make a fresh effort to see all things synoptically, combining facets old and new. Dedicated to their ideals, the Jews can once again assume the destiny of a prophet-people. In liberal Judaism, the hero-image of the spiritual leader was shifted from that of priest-sage-scribe to that of sage-preacher-prophet. It was no longer to be the function of the rabbi to be the custodian of the laws and the guardian of the tradition, but like the prophet of old, he was to become the instrument through whom God manifests the forward thrusts of His Purpose.

The proponents of "historical Judaism," Frankel and Graetz, entered the lists against Reform. Yet, when seen from the distance of a century, their efforts served to fill in the details of the prophetic hero-image. While the Reform wing emphasized the rational and assertive elements of the prophetic mentality, the Conservative wing stressed the passive situation of the individual within the massive processes of history, which include the fortuitous, the irrational and the national elements. The historians uncovered the connecting tissue between prophetism and rabbinism, proving the existence of an organic unity between prophecy and peoplehood, between inwardness and reverence for Divine Law. Thus, while one wing of modern Judaism stressed the message of the prophets to mankind, the other called attention to the psychic background of national soil and cultural context, out of which prophecy emerges. Later, Conservative writers were to complete the prophetic image by focusing the spotlight of research on the mystical elements which enter into the prophetic consciousness.

Thus, the fulness of the prophetic hero-image was reconstructed. Once again, the Jewish people could be seen against the backdrop of past and future and within the context of competing cultures and clashing ideologies. The Jew was to live not merely by the compulsions of a Divine mandate which, for the doubting and the hesitant, begged the question, but for the sake of a high purpose which could be read out of the historical experiences of mankind. And this purpose was conceived in terms so lofty as to transcend the actual reach of any generation. New this concept of a prophet-people was, in its non-ritualism and its non-dogmatism. The content of the prophetic message was not a list of commandments but the spirit of love, faithfulness, and truthfulness. The appeal of this vision was direct and immediate. Liberated from the dross of the ages, it evoked fresh loyalty and renewed enthusiasm among the Jews of the Western world.

In Krochmal's philosophy of Jewish history, this revived conception of a prophet-people was projected, albeit sketchily and vaguely. A people is formed by loyalty to a great ideal. In the unfolding of the Divine Purpose, one ideal after another enters into the actual process of history and merges gradually into the total, eternal treasury of mankind. Along with the rise of an ideal, the people embodying and representing it emerges upon the stage of history, and when the ideal sinks into eternity, the people lose their inner cohesion and descend from the stage. The Jewish people, in their worship of the Absolute

Spirit, containing the totality of ideals, is as eternal as the divine plan for mankind. Subject to the laws of nature and history, they too rise and fall, along with the ideals of their faith, but phoenix-like they emerge from the ashes and rise again with the dawn of the new ideal, that is for them but a fresh facet of Him whose seal is truth. For every ideal is but a revelation of the Divine Truth to which the Jewish people are dedicated.

In the progressive emergence of new ideals, the Jew constantly rediscovers his own faith.

The steady and massive growth of the new concept of "prophetic Judaism" in Germany and Austria slowed down, though it did not completely halt, the tide of frustration and despair in the Western world. The influence of this concept was also felt most powerfully in Russia. There, however, for many sociological and ideological reasons, the focus of attention was shifted from the message of the prophet to the national base for his pedestal. And this shift of focus was occasioned, at least in part, by the rise of romantic nationalism among the nations of Europe.

Romantic nationalism is the ideal of the prophet-people reversed and stood on its head. The seductive suggestion is put forward that the healthy and abundant life of the people produces authentic life-giving ideals, as a healthy tree produces the fruits of its own peculiar kind. This apparently innocent observation converts the prophetic ideal into a self-righteous, jingoistic slogan on the banners of the nation. The life of the people, not its ideals, becomes the supreme purpose. We need to concern ourselves only with the cause; the effect, it may be assumed, will take care of itself. Thus, we move from the realm of ideals to that of sociology. Since the ideal is the natural product of the life of the people, the vitality and purity of the nation are elevated to the highest moral rank. The national message or ideal seldom checks the excess of chauvinism, for its nature is shrouded in the mythical vagaries of intuition and its time is in the future. But the self-righteousness and the self-exaltation of the prophetic posture remains. The life of the nation itself is magnified and sanctified, instead of the Name of the Lord. The nation itself is glorified, not made to serve an ideal or the Glory of God. So subtle is the distinction between the prophetic and romantic concepts that it frequently escapes detection. And, in certain circumstances, they coalesce for, on occasion, what makes the life of a people possible must take precedence over what the life of that people makes possible. Indeed, the paradox is inherent in the very nature of prophecy. Since the prophet speaks for God, how can he, save by his uniquely keen conscience, avoid self-exaltation and self-sanctification? Must not his powers of self-criticism be fully as great as his intuitive vision? Objectively, the only acid test of authentic prophecy is the relation of a person to other individuals and of a nation to other human groups, the capacity to rise above the narrowness and blindness of sheer nationalism. The true prophet demands more from his own than from other nations, loving his people passionately but with open eyes and a generous spirit. The inner life of a prophet therefore balances on a hairline drawn taut between heaven and hell. Thus, the Baal Shem Tov was uncertain to the end of his life whether he would land in highest heaven or in deepest hell.

Romantic nationalism appears to be a modern recasting of the Biblical concept of prophet-people but, in actuality, it is a radical inversion of the heavenly ideal. Ends and means are subtly reversed, and the pretentious stance of the prophet takes the place of the substance of his message.

How penetrating was the insight of the cabalists when they maintained that the archetypal hierarchy set up by Satan parallels in every respect the one set up by God, except that the arrangement is reversed!

Whether it is Mickiewicz writing for the Poles, or Mazzini for the Italians or Fichte for the Germans or Dostoyevsky for the Russians, the emphasis is uniformly on the life of the people, on the assumption that its concrete prosperity will redound in a general way to the benefit of humanity in the abstract. The concept of a prophetic mission is employed not as the standard and measuring rod of the acts of the nation, but as a fig leaf hiding the nakedness of sheer national aggrandizement. And so clever is the camouflage on occasion that only the keenest analysis can separate prophetism from its Satanic counterpart.

At one and the same time, the romantic and prophetic conceptions of peoplehood burst upon the horizon of Russian Jewry. And the tension between these conceptions is the major theme of Hebrew literature from the time of Aḥad Ha'am and down to the present day.

VI

Aḥad Ha'am was looked upon by contemporaries and disciples as a veritable prophet, announcing a fresh revelation. Ḥayyim Naḥman Bialik articulated the feelings of all Hebraic intellectuals, when he wrote:

ותלויים באמצע בין שני המגנטים הללו

כל רגשות לבנו הסתומים אז נביא שאלו

נביא אמת, שיגע בצנור לבנו ויבא

וידליק מלמעלה, מעל לראשנו כוכבו.

ורוחו יהי המבוע לכל ההרהורים

הכבושים בהרבה לבבות כחלומות לא ברורים

ובעוד מבטנו בתוך הערפל תקוע

ובעוד אנו תועים, נואשים וקטני אמנה

מתמהמהים על פרשת דרכים ושואלים: אנה? —

וינצנץ כוכבך, מורנו, וברמז צנוע

קראנו מתוך הערפל וימשך אותנו —

ואל תחת כוכבך היחידי נזעקנו כלנו.

And suspended midway between these twain magnetic poles
The vague inchoate feelings of our heart then yearned for a prophet,
A true prophet who would touch the channels of our heart,
And kindle on high, above our heads his star,
His spirit becoming the fountain for ruminations
In many hearts hidden as dreams, vague aspirations.
While still toward the clouds our looks were fixed,
While still we wandered, desperate, disbelieving,
Loitering at crossroads, inquiring, "whither?"
Behold, your star appeared and modestly beckoned,
Calling and leading us out of the darkness,
And under your single star all of us were gathered.

Several writers maintain that Aḥad Ha'am regarded himself as the
modern incarnation of a Biblical prophet, standing at the crossroads
and pointing the way leading to salvation (*Aḥad Ha'am*, by Simon
and Heller, p. 97). While this assumption is unwarranted, we cannot
doubt that Aḥad Ha'am regarded the prophet as the ideal exponent
of the spirit of the nation. He founded the secret society of "Sons of
Moses," as an instrument for the revival of the prophetic ideal
of Jewish life and, in his essays, he wrote of the prophet as the one
who, in his search for absolute truth and justice, gives expression to
the underlying spirit of the people (*Navi Vekohen*). In keeping with
the prophetic and Ḥasidic tradition, Aḥad Ha'am stressed the
"inner Torah" (תורה שבלב) in contrast to the visible Torah of precepts
and commands, and insisted that spiritual redemption preceded, as
an indispensable condition, the redemption of the people. Like Isaiah,
too, Aḥad Ha'am argued for a return, not of all the people, but of
the chastened remnant. Like Jeremiah and Ezekiel, he looked forward
to the birth of a "new spirit" and a "new heart" in the land of Israel,

which will generate new ideals and life-giving forces throughout the Jewish Diaspora and among all men.

In striking contrast to the nationalists of his day, he recognized the marks of the prophetic spirit in the passionate devotion of the Talmudists and Medieval scholars to every detail of the Law. While he disapproved of the pedestrian piety of the Shulḥan Aruch, he saw in its very extremism proof of the continued vitality of the prophetic spirit. For the prophet is an ethical absolutist, unyielding and uncompromising.

But, the prophetic tone and message constituted only one side of the complex thought of this philosopher of Hebraic renaissance.

Actually, the philosophy of Aḥad Ha'am was a synthetic union of Hebraic prophetism and nationalistic romanticism. Like all the romantics, he maintained that the nation as a biological organism, (not the Torah) is the "tree of life" producing the ideals and ideas of its own peculiar kind, and giving good and ripe fruits only when the conditions of soil and climate are ideal. He even spoke of a "nationalistic pantheism," as if all things produced by the nation were holy (Teḥiyah and Beri'ah). His central emphasis on the building of a homeland, which would function as a "spiritual center" of world Jewry, is essentially romantic, i. e. — it operates with the image of Israel as a biological organism. Only in its own native soil can the tree of Israel strike roots, and only when the tree is healthy and secure will its fruits be ripe and life-giving. It is important to note that Aḥad Ha'am did not believe that any ideal presently conceivable could endow Jewish life in the Diaspora with the golden radiance of a supreme purpose. He criticized caustically the "mission-theory" of Reform, on the ground that the ideas of monotheism were in modern times the possession of mankind. But he advocated a "mission-theory" of his own, founded on the romantic principle of the essential unity of blood, soil and spirit. Out of the reconstituted homeland, a new ideal will emerge that will correspond to the instinctive character of the Jew, awaken the loyalties of the scattered people, who no longer believe in the Jewish faith, and also bring fresh vision to mankind. While the liberal rabbis of the West thought of the Jewish mission in terms of religious teachings presently understandable and available in classic formulations, Aḥad Ha'am thought of the "mission" as the emergence of a doctrine, presently inconceivable. And this fresh dawning of a new light will be made possible through the efforts of national rebirth. While the nature of the new ideal cannot now be foretold, we may safely assume that it will constitute a fresh embodiment of ethical absolutism, devoid of the mystical fetters of religion. For religion was to him, in his positivistic moods, both futile and outworn, the discarded "garments of exile." The "national spirit" needs fresh garments, and these will be found only in the national homeland. "For only where the national ideal was first created can we look for it again." In exile, "a living national idea, a great national ideal, cannot be created" (Introduction to second edition of first volume, *Al Parashath Derachim. Golah Venechar*, by Y. Kaufmann, IV volume, p. 370).

If Aḥad Ha'am had been only a romantic nationalist, he could not have awakened the quasi-religious fervor of the Zionist movement. To the pious sentiments of nationalism, he added the modernized conception of a prophet-people, blending the two so skillfully that they could hardly be told apart. Adopting the Reform-Conservative conception of "ethical monotheism" as the heritage of the prophets and the living kernel of the Jewish faith, Aḥad Ha'am carried the process of discrimination one step further, asserting that religious faith in its totality was the shell, of which the living kernel was the "national ethics." Loyalty to this ethical ideal is the first duty of a national Jew.

As to the nature of this ethical ideal, Aḥad Ha'am attempted to define it more than once. It was the spirit of absolute justice, perfectly abstract and unemotional, concerned with the welfare of the group as a whole, not with the happiness of the individual, and disposing society so as to produce from time to time "saints" that, like the Nietzschean "supermen," stand beyond "good and evil," beyond the ordinary rules of ordinary people.

Though he reiterated this formulation time and again, he remained dissatisfied. For well he knew first, that there was nothing Jewishly distinctive about any aspect of this formulation, and second, that other scholars had formulated Jewish ethics in exactly opposite terms.[8]

At this point, Aḥad Ha'am again had recourse to instinct. Jews know by instinct that their ethics is different. Scholars may define this difference in various ways, as they choose, but they are obliged to maintain that a deep and impassable gulf yawns between the ethical insights of Jews and gentiles. This obligation to believe in Jewish difference is a kind of "national imperative," a patriotic form of thinking. Thus, the romantic nationalist dogma of being somehow and essentially different was substituted for the dogmas of religion (*Aḥad Ha'am* by Aryeh Simon and Yoseph Eliyah Heller, p. 189).

The prophetic side of Aḥad Ha'am was manifested in his being

---

[8] Thus, S. D. Luzzatto regards the quality of pity as the essentially Jewish contribution to ethics, while Kant is the great expounder of ethics as absolute justice.

the first leading Zionist to recognize that Arabs too live in Israel, and that the early colonists were occasionally unjust in dealing with them (*ibid.*, p. 15). Along prophetic lines too, was his insistence on the need to choose for colonization in Palestine men and women of the highest idealism and moral integrity. This principle, only partially implemented, was doubtless instrumental in setting a high moral tone for the early pioneering colonies. A. D. Gordon's "religion of labor," expressing the mystical and devotional spirit of the self-sacrificing Ḥalutzim may be considered as a continuation of the prophetic phase of Aḥad Ha'am's philosophy. Productive labor takes the place of "mortification of the flesh" in mystical piety and the surrender of personal ambitions the place of the Biblical "we shall do and we shall listen." However, it was in the Hebrew University of Jerusalem that Aḥad Ha'am's moral heritage was most zealously guarded. And the greatest proponent of his prophetic ideal of "absolute justice" was a stranger from the West, a rabbi and a rebel, a man of peace who was always at war with the people he loved most, for he could see the ideal towering above them — Judah Leib Magnes.

In the progressive descent of the Zionist ideal from heaven to earth, it was Rabbi Magnes who for a full generation protested against the subversion of moral principles to the pressures of political expediency. While, in any study of modern Hebrew literature, the name of Magnes is not likely to be mentioned, his voice and personality cannot be ignored in any analysis of the struggles within the soul of the modern Jew. Amidst unparalleled desperation and against a rising tide of violence, he stood for the right, boldly and immoveably clinging to the prophetic banner at all costs. Round him, the remnants of a prophetic conscience in Israel were gathered, building up a claim on eternity for the Jew, more enduring than any army or any government. While patriots around him glibly employed the prophetic posture as a cover for the resurgence of "sacred, collective egoism," he cherished the soul of prophecy and nurtured it with his life's blood, even when like Jeremiah he was assailed as a traitor. (For Magnes' leadership and prophetic character, see Norman Bentwich's *For Zion's Sake*, chaps. 12, 13.)

VII

The brilliant essays of Aḥad Ha'am dominated the intellectual horizon of his generation. But, the prophetic hero-image which he recreated and imposed upon the substructure of romantic nationalism was not captured in its fulness by any one of the writers in modern

Hebrew literature. Once again, the dazzling vision illuminating the skies for a brief moment came crashing down to earth in fragments. The cabalists peered deeply into the tragic mystery of human nature when, in describing the process whereby a heavenly ideal is clothed in the flesh and blood of reality, they spoke of the "breaking of the vessels." For, as in the mid-eighteenth century, the prophetic vision was fragmentized in the post-Aḥad Ha'amist era, with only broken facets of it being found here and there.

Ḥayyim Naḥman Bialik believed himself to be a faithful disciple of Aḥad Ha'am. His wondrous poems of national resurgence betray the posture, tone, and pathos of a prophet. His earnestness was so overpowering that the Hebrew reading public did not resent his wrathful rebuke of the Jewish people for their defenselessness and passivity during the pogrom in Kishineff. His readers felt that the national poet spoke for the newly born sense of dignity in their own hearts. Seldom, in history, did a poet exert as much influence as Bialik did in the first decade of the twentieth century. (See Sh. Niger's introduction to the collection of Bialik's Yiddish poems.)

Several of his poems were written in conscious emulation of the style and stance of a prophet (his Hebrew poems, *Davar*, *Achen Gam Zeh Musar Elohim*, *Ḥozeh Lech Braḥ*; his Yiddish poems in *Lieder*, pp. 18, 19, 20). In his *Songs of Wrath*, he protests against God, in terms verging on the blasphemous, but in the spirit of one who finds it impossible to assume His indifference to human woe. Like Jeremiah, he pleads, "Righteous Thou art, O Lord, but judgment I shall speak with you" (Jer. 12.1), though unlike the ancient prophet, he fails to state his basic premise. As the poet of national continuity and rebirth, he both glorifies and lays to rest the ideal of the *Mathmid*, the hero-image of a bygone generation. For the guidance of his contemporaries, he recreates and transfigures the legend of the "Dead of the Desert," the heroes who dared defy Moses and God. Though they failed and perished, a magical aura of heroism pervades their camp and evokes the tribute of awed reverence from the wanderers of the wilderness. This glorification of the impatient rebels against the authority of Moses was intended to inspire a similar rebelliousness in his own day against the spirit of pious resignation to the Will of God. The message of the poem is a call for the substitution of aggressive force for quiescent piety. Thus, the dead, momentarily revived in a storm, shout

We who are heroes,   אנחנו גבורים!

Last of the enslaved and first of   דור אחרון לשעבוד וראשון לגאולה

   the redeemed are we!   אנחנו!

Our hand alone, our mighty
hand,

ידנו לבדה, ידנו החזקה

From our proud neck the heavy
yoke hath removed.

את כבד העול מעל גאון צוארנו פרקה

But, the spirit of rebelliousness is tempered by the feeling of belonging inescapably in the entourage of the Shechinah. The poet sees the Divine cause as being nearly defeated and deserted, but he remains with God even if only to bemoan the tragedy and to lament over the desolation of His Kingdom (*Al Saf Beth Hamidrash Hayashan* and *Levadi*). The cause of God may suffer temporary setbacks. The Almighty, as it were, may be "wounded," but He cannot be defeated (*Yadati Beleil Arafel* and *Lo Timaḥ Bimherah Dime'athi*).

Within the soul of Bialik the earthly spirit of romantic nationalism vied for supremacy against a genuine spark of prophetism. This titanic struggle within him, he represented symbolically in the beautiful prose-poem, *Megillath Ha'esh*. The young refugee from Jerusalem is torn between two fiery forces, the one deriving from the last flicker of holy fire on the altar of the Temple, the other issuing out of the subterranean black flames of hell. With this titanic turmoil in his restless soul, the young hero wanders disconsolately, unable to achieve inner harmony and peace.

Bialik failed to represent the prophetic vision in its fulness, chiefly because he did not rise above the immediate, national needs of his people and did not glimpse the human and the universal vistas of existence. In his poem, *Be'ir Haharegah*, he does not attempt to look beyond the horrors of the pogroms to the people that perpetrated them. To him, the rioters were simply inhuman beasts. He fails to take note of the tragic conflict of ideas, the whirl of interests, malice and misunderstanding that led to the slaughter. In the "Dead of the Desert," he ascribes the defeat of the defiant rebels to God, not to the Canaanites, defending their homes, while the exodus from Egypt he attributes to the "strong hand" of the Israelites, thereby reversing the order of explanations in the Torah. For him, the Canaanites (read: Arabs) did not exist. Though he sensed the prophetic hunger for inner purity in the sight of God (see especially his poem, *Ḥalfah 'al Panai*), he lacked the prophetic passion for universal ideals and the moral strength to behold mankind as a whole.

In Saul Tchernichovski, we encounter Bialik's rebelliousness without the latter's firm faith in and reverence for tradition. Like that lonely rebel of the Mishnah, Elisha, son of Abuya, Tchernichovski knows the Jewish hero-image and rebels against it. In behalf of his people, the poet apologizes to the Greek god, Apollo (*Lenochaḥ*

Pessel Apollo), for the sin of rejecting "the light of life" and the crime of binding with thongs of *Tefillin* the primitive impulses of the flesh. In contrast to the enfeebling piety of the true prophets, he extols the unabashed love of life of the so-called "false prophets." Above the (*Meḥezyonoth Nevi Hasheker*) crown of Torah and heroism, he sets the crown of beauty (*Sheloshah Ketharim*). In his version of Dinah's parting words, he reverses the scale of values in the Blessing of Jacob (*Parashath Dinah*), praising natural vengefulness and raw courage rather than quietude, ethical principle, and moral restraint.

In the massive writings of M. J. Berdichevski, the spirit of rebellion against the prophetic hero-image is given poignant and moving expression. Yet, in his passionate avowal of the supreme worth of the individual, we can hear a distinct echo of the prophetic voice. Since Aḥad Ha'am attributed to prophetism an exclusive concern with the community, Berdichevski believed his own emphasis on individuality to be a revolt against the tradition of Hebrew prophecy. Actually, the reverse was true. The Hebrew prophets rejected the totalitarian tendency of paganism, insisting on the responsibility of the individual, the supremacy of the ethical imperative, the sole rightness of the "still, small voice" of conscience, the substitution of the holy remnant for the holy people and the duty to oppose the national interest in the Name of God. Deeply steeped in the mystic lore of Ḥasidism, Berdichevski centered attention on the direct bond between man and God. By arguing for the fulness of the life of the individual, he, for all his avowed rebelliousness, articulated a genuine prophetic demand. In all his writings, one senses the horror and mystery of "the hound of heaven" theme. He rebels against "monotheism," against Judaism, against "spirit," against "the book"; but, even when he strikes the pose of a "blonde beast," he remains inescapably a man of the book and a son of the prophets. His heroes find themselves held fast by the chains of Israel's peculiar, prophetic destiny, even when they set out boldly to act the part of Nietzschean "supermen."

Another broken fragment of the prophetic soul, we find incarnated in the writings of J. H. Brenner, who combined supreme emphasis on the free individual with the ideals of socialism. In addition to its inherent apocalyptic elements, socialism hit Jewish youth with the impact of a pseudo-messianic movement, promising the glory of regeneration through identification with the proletariat. All that is ugly and unworthy in Jewish life will be magically transmuted, all problems will be solved, all yearnings will be stilled. For the "national theology" of Brenner and his fellow-ideologists of the Histadruth, socialism spelled inner and outer redemption. "The new Hebrew individual of our generation enters with but one simple word on his lips — 'labor' " (*Baḥayim Uvasafruth*, Vol. VI, p. 325). The magic of labor will cleanse the Jewish soul of its "sin" and of its "shame," incurred through centuries of a capitalistic life in "exile" (*Golah Venechar*, vol IV, p. 408).

Labor assumed a quasi-messianic guise in the life and literature of the new Israel, and the Ḥalutz, with open blouse and khaki pants, spade in hand and song at heart, was its forerunner. The intellectual who, surrendering individual ambitions and the modern cult of success, bows his back to the unyielding soil and sacrifices the joys of privacy to the rigors of communal discipline is the hero of the "religion of labor." Originally, Tolstoyan in inspiration, the new "man with the hoe" became the bearer of the promise of national rebirth and fulfilment. His renunciation of bourgeois comforts offered a psychological equivalent to the saints' fasting and ascetic exercises, the prophet's escape into the wilderness, the artist's retreat to the garret and the knight's donning of his heavy armor. "This love of Zion movement is to embrace all the parts of the nation that are capable of repenting of the sins of exile and to accept the penance of labor" (Quoted from Brenner in Fichman's *Lashon Vasefer*, vol. V. p. 69).

Still another tattered shred of the prophetic soul is incarnated in the muscular verse of Uri Zevi Greenberg, the favorite poet of the Revisionists. Greenberg mourns over the fate of Hitler's victims, calling for bloody vengeance. He evokes the saintly figure of Levi Yitzḥak which, brooding over the devastation wrought by the Nazis, gives up prayer and demands revenge. For him, "the nations," all mankind with hardly a significant distinction, is embraced in one category. And Israel, the "holy people" is the perpetual victim of "the nations" (*Rehovoth Hanahar*, pp. 169; 291). In the ardor of longing for national dignity and power, Greenberg attains lyrical climaxes of purest chauvinism,

אין טהורים לשלטון מהיהודים, אין יפים מהם בעולם!
אין אצילים, עמוקים, נגוניים, ואין גבורים וננהים מהם בגויים!
אין ראויים מהם לשאת על קדקד כתר מלכות בעולם.

(*Rehovot HaNahar*, p. 165)

None are purer for dominion than Jews, none more beautiful
None nobler or deeper among the nations, more heroic, melo-
        dious or brighter,
Not one in the world more worthy of carrying a kingly crown.

74 INTERPRETING THE PROPHETIC TRADITION

The saintly figure of the Berdichever Rebbe, Levi Yitzḥak, is utilized by another great poet, Jacob Cohen, for the purpose of symbolizing the rejection of the prophetic mission for the Jewish people. The poet makes use of the legend concerning the ten martyrs, who learned that their death was decreed by God Himself. If they cry out against this decree, the Lord will return the world to chaos. The ten martyrs accept God's Will and do not protest. They know that up in heaven the Archangel Michael offers the souls of saints in sacrifice in order that the Divine Purpose may be fulfilled. The poet knows that the prophets have taught the Jews to look upon themselves as the suffering servants of the Lord, the "martyr race," who bear upon their pain-racked backs the sins of mankind. But, he also knows that, in his generation, the ten martyrs have grown into a vast mass of nearly six million hapless victims of the Satanic rebellion against the Divine Kingdom. Levi Yitzḥak, the loving advocate of Israel, is prepared to utter that "third cry" which might turn the world into chaos. For even chaos is preferable to so colossal a crime (*Modern Hebrew Literature* by S. Halkin p. 135).

In Greenberg's verses, rebellion against the prophetic spirit attains its acme. The garments of the prophet-people are still worn by Israel, but only as drapery and disguise for the newly raised national flag.

The anti-prophetic outbursts of Greenberg can hardly be matched in recent Hebraic literature. However, he is by no means alone in his endeavor to substitute resurgent nationalism for the ancient faith. Significant is this final verse in the popular poem by the recently deceased David Shimoni:

> And in this dreadful darkness, in this darkest of all nights,
> Let our exultant song go up out of the night:
> "Hear, O Israel: Israel is our fate, Israel is One."

In the last line, the most fundamental assertion of Jewish faith by prophets and martyrs of all ages and climes is transformed into a slogan of national unity. Israel takes the place of God in the Scriptural declaration of faith (Deut. 6.4).

A glowing spark of the prophetic flame shines out of the mystical writings of Chief Rabbi Kuk. While the fulness of prophetic stature cannot be ascribed to this gentle saint, since he lacked a clear comprehension of reality, a genuine vision of mankind and a deep appreciation of its universal values, we can see in him the man who lives in "two-aloneness" with God. The prophets were more than mystics; for, disdaining to speak of their intimate feelings, they concentrated on bringing the Divine message to mankind. The Jewish literary tradition, following the example of the prophets, discouraged any descriptions of the ineffable ecstasies of mystical delight and terror. In Kuk's writings, this literary genre makes its appearance. (For examples, see *Banner of Jerusalem*, Bloch, 1946.) A charming note of freshness pervades his poetry in prose, reflecting a remarkable synthesis of Hasidic mysticism and Western romanticism. Perhaps, the central message of his books is best conveyed by the motto which he coined, "the old shall be renewed, the new shall be sanctified."

Motifs of religious mysticism occur frequently in the Hebraic poetry of our generation, reflecting the unspoken yearning of the Jewish soul for the reconstruction of its prophetic hero-image. The union of people and land inevitably makes the storied characters of the Hebrew Bible take on the vividness of flesh and blood. The great theme of our Holy Scriptures, the eternal dialogue between man and God, becomes inescapably the fundamental theme of Hebrew literature. Though we have now scarcely passed beyond the threshold of the new Israel, we can already discern beautiful expressions of longing for the wholeness of the Jewish soul through its service of God.

Abraham Shlonsky expresses the inchoate, vague piety of a whole generation in this hymn to labor in the new land:

> Clothe me, purest of mothers, in the resplendent coat of many colors.
> And lead me to toil at dawn.
> My land wraps itself in light as in the prayer-shawl.
> New homes stand forth as do phylacteries.
> And like phylactery-bands, the highways, built by Jewish hands, glide.
> Thus, a town beautiful recites the morning prayer to its Creator.
>
> (From *Modern Hebrew Literature*, p. 205 by S. Halkin.)

Except among the Orthodox writers, who are separated from the rest of the population by a forbidding barrier of dogma, the sense of dedication to high ideals is still restrained by the rebelliousness of the preceding generation. The literary world of Israel has not yet experienced the stirring phenomenon of the return of the "third generation" to the spiritual wellsprings which were repudiated by the second generation of immigrants. The contrast between two poetic treatments of the same theme is instructive. Richard Beer-Hofmann, living in Vienna, celebrated the wondrous destiny of the Jewish people in the hauntingly beautiful, dramatic poem, *Jaakob's Traum*. Jacob is warned by Satan that his children will be "chosen" for untold agonies

and be marked for lonely wretchedness, if they should accept the
proffered Divine mission to be "a prophet unto the nations." Yet
Jacob in full realization of the immensity of the price and the multitude
of yawning pitfalls, accepts the Divine command, even as every poet
and every great man accepts the obligations implied in the insights
granted to him. Yitzḥak Lamdan, expressing the spirit of a sadder
generation, makes Jacob protest against the imposition of a yoke
which deadened his senses to the joy of life and made him an orphan
among the nations:

But now heavy are the heavens of a sudden;	ועתה כבדו שמים עלי ראשי פתאם
The soil burns my soles, till they hurt;	האדמה תלהט רגלי, תכון עדי כאב,
Like a serpent biting heels, every path in it and trail.	כל נתיב בה ומשעל — כנחש ישך עקב
Uplifted with bigness I awoke and bowed down by fear and orphanhood.	הקיצותי זקוף גדולות וכפוף יראה ויתם.

In Lamdan's version, Jacob is quite willing to accept a revelation
of God in nature, but not a special human task that will set him
apart and single him out.

> Let me be! I will not be dragged perforce any more
> To the gallows of thy love, O Lover and Seducer!
> As one, the only chosen one, I am called to thee,
> And by the time I come — I am misshapen — crippled;
> "Jacob, Jacob!" No I will not come and listen,
> And be once more scorned of man, yet beloved of God.
>   If you have some matter to impart to me, a great and
>   precious matter of love —
> Stretch it at my feet as a verdant carpet of spring;
> Light it up over my head as a blazing morning-rose.
> Let its music sing in a myriad voices that all, that all, may
>   hear:
> Bejewel it with thy stars at night; thy sun by day,
> And let the butterflies of all the world frolic with it.
>   (S. Halkin, *Modern Hebrew Literature*)

But even when the prophetic mission is repudiated, its haunting
spell remains pervasive and powerful. The peculiar tragedies of
Jewish history hammer home the realization that, bereft of the
prophetic garb, we stand before the world naked and shamed. Caught

in the serpentine coils of romantic nationalism, the prophetic vision may be perverted, but not utterly dissipated.

The dramatic poet, Matithyahu Shoham, recreates the image of the prophet Elijah. Addressing the dying King Ahab, who was sincerely devoted to the military greatness of the Northern Kingdom, Elijah says, "Forgive me, my king, but the Lord has led me far beyond the boundaries of your Kingdom." Contrasting Ahab's vision of national power with the prophetic vision of Israel's true greatness, the poet asserts:

נתבענו לנצחון	We are called to triumph, as a nation
מאדם ואלהים, לפדות נשבענו;	within man and before God, sworn to salvation.
וארור כל מתחמק, כל הכופר	And cursed be all who sneak away, all who deny
בטהר ראשית ובגאולת אחרית.	Pristine purity and ultimate redemption.
מי נבהל לב בנביאי עמים ישא	Let the panicky prophets of other nations
חזון המנוסה — לנו	preach their counsels of escape for us
דבר הגאון	the word of greatness,
לדורות אדם על אדמות.	for the generations of man on earth.

(*Zor and Yerusholaim* by M. Shoham)

VIII

Our survey of the prophetic image in modern Hebrew literature ends on a mixed note, trembling uncertainly between the haunting spell of the ancient vision and its rejection in whole or in part. The debris of the mighty Biblical figure lie littered in all directions, but its organic unity is lost. And the voices of anti-prophetism are as loud in the land as the scattered echoes of prophecy.

Since literature is the mirror of life, we can hardly expect any other result. For, the world-wide mass movement of Zionism, which revived Hebraic literature and created the state of Israel, was compounded of two spiritually contending forces — the one quasi-prophetic in nature, the other, opposing and contradicting it. Also, the mentality of those Jews who aimed to root themselves heart and soul in the lands of the Diaspora was similarly compounded of the same opposing forces.

Within Zionism, the heritage of Aḥad Ha'am was opposed by the "realists" who thought of the goal of the movement as the attainment by Jews of "normalcy," so as to become "like unto the other nations." A stateless people takes on the aspect of a ghost, evoking fear and hatred from the naïve masses. To become "normal" once again, the Jews should learn to fight for the things of this world and give up all pretensions to the mission of prophecy which made of them a "peculiar people." The one cure of all afflictions consisted in the dissociation, clean and complete, between people and prophecy, between the nation and its faith. In the land of Israel, the people would attain earthly salvation by ceasing to strive for heavenly bliss and by arising to confront the world as just another secular nation. The world refused to honor the people with the Book; they will be forced to respect the people with the sword. This anti-prophetic mood was obscured at times by the ambiguous verbiage of romantic nationalism, which tended to employ the prophetic posture and occasionally to use its central symbols though with opposite intent. Self-glorification and self-sanctification, to the point where the nation takes the place of God is altogether in keeping with the "sacred egoism" of modern nationalism. And, of the subtle seduction of this malady of the spirit, both life and literature offer ample substantiation.

In Diaspora Judaism, too, we recognize a similar tension between prophetism and rebellion against the Divine mission. On the one hand, the ideologists of classical Reform and Conservatism recreated the image of the prophet as the protagonist of "ethical monotheism," proclaiming its "eternal verities" unto mankind. On the other hand, Zionist critics were not altogether off the mark in pointing to the assimilationist trends within modern Judaism. For, it cannot be denied that this domain shades off gradually into the no man's land of indifferentism and ultimate disappearance. A liberal faith does not delimit itself by rigid boundaries and does not impose sanctions upon its marginal adherents. Hence, the outside boundaries of its following are not defined. Conversionist assimilation blends insensibly into its opposite, prophetic Judaism, and the two forces are interlocked in an embrace which is also an unending struggle. In the Diaspora, it is not the group as a whole, but many an individual who seeks the Nirvana of "normalcy" by dissociating himself from the faith and destiny of the Jewish people. These seekers of oblivion employ the symbols and banners of prophetic religion, though their purpose is to reduce Jewish loyalty to the minimum. And the tensions of Diaspora

Judaism are, of course, sensed and interpreted by the Hebrew writers in Israel.

If we hazard a guess concerning the future, it is this very contact between Hebrew literature and Jewish life in the Diaspora that leads us to foresee the possibility of a revival of the prophetic image in Israel. Twice in the period of two centuries, the vision of prophecy was recreated through the stimulating influence of an outside cultural force. Humanism in Italy helped to produce the peculiar genius of Luzzatto, and Nineteenth Century rationalism brought into being the philosophy of modern Judaism. May it not be that the same event will be repeated once again, the re-emergence of prophetism in the Diaspora being followed by a corresponding resurgence of the prophetic image in the literature of modern Israel?

Two factors appear to make for such a revival. First, to recapture the synoptic vision of prophecy is indispensable for the very life of the Jewish community. Without the dynamism of a supreme purpose, that is universal in scope and transcendent in quality, the Jewish community cannot long continue to thrive. Second, the overwhelming majority of Diaspora Jewry reside in America, where the spell of romantic nationalism, that Satanic counterpart of prophetism, is bound to become progressively weaker. America is the classic land of liberal statism as Germany was the classic land of romantic nationalism. Furthermore, American culture is more hospitably disposed toward the Hebraic prophetic image than toward the competing images of saint or mystic, artist or philosopher. In this land, there is no conflict between Judaism conceived in prophetic terms and Americanism interpreted in the light of its prophetic tradition. Hence, the prophetic miracle is, to say the least, a possibility in this country — the miracle of being so authentically true to one's own being as to reflect at the same time the soul of mankind.[9]

If American Judaism rises to the magnificent challenge of its time and circumstance, modern Hebrew literature will be sensitized to discriminate between the stance of prophecy and its substance, between the allurements of romanticism and the call of God.

In the world-wide struggle of the Jewish soul to recapture its heroic vision, the decisive engagement is being fought here and now.

---

[9] However, the prophetic spirit is here held down chiefly by the dead weight of "crowd psychology," that crushes all idealistic efforts. When the several hero-images fail to inspire and to evoke emulation, the fickle mob with its tinsel idols achieves predominance, so that popularity takes the place of moral authority, conformity the place of rightness, the statistical Mr. Average the place of the ideal hero.

It will not do for us to imagine that the prophetic fire is rekindled in us automatically the moment we recount the achievements of the prophets of old. Salvation is not "over there," in the past, all packaged and ready. We are not the proud custodians of "eternal verities" unavailable to others, but only the humble seekers of a Divine mystery that is never fully grasped. The genius of prophecy may be described, the mantle of prophecy may be institutionalized, but the spirit of prophecy cannot be manufactured at will. In keeping with the cabalistic ideal of gathering the scattered sparks of divinity, we should aim at that synoptic vision that is always being built but that is never completed. We cannot claim to be among those who know all about God, but we can proclaim the supreme virtue of the unending quest. Let our motto be, "Those who seek the Lord shall not lack ought that is good" (Ps. 34.10).

Nor will it do for us to await complacently the rebirth of a new prophetic vision in the land of Israel on the romantic assumption that prophecy is like the fruit of a tree, ripening best in its own native climate. Salvation again is not "over there," in the storied rocks and freshly poured cement of Israel. Always and everywhere, salvation comes from within, consisting in the sparks that fly when the hammer of God beats upon the anvil of the soul.

PROPHETS AND PHILOSOPHERS:
THE SCANDAL OF PROPHECY

Lou H. Silberman

Hillel Professor of Jewish Literature and Thought
Vanderbilt University

THE GOLDENSON LECTURE OF 1958

℘HE POINT OF DEPARTURE FOR THIS PAPER is the postscript of a letter written by a distinguished British theologian who is at the same time personally and deeply involved in the current day to day political life of the British Isles. He wrote: "My puzzle: as a minister of religion I used (with what terror of heart) to say 'thus saith the Lord;' as politician (with a light heart) I say 'I think.' But the true prophet giving his political message could say *Koh 'amar 'Adonai*. Have you light on that?" Fortunately, he did not ask for an answer to his question, but only some light on it. Thus can I avoid the sin and danger of presumption, speaking to the matter without the necessity of pontificating or absolutizing. I mean to take the puzzlement seriously, in the serious meaning of that word, for its real intent is, of course, what do we mean when we say prophet? what is prophecy?

The justification for such an inquiry, or rather for indicating that there is need for the inquiry, is quite the same as that offered by Leo Strauss at the beginning of his essay "How to Study Spinoza's Theologico-Political Treatise." There he wrote, "A glance at the present scene is sufficient to show one that the issue [belief in revelation] which, until a short while ago was generally believed to have been settled by Spinoza's nineteenth-century successors once and for all, and thus to be obsolete, is again approaching the center of attention." He goes on to say, however, "The issue raised by the conflicting claims of philosophy and revelation is discussed in our time at a decidedly lower level than was customary in former ages."[1] Indeed, one may add, most philosophers refuse to take revelation seriously, while confessional theologians find in philosophy the flower and fruit of sinful pride. For both, prophecy, as another way of defining revelation, is a scandal. For the latter it is the stumbling block on which proud human reason falls; for the former, an offense to reason which must be thrust down and demolished again and again.

But do these antagonists have the last word? May not Emil Fackenheim's suggestion point toward a more creative situation? "If man's concern with the divine is perennial, and if it is at least in part rational, then what is needed in our time is renewal and rejuvenation."[2]

Beyond, however, the warrant of our own needs, we recognize an enduring tradition which, if it does not offer us a made-to-order answer for our puzzlement, at least makes clear that our striving is not necessarily foolish or blasphemous. In a sense the attempt to understand prophecy is coexistent with the phenomenon (a necessary weasel word) itself. To seek to understand is to philosophize, that is, to bring reason to bear upon the object at hand. The crescendo of Amos' argument from effect to cause in Chapter III, while indeed "no mere general disquisition on this oft-discussed philosophic question," as Dr. Morgenstern has pointed out,[3] is a justification of the prophet's words by indicating the naturalness of prophecy, of its understandability side by side with other understandable events. Even Jeremiah's agonizing,

"Thou, O God, hast enthralled me, and I am enthralled,"

echoes his understanding of the situation of prophet and prophecy; an understanding not to be thought of as part of a system yet, nonetheless, a philosophy of prophecy in a real although rudimentary sense.

It would be unwise to belabor this point and thus prove more than can be demonstrated. Philosophy as a discipline belongs to a realm of experience and thought at a distance from the Bible, but so saying does not exclude from its pages philosophy as a seeking-to-understand.

The same is true of the rabbinic world. The imposition of philosophic abstraction is not only an ever present danger but constantly distorts meanings even in the hands of those whose devotion to the tradition is unquestioned. Yet even among those so cavalierly lumped together as "the Rabbis," the attempt to understand prophecy was not absent. The very discussion of the requisites for the prophetic gift, both personal: "The Holy One, blessed be He, causes His Divine presence to rest only upon him who is strong, wealthy, wise and meek;" and communal: "There is one amongst you who is worthy that the Shekinah should rest on him as it did on Moses, but this generation did not merit it," points clearly to the fact that in part, at least, prophecy was comprehensible by reason. It could to some degree be understood.[4]

What was tentative and anticipatory in the Bible and rabbinic writings, became one of the great themes of medieval thought. Human reason, daughter of Olympian Zeus, found shelter in the tents of the children of Shem. Philosophy not merely as understanding but as discipline and system soon was at home in Islam and Israel. So widely and so imperiously did philosophy hold sway and so far-reaching were its demands that Abu'l Ala could write: "Moslems,

Jews, Christians and Magians, they are all walking in error and darkness. There are only two kinds of people left in the world. The one group is intelligent, but lacking in faith. The other has faith but is lacking in intelligence." To which Saadya Gaon sadly echoed, "I saw in my time many of the believers clinging to unsound doctrine and mistaken beliefs, while many of those who deny the faith boast of their un-belief and despise men of truth . . ."[5]

It was to the support of sound doctrine (*Emunot*) that Saadya brought rational demonstration (*De'ot*). They were, he held, not adversaries but sisters whose misunderstandings and falling-out were engendered by the human will, im-patient and frail. Indeed, said Saadya, reason confirms not only the content of revelation but revelation itself. Even the rational laws *halakhot sikhliot* as contrasted with the *shim'iot* (those matters on which reason has no judgment) point to the necessity of revelation. Not only does revelation fill in the details that are beyond the scope of reason—which deals only with the general—but it is made necessary by the very nature of the Creator. Revelation exhibits God's grace, for it enables man to serve Him even before reason has discovered the true pattern of human behaviour. Further, Saadya suggests, revelation provides the means by which God may bestow upon man that reward which is deserved through obedience.[6] Actually the question of revela-tion and prophecy as such is not central to Saadya's thought but is clearly ancillary to his discussion of the divine nature, and serves particularly as justification for God's justice.[7] In this sense prophecy in *Emunot v' De'ot* seems to be a dialectic necessity rather than an obdurate fact. Its reality is less palpable than the historical concreteness it possesses, for ex-ample, in Judah ha-Levi's thought.

Here indeed one faces the paradox that the medieval theologian who may be called the most confessional, the most antagonistic to the claims of rationalistic philosophy, provides a most elaborate interpretation of the phenomenon of prophecy. Far from insisting upon revelation and prophecy as mysteries beyond the approach of understanding, ha-Levi argues their naturalness and comprehensibility in terms of what may be called philosophic biology. Basing himself squarely upon medieval biological concepts, ha-Levi challenges the philosophers to explain the actuality of religion. Against the claims of philosophy as adumbrated at the very beginning of the *Kuzari* that "the highest grade of humanity (the prophet) is attained by the perfection of our spiritual powers and that therefore philosophical training brings us to it," ha-Levi retorts witheringly through the king of the Khazars. ". . . one might expect the gift of prophecy to be quite common among philosophers, considering their deeds, their knowledge, their researches after truth, their exertions and their close connection with things spiritual; one might expect that wonders, miracles, and extra-ordinary things would be reported of them. Yet we find that true visions are granted to persons who do not devote themselves to study or purification of their soul. This proves that between Divine power and the soul are secret relations which are not identical with those thou mentionest, O Philosopher!"[8]

But this rejection of the claims of rationalistic philosophy is not meant to suggest that prophecy cannot be understood. It is the direct relation of God to a natural species, the *homo religiosus*. It is made possible by a native endowment, the form of the species *ha'inyan ha-elohi* which enables man, when God so wills, to "see" those "temporary visible manifestations created by God during the process of His communication with men." This openness to divine influence possessed by one species only, stands at the summit of creation. It is, to use David Neumark's phrase, "the fifth kingdom of being." It is, however, only the ultimate expression of the divine activity at every level of being. ". . . even the highest life is still life, indeed life in intensified form and subject to the same laws as all other life . . ." "Thus belief in the reality of the facts of religion in no way requires of us a 'sacrificium intellectus;' the miracle that came to light in its lowest form of development in plant life becomes more and more apparent as it passes through the animal to the human and thence to the prophetic life; but the domination in the highest spheres of the same laws as were seen to govern in the lower realms of life is consistent with the analogical schools of thought and is corroborated by the testimony of history."[9]

The actual appearance or non-appearance of prophecy can be explained—from the human side—in biological terms. It is a recessive characteristic whose manifestation requires both proper environment—the land of Israel—and proper nurture — not philosophic contemplation, but observance of Israel's religious duties. Thus prophecy is, for ha-Levi, susceptible of rational understanding, although it is not reason's off-spring. Its actuality is demonstrated by the intersection of history and biology. The former exhibits it; the latter explains its appearance.[10]

It is in Maimonides, however, that the philosophic attempt to understand prophecy reaches its most subtle climax. Both Diesendruck and Strauss argue that it is a central theme in the Moreh Nebukhim; and more, that it is not, as some have claimed, a mere "inadequate presentation of a long-held theory." The broad sweep and the closely argued details of this Maimonidean prophetology as elaborated with varying emphases and interpretations by the scholars just mentioned, and quite beyond the areas of sharp disagreement between them, provides an intellectual joy that is not always the reward for submitting to scholars' demands.[11] Nonetheless, it is not to a delineation of the theory of prophecy that we turn our attention but to Maimonides' insistence that revelation itself calls man to philosophize and the reciprocal insistence that philosophy provides revelation's certainty. Strauss puts this succinctly: "Revelation itself summons those men suitable for the task to philosophize. The divine law itself commands philosophizing. Free philosophizing based on this authorization, takes all that is as its object. Revelation as the Law given by God through a prophet becomes the object of philosophy in prophetology." And further and most crucially: "Were revelation *merely* a miraculous act of God it would be entirely beyond man's comprehension. Revelation is then understandable only insofar as God's act occurs by means of intermediaries, taking place in creation, in created *nature*. In order *fully* to be understandable it must be plainly a *natural* fact. The means used by God in the act of revelation is the prophet, i.e., an unusual and superior human being, but nonetheless a *human being*. Philosophical understanding of revelation, philosophical confirmation of revelation is thus the elucidation of prophecy from the *nature of man*."[12]

As long as the reality of prophecy, of revelation, was the situation in which he stood, the philosopher was free or perhaps even more, was required to philosophize. The philosophers in an age of belief, says Strauss, "justified their philosophy before the forum of the Law; they derived

from the Law's authorization to philosophize, the duty to
do so." But their world was torn asunder. Spinoza, among
others, ground away at the foundations of revelation and
brought its structure down in ruins.[13]

The attack was two-fold. On the one hand, the documents taken as the objective statement, the content and form
of revelation, were subjected to such critical literary analysis
that the claims made on their behalf could not be upheld
with any real intellectual assurance. On the other hand,
the very idea of revelation as argued by the medieval
philosophers, the very "philosophische Begruendung des
Gesetzes," was attacked by the new philosophical positions
emerging in the seventeenth and eighteenth centuries. In
the face of the attack, the scholastic system of Jewish
philosophy collapsed, with no new synthesis to take its
place. Guttmann comments concerning Jewish participation
in the European philosophic enterprise from the eighteenth
century onward: "The predominant part of this philosophical
endeavor had no connection with Judaism as such . . . The
sphere of Jewish existence encompassed the religious in the
narrow and particularist sense from which all other spiritual
concerns and with them philosophy were excluded."[14] Moses
Mendelssohn's philosophy of reason clearly moves along
lines laid out by European thought, and revelation is saved
by him at the expense of its universal meaning. For Mendelssohn, religion, true religion, is the same everywhere and
for all men. It cannot be dependent upon an act of revelation. Judaism is, therefore, not revealed religion but revealed
law. The Bible is for him somewhat as for Spinoza a political
document governing the life of the Jewish community; at
most its laws "allude to or are undergirded by the eternal
truths of reason or they recall and stimulate thought about

such." As Guttmann puts it: "Thus the two worlds in which Mendelssohn lived are joined together. Through faith he belonged to the universal religion of reason; through observance of the ceremonial laws, to the Jewish community." That they were no more than juxtaposed, despite Mendelssohn's endeavor to bring them together in theory as well as act, seems a tragic truth lived out in his own family.[15]

From this point onward, for the most part, the entire meaning of revelation and prophecy underwent a radical revision. As Fackenheim says: "Religion is no longer understood as the attempt of man to relate himself to a God outside himself. It is a self-transformation of finite into infinite spirit . . ."[16] Thus in the thought of Solomon Formstecher, historical revelation is the coming to self-consciousness in man of the ideal of his spiritual life. "At first as in prophecy man's spirit does not realize that it has its content within and so assumes that it comes from without, that it is something objectively given. But at last, after passing through intermediary stages in which truth is transmuted from the stage of objectivity to that of subjectivity, the spirit recognizes that it is in itself the bearer of truth, that the objective fixing of prophetic revelation is but a preliminary stage in the movement toward subjectivity." Thus for Formstecher, "revelation is but an hypostasis of the immanent processes of knowledge, to be recognized by mature self-knowledge as the product of the human spirit."[17]

But Formstecher and with him Samuel Hirsch raised solitary voices on behalf of a philosophic justification of Judaism as the true disclosure of the movement of the spirit. The only other writer who took the task seriously, although diametrically opposed to their formulations, Solomon Ludwig Steinheim, was rewarded for his insistence on revelation as a "divine communication made to mankind in a once and for all event at a particular time" with the epithet "free-thinker" in the Jewish Encyclopedia.[18]

For the nineteenth century it was a self-evident fact rooted in a union of Kantian philosophy and historical evolutionism that *Das Wesen des Judentums* was the purest and most complete formulation in history of the universal truth of the ethical faith of reason. This self-congratulatory assumption made "any further philosophical analysis and justification of Judaism unnecessary."[19] Jewish history took philosophy's place and demonstrated over and over again to its own satisfaction that this assertion was true. That this required radical judgment on many elements of the Jewish past was inevitable, but the task was faced boldly and such embarrassing movements as Kabbalah and Hasidism were treated clinically, although at times passionately, as aberrations and pathological formations whose existence impeded but did not hinder the course of rationality.[20] Even the fading away of certainty about the exact nature of the religion of reason has not shaken this self-assurance. That it is possible to assert the complete congruence of Judaism with any and every philosophical or non-philosophical or anti-philosophical position is a basic postulate of contemporary Jewish discussion. It needs only to be proclaimed and provided with a few well-chosen proof texts to sweep the field and win the day.

It was to the remedy and repair of this ultimately self-denying situation that Hermann Cohen, dominant spirit of the Marburg neo-Kantian school, devoted his continuing effort, culminating in his posthumous work *Religion der Vernunft aus den Quellen des Judentums*. Here are no bland assumptions, no fatuous claims, but rigorous and demanding analysis. The lofty structure of a reformed and revitalized Kantian epistemology is offered as the dwelling place of prophetic Judaism. It is not necessary for our purpose to attempt a description of this vast and soul-stirring enterprise; what is required is the recognition in and through it that one cannot be satisfied with mere words, but needs, desperately needs, meaning. Whether or not one accepts as his meaning the crucial sentence: "This eternal (law) which is reason's basis for its own content is called revelation by the Jew,"[21] is in our context immaterial. What is of concern is Cohen's undeviating perception that such a word has a meaning, which meaning is determined by its larger context. Thus one finds within this work the continual and unflagging attempt to demonstrate what indeed such meanings are. Prophecy as the proclamation and working out of the meaning of correlation between God and man, as these terms are understood philosophically, conveys to him who is willing to take the matter seriously, a real content. If in the end the effort failed, it was not out of philosophic incompetence nor religious indifference. Cohen took his task to heart; indeed, he went far beyond the demands of his system and sought a place and a meaning for religion within it. What actually happened was that in the end faith conquered philosophy, but not without philosophy's earnest challenge. Thus we are not liberated from our task but thrust back into the midst of the problem.

The conclusion to be drawn from this noble attempt which began with reason alone and unaided is that revelation and prophecy are more than the heroic strategems of the human spirit to personalize the abstract system of rational thought. They are ineluctable facts to be dealt with and understood. They are the challenge to Jewish philosophy. They are part of the given of our situation. We do not come to them as conclusions; we begin with them as of the stuff of our existence, our Jewish existence.

We can, of course, avoid such a conclusion by accepting for such words as these what Professor Cronbach calls dramatistic rather than cognitive meanings. In all candor, however, one wonders how satisfactory this solution really is. Does not the very dramatistic value of prophet or revelation lie in the recollection, be it ever so faint, of a cognitive meaning? More than this, one discovers in the most consistent transvaluation of the entire cognitive body of tradition into dramatistic terms, that of Mordecai Kaplan, not only a residue of cognitive meaning which is the effective dynamic of his system, but a real although diffuse and inconsistent metaphysic. As pragmatic instrumentalism has learned over the years, ontology continues to assert itself even after banishment from the vocabulary.

Thus the question cannot be avoided: what do we mean when we speak of prophets and prophecy? Is it at all possible to give these words any substance within our contemporary universe of discourse? Are we permitted no more than a descriptive approach to a past phenomenon that is to be taken as a more or less primitive stage in the assumed unfolding of man's religious consciousness? Are the men behind the words yet read as conveying potent meaning for us to be thought of in and of themselves as self-deluded, or psychotics with auditory or visual hallucinations? Quite frankly we cannot have our cake and eat it. Either we take seriously as the basis of our discussion the prophets' self-understanding, as for example A. J. Heschel has set it forth, or we might as well close the book at once and move on to weightier matters. Heschel wrote: "The consciousness of the prophets that they were inspired by God is the foundation of their vocation. The very right to engage in prophetic activity, the claim of authority for their words, begins with the fact of being-given-ness (Eingebung). Their words claim neither respect nor value on the basis of their aesthetic or logical qualities, or even because of their in-dwelling content but only because of their transcendent origin. It is this point of origin they proclaim over and over again in many ways: they are not bringing to the people the formulation of their own consciousness . . . but that which has been given. The vigorous and emphatic certainty that their messages are not inventions . . . but communi-cations . . . as well as their condemnation of the deceit and error of the false prophets . . . constrains us to regard the form of their proclamation—'God has spoken to me' as unequivocal explanation of the source of that which is given to them."[22]

This fact, which may be for them ultimate, is for the philosopher primary. It is the point from which, not toward which, he moves. His task, as we have seen, is to discover a total frame of reference in which this fact finds its place. For ha-Levi the very hierarchy of nature and the immediate and continuing act of God in creation made prophecy un-derstandable. For Maimonides it was the influence of the Active Intellect upon the imagination and the contempla-tion by reason of the imagery thus produced which justified the prophet's assertion. The task of any Jewish philosopher cannot then but include the search for such understanding as a primary concern. Prophecy belongs to the structure of Israel's experience. The attempt must be made to under-stand it, not explain it away.

Within contemporary Jewish thought this beginning

with the fact, this existence within the community of revelation, in contrast to nineteenth century formulations, has assumed an ever more central position. The statements of those who have addressed and are addressing our present day community with true seriousness are written from within what Leo Baeck in the subtitle of his concluding work *Dieses Volk*, called "juedische Existenz."[23] This is not to suggest that such thinkers as Baeck, Buber, Rosenzweig, Heschel and others belong together as a school or as a movement. Despite the tendency to throw some of them together for the purpose of derogation, it ought to be clear that these are independent attempts to understand the revelation under which they stand and which thus unites them. What is important is the recognition that these thinkers take revelation and prophecy with utmost seriousness and attempt to do what the great medieval thinkers did, construct a total statement which will enable us to understand, to comprehend what these words may mean in contemporary rational discourse. The following words of Rosenzweig make the implications of this task clear and present: ". . . [philosophy] must cling to her new point of departure, to the subjective, extremely personal unique self, absorbed in itself and the standpoint of self, and still attain to the objectivity of science. Where is the bridge to connect extreme subjectivity, one might even say, deaf and blind subjectivity, with the luminous clearness of infinite objectivity? The answer must anticipate developments and, even so, stop halfway, stop at mere suggestion. The theological conception of revelation must provide the bridge from the most subjective to the most objective. Man, as the recipient of revelation, as one who experiences the content of faith, contains both within himself. And whether the new philosophy admits it or not, such a man is the only thinker fit to deal with it . . ."[24]

Were this a series rather than a single lecture, it would indeed be the responsibility of the lecturer to clothe the bare bones of mere assertion with the living flesh and sinew of demonstration. As it is, all that can be done is to indicate the reality of the problem and the directions from which the answers appear to be coming. Prophetology as the focus of the question of man's dealings with God is the crucial and demanding challenge to Jewish religious thought today.

But in so projecting the task, we need to remember that the absolutizing of whatever structure we may erect must be ruled out from the very start. The scandal of prophecy must ever and again reassert itself lest *our* understanding become *the* explanation, and as explanation thrust the fact aside. It is to this danger that Gabriel Marcel addresses himself, although he speaks in terms of his own Christian tradition and to another point: "It seems certain to me . . . that if we consider the evolution of moral thought, Christianity has tended to attenuate this paradox progressively, to withdraw the scandalous from its character." If this then be our danger as well, we will find hope in his continuing words. "It is no less certain that periodically spiritual upheavals have appeared, violently to re-open the breach that attempts had been directed toward closing; and to denounce the work of smoothing over, indulged in more or less consciously by the doctors of the previous age."[25]

The shattering no less than the building belongs to our striving. Though we tend "to withdraw the scandalous" the scandal will not be gainsaid. Buber's valedictory for his opponent Hermann Cohen puts the matter with poignant beauty: "Cohen did not consciously choose between the God of the philosophers and the God of Abraham, rather believing to the last he could succeed in identifying the two. Yet his inmost heart, that force from which, too, thought derives its vitality, had chosen and decided for him. The identification had failed, of necessity had to fail. For the idea of God, that masterpiece of man's construction, is only the image of images, the most lofty of all the images by which man recognizes the imageless God. It is essentially repugnant to man to recognize this fact and remain satisfied. For when man learns to love God, he senses an actuality which rises above the idea. Even if he makes the philosopher's great effort to sustain the object of his love as an object of his philosophic thought, the love itself bears witness to the existence of the Beloved."[26]

And so too for us with prophecy. One is always driven to go beyond his understanding.

Sailors use the phrase "the loom of the land" to indicate the sense of the shore's presence even when it lies beyond their vision, even enshrouded in the dark of night. We too who have in our day experienced the shattering of the system, sense the loom of prophecy's vast reality below the horizon of our lives. Yet neither the hard unyielding fact nor its understanding is clear within our spirit's sight. All one dares, crying the landfall, is to attempt in fog and gloom neither to run aground on shoal or reef nor doubting, turn and sail away, but sounding with reason's lead and line, come at last unto the land.

NOTES

[1]*Persecution and the Art of Writing,* (Glencoe: The Free Press, 1952), pp. 142-143.

[2]"Schelling's Philosophy of Religion," *University of Toronto Quarterly,* XXII, No. 1, (Oct. 1952), 17.

[3]*Amos Studies,* (Cincinnati: The Hebrew Union College Press, 1941), pp. 15-16.

[4]b. Ned. 38a; b. Sanh. 11a.

[5]Saadya Gaon, *The Book of Doctrines and Beliefs,* ed. A. Altmann, (Oxford: East and West Library, 1946) pp. 11, 29.

[6]*Ibid.,* pp. 94 *et seq.;* pp. 103 *et seq.*

[7]Julius Guttmann, *Die Philosophie des Judentums,* (Muenchen: Ernst Reinhardt, 1933), p. 80; see also, H. A. Wolfson, "Hallevi and Maimonides on Prophecy," *JQR,* n. s., XXXII (1941-42), 345.

[8]Judah Halevi, *Kuzari: The Book of Proof and Argument,* ed. I. Heinemann, (Oxford: East and West Library, 1947), pp. 13, 30; see also Wolfson, *op. cit.,* p. 345-353; and Strauss, *op. cit.,* p. 141.

[9]Wolfson, *op. cit.,* XXXIII, 357-358, 368; David Neumark, *Jehudah Hallevi's Philosophy,* (Cincinnati: Hebrew Union College Press, 1908), pp. 36 *et seq.; Kuzari,* pp. 14-15.

[10]*Kuzari,* pp. 64-72.

[11]Z. Diesendruck, "Maimonides' Lehre von der Prophetie," *Jewish Studies in Memory of Israel Abrahams,* (New York: Press of the Jewish Institute of Religion, 1927), p. 74; L. Strauss, *Philosophie und Gesetz,* (Berlin: Schocken Verlag, 1935), p. 87.

[12]*Ibid.* pp. 76-77, 89, 90.

[13]*Ibid.,* p. 122; Guttmann, *op. cit.,* pp. 296-300.

[14]Strauss, *Persecution,* pp. 194-195; Guttmann, *op. cit.,* p. 302.

[15]Guttmann, *op. cit.,* pp. 313, 317; Eric Werner, "New Light on the Family of Felix Mendelssohn", *HUCA* XXVI (1955).

[16]*op. cit.,* p. 3.

[17]Guttmann, *op. cit.,* p. 324; Albert Lewkowitz, *Das Judentum und die geistigen Stromungen des 19. Jahrhunderts,* (Breslau: Marcus Verlag, 1935). pp. 407, 416.

[18]S. L. Steinheim, *Die Offenbarung nach dem Lehrbegriffe des Synagoge,* III (Leipzig: Leiner, 1863), 319; Guttmann, *op. cit.,* p. 338; *J. E., s. v.* Steinheim, XI, 544a.

[19]Guttmann, *op. cit.,* pp. 317-318.

[20]See for example Graetz' discussion of Kabbalah and Hasidism throughout his *History of the Jews.*

[21](2nd ed.; Frankfurt a.M.: J. Kaufmann Verlag, 1929), p. 97. "Dieses Ewige, als die Grundlage der Vernunft fuer allen Inhalt der Vernunft, nennt der Jude Offenbarung."

[22]*Die Prophetie,* (Krakow: 1936), p. 7.

[23]*Dieses Volk: Juedische Existenz,* (Frankfurt a.M.: Europaeische Verlagsanstalt, 1955).

[24]N. Glatzer, *Franz Rosenzweig:* *His Life and Thought,* (New York: Farrar, Straus and Young, 1953), pp. 208-209.

[25]*Le declin de la Sagesse,* (Paris: Plon, 1954), p. 109. I am indebted to my colleague James Sellers for bringing this passage to my attention and allowing me to quote it in his translation.

[26]*Israel and the World,* (New York: Schocken, 1948), p. 65.

THE VOICE OF PROPHECY
IN THIS SATELLITE AGE

___

Edgar F. Magnin, D.D., L.H.D., S.T.D.
Rabbi, Wilshire Boulevard Temple
Los Angeles, California

THE GOLDENSON LECTURE OF 1959

THERE ARE TWO APPROACHES TO ANY FIELD of knowledge. One is the purely academic and theoretical. The other is dynamic and practical. The former deals with data per se, the amassing of knowledge for its own sake; while the latter applies to what has been discovered for the general use and welfare of the individual and society.

In this paper, I am concerned with the practical and the dynamic influence of the Prophets of Israel as it affects our lives today. I shall leave the area of pure scholarship to the exegetes, the critics, the historians, the psychologists, and the theologians, who are the specialists in their respective fields.

I am mindful of the fact that I am speaking as a rabbi to rabbis and rabbinical students. Our calling—and I prefer to think of it as a calling rather than as a profession—imposes upon us the obligation and the privilege of suggesting to individuals and to the nation at large a way of life that patterns itself after the will of God. Our preachments should tend to direct people into the paths that will enable them to avoid sin and stupidity, the causes of misery and destruction, of unhappiness and chaos, and thus should lead them into the way of decency and sanity, so that they may be assured of survival, of a greater sense of security, and enrichment of soul.

We are living in turbulent times. Civilization and possibly also the survival of the human race are in the balance.

Technology has made the world in which we live more comfortable physically. It has lengthened life, assuaged pain, and bestowed upon us a series of luxuries such as the world has never known or could possibly have dreamt of previously. It has reduced space by increasing speed to an unimagined pace. Ours is truly an age of scientific miracles.

Yet with all of our progress, we are not secure. We are confused and bewildered. Our nerves are on edge. The tempo of the times is consuming us. We are lost, like the victims of the old legend, in the labyrinth of a highly complex society. Within it dwells the Minotaur, half man and half monster, the symbol of our dual nature.

Like Theseus, we must follow the thread that will lead us out into the fresh air and sunlight of freedom: freedom from our own enslavement, from the possibility of a war which threatens to blot out so many lives and so much property, not to speak of our cultural and spiritual heritage; freedom from the iron shackles of a materialism which has indeed become a modern worship of Baal.

With all our wealth, we are poor. With all our speed, we can find no pillow of security on which to lay our heads. With all our miraculous means of communication, we are unable to hear the still small voice that alone can bring comfort and hope to our bruised spirits. We are beggars sitting on bags of gold. Or should we say, bags filled with explosives?

Fortunately, Ariadne's thread, which can lead us out of the dilemma, is close at hand. All we have to do is reach for it. Is was spun out of the minds and hearts of the greatest spiritual geniuses who ever lived—the Prophets of Israel.

Those Galileos of the spirit discovered the noblest religious teachings that the world had ever received up to their time and, I believe, after it. In fact, they were centuries ahead of their day and age. They brought religion to its highest peak. To ignore them is to court death and destruction in any era. To accept their message and apply it individually, nationally, and internationally is to embrace salvation and survival.

Whether we will exercise the wisdom, the patience, and the strength of will to follow their revelations, only time will reveal. But meanwhile, as rabbis—and this applies to all ministers of religion, irrespective of creed—who are concerned with the welfare of men and women and who pray for the future progress of the society of nations, we must become filled with their spirit and endeavor to transmit their teachings in the most potent and effective manner possible.

No two of the Prophets were exactly alike, nor did they express themselves in precisely the same way. Each was confronted by a set of different situations, and each one of them employed, in a most colorful and forceful manner, the imagery that represented his inner thoughts.

They spoke in the language and used the symbolism of the land and age in which they lived. They referred to chariots, not to motor cars or airplanes. They had no concept of the size and nature of this planet, much less of the extent of the far distant galaxies and their nature.

They spoke to kings and queens and the people of Israel and Judah. They referred to alliances with Egypt, Assyria, and Babylonia. But they are not outdated. They are as much alive today as they ever were.

Religious truth, like all truth, is eternal and applicable in every era. And let us not forget that while customs and costumes change, human nature remains basically the same. Whether it is Ahab or a modern despot, ancient Israel and

Judah, or Russia and Germany, or any other nation, the problems remain much the same, and likewise the solutions.

Human Nature

The evils of society are largely the result of faulty thinking and of the basic, primitive, bestial, and savage urges that lie deep down in the unconscious mind. The catastrophes of nature, so-called acts of God, are nothing in magnitude compared with wars caused by anger, fear, and the love of power. We are endowed with a dual nature. The expressions *yetzer hatov* and *yetzer hara* may seem rather naive and an oversimplification in the light of modern psychiatry and analysis, but they still hold good.

We pull ourselves up by one set of forces within us, and then hurl ourselves down by the other. We build cities, and drop bombs on them; we teach love, and then proceed to hate; we spread prayers about the Fatherhood of God and the brotherhood of man, and then become chauvinistic religiously and racially exclusive.

There is little consistency between our education and our daily living. We place our ideals in compartments, lock them up, and then throw the key away. We find it easy to be law-abiding, loving, just, and gentle, just so long as nobody seems to be stepping on our toes.

Since our problems are rooted in human nature, human nature must be controlled and our impulses rechanneled constructively so far as this is possible. Analysis, psychiatry, and formal education alone cannot do this, at least on any large scale.

Political freedom which is based on charters, covenants, written laws, and constitutions, unless backed up by the will of the people, is destined to be thrown out of the window as it was in Germany under Hitler, in Italy under Mussolini,

and in Russia today. Treaties and covenants to prevent war
are not worth the paper they are written on unless men and
women love peace and demand it from those who sit in the
seats of authority and create wars.

We require an entirely new method of education. The
present one is a failure. The future one must not be the union
of church and state under any circumstances, for reasons
that are perfectly obvious. But unless we can devise some
manner of changing the hearts and minds of people so that
they will act in accordance with the highest religious principles, as enunciated by the Prophets of Israel and by others
who have possessed their great spiritual insight, there can
be no hope for the future.

The Prophetic Message In Essence

An analysis of the writings of the Prophets reveals the
following basic ideas:

1. There is one God of the entire universe. He is spiritual,
and the essence of perfect justice and love. He is the Father of
all humanity irrespective of race, creed, or color. Therefore
it behooves individuals and nations to live in peace and
brotherhood and to co-operate for the welfare of all mankind.

2. Morality is absolute, and not relative. It is rooted in the
divine commandments. Every individual is endowed with
free will to choose the right or wrong path, and there is a
penalty for the sinner. There is a law of justice that prevails
for individuals and nations, but this does not exclude salvation and ultimate redemption. Repentance, which means a
change of heart in order to live in accordance with God's
law of righteousness, not only can avert the day of doom,
but, should that day arrive, repentance also causes the individual and the nation to be restored.

3. The vision of the Messianic age, laying aside theo-

logical considerations, affords us a hope for a better tomorrow. This vision does not necessarily mean the attainment of perfection, but it must be aimed at nonetheless. The remnant will survive and build a better future.

4. The causes of much of the distress in the world are the false prophets and the selfish rulers. The selection of leadership is extremely important. Sincerity and character are essentials. Leaders of the people must pursue the will of God.

5. While all individuals and nations are children of God, Israel is still His servant to carry out the message of ethical monotheism in its own particular way and to help usher in an age of peace and justice.

6. The knowledge of God comes from within. Religion transcends ritual, traditions, and forms. God is a living entity, closer than one's hands and feet, not a philosophic or theological abstraction.

Let us examine these thoughts a little more closely.

Justice Today!

Man is created in the divine image. Each life is sacred, and every person has the right to a sense of dignity. We are all here on earth for a purpose, and every one is entitled to respect and consideration, whether he is black or brown or yellow, or whatever be the color of his skin.

It is because we are all children of God that we dare not practice injustice against one another, that we have no right to exploit, humiliate, and subjugate our fellow creatures.

Amos refers to the selling of the righteous for silver and of the needy for a pair of shoes; Isaiah mentions the abuse of the widow, the orphan, and the poor in the land.

It is not difficult to guess what they would think of those who consider Negroes inferior just because of their skin, or who heap abuses and discriminations upon them, whether in the South or, as it sometimes happens, even in the North. We know what the prophets would say to the followers of Apartheid, if they were living in South Africa. They would hurl invectives at the Soviet leaders for the atrocities in Hungary and for the despotism and terror in their own country. The Nazi and Fascist treatment of human beings would have horrified them. Hitler committed more atrocities in his day than did all the nations during the years in which all the Prophets lived. Mussolini was little better.

The sad part about it all is that we are living long after them, in a period of history in which the world has acquired more knowledge, and civilization has greatly advanced scientifically and culturally; in a period in which democracy does exist and much progress has been made in human relations.

Morality Is An Absolute

To the Prophets of Israel, morality was an absolute. God condemned sin—"Thus saith the Lord. . . ." Good is good and evil is evil, and there is no excuse for the latter. The Prophets would not accept our modern attitude of laxity toward sin on the ground of certain pseudopsychological theories or of a relativistic philosophy.

Today, nobody is good or bad. We find excuses for everything. Youngsters are not bad even when they hold people up with guns. They are disturbed. Every excuse is found by sob sisters and theorists for murderers, thieves, and rapists.

Now, it is all very well to be "modern," "progressive," "intellectual," "liberal," so long as one's own house is not robbed or one's own children are not killed by a fiend.

I long ago discovered that much that comes under the heading of idealism is little more than frustration seeking an outlet in some heroic form, heroic mostly by way of mouth. Some of the most "charitable" people I know have no heart, and some of the "humanitarians" hate people as individuals.

Understanding and sentiment have their place. We are told that the Lord requires that we love mercy, but in the same verse Micah informs us that we must do justice. Justice and mercy are two sides of the same shield. It is the proper intermixture of both that makes the ideal way of life possible. Moses represented both aspects. So did Isaiah, Amos, Hosea, and Jeremiah. All taught punishment and forgiveness through repentance, but none of them ignored evil as a factor that exists in the human mind and heart or excused it.

Sin was sin, and sin brought punishment, even to nations. There can be no compromise with the cardinal evils. They wreck the individual and society.

So the Day of Doom was threatened, and the Day of Doom hangs over us today like the sword of Damocles.

We have been shown the way to live. We have been given the choice between life and death, and told to seek life.

This is no time for excuses, alibis, empty and superficial theories relating to human behavior. Sin is sin now and always, and it is sin not because of a man-made morality which is relative, but because God has established the right in the world and has shown us the way through His servants, the Prophets.

The Vision of Peace

Isaiah envisioned the day when the lion would lie down with the lamb; when swords would be turned into plowshares and spears into pruning hooks; when every man would dwell under his own vine and fig tree and none would be afraid.

Since God is the Creator of the vast cosmos, the Father

of all mankind irrespective of race, color, or creed, He desires the peace of the world, and not war.

God tolerated no cruelty. Amos hurled his invectives and prophesied doom for Damascus, Gaza, Tyre, Edom, Ammon, and Moab because of their atrocities. And please note that God, who up to the time of the Prophets was thought of as the special Deity of the Hebrews, has an interest in the welfare of all nations and holds them all responsible for their sins. He sends Jonah to Nineveh to save the wicked city. The Ninevites, too, have bodies and souls. They are also human beings.

If the Prophets were shocked at the atrocities of Damascus, Gaza, and Edom in a day of limited warfare, what would they have to say, if they were living today, about the millions of casualties in World Wars I and II and about the inestimable damage to life and property from the latest hydrogen bombs and missiles that can be hurled across the seas and over vast continents? In such an age as that in which we are living, nothing less than the dynamics of a profound faith in a Spiritual Creator and in the sanctity of human life, because we are endowed with souls, can suffice to hold us back from exterminating millions of men, women, and little children.

Bombs have no heads or hearts. A missile has no conscience and cannot reason, but those who wield them have, or should have, a moral sense and can think things through. Unless we want to hurl all society into chaos and exterminate much of our present civilization, burn up the libraries, crumble every college building into ruins, and send man back to the caves out of which he emerged, we had better read the words of the men of God—the God of love and justice and peace.

We stand today in the position of the ancient Samson.

who used his strength to pull the Temple of Dagon down upon the heads of his enemies, but committed suicide at the same time.

The Messianic Dream

The Day of Doom enunciated by the Prophets did not spell out the last hope of the nation. Basically, the Prophets were optimists.

"Comfort ye, comfort ye, my people," said Deutero-Isaiah, "in the name of God. Every valley shall be exalted, and every mountain and hill shall be made low. The crooked shall be made straight, and the rough places plain. And the glory of the Lord shall be revealed. And all flesh shall see it together."

The spirit of this passage is repeated many times not only in Isaiah, but also by most of the other Prophets of Israel. After punishment would come the hour of redemption. The nation would rise from the ashes like the phoenix.

The same thought is embodied, in a sense, in the prophetic concept of the millennium. The Messianic ideal gives humanity a hope for a better tomorrow. Lay aside the differences of opinion theologically concerning the Messiah. The important thing to remember is that in the end of days, peace and justice will reign on earth, and as long as mankind can hold on to this ideal, we can and will survive and go forward.

The Messianic concept, unlike the utopian Republic of Plato and the utopias of those who followed him, presents no sociological or political theories. It does not concern itself with economics. There is a mystic quality about it. Again, let us remember that these men were prophets, not fortune-tellers; seers, men of vision, not experts in some academic field; dreamers filled with emotion, not philosophers.

The concept of a Messianic Day, however vague, affords comfort in an age of despair and frustration. There are too many people these days who cry: "Woe unto us, woe unto all the world! There is no hope! The human race is doomed! Human nature cannot be changed! Mankind will always repeat the same mistakes! History is testimony of the fact that we can never learn!"

It is too easy to fall into this trap, just as it is easy to move in the opposite direction and, like the cultists, whistle in the dark and hide our heads in the sand like the proverbial ostrich.

Either extreme is bad, and both extremes are dangerous. We must live realistically. If we do not face facts honestly, even the fact of our own weaknesses, we can easily succumb to failure. But by facing the actual facts, we can still have within us the will to survive. We are more than mere animals. We have never lived by bread alone. Slowly, but stubbornly, and by a tortuous, long route, but nonetheless going forward, we have conquered many of our problems and will conquer many more if we cling to the hope of Isaiah.

This is what is meant, to my way of thinking, by the remnant which shall return. This is the stump that remains rooted and will send forth new branches.

Synagogues and Rabbis

At this juncture, I should like to introduce the question of what the Prophets would have to say about our religious institutions, ritual, traditions, and the like, were they to come back to earth.

The subject of their attitude toward the established Temple in Jerusalem and the sacrifices is scarcely debatable. Some few scholars have taken the position that they were utterly opposed to sacrifices. Most scholars maintain, however, that it was not the sacrifices themselves to which they objected, but the substitution of the sacrifices for real religion, meaning, of course, morality and social justice. They opposed hypocrisy, formalism, for its own sake; in other words, the outward trappings of faith.

Certainly, if they did have any objections to sacrifices, they could display no opposition to prayers, provided that they were from the heart and were uttered by people who loved God and their fellow men.

We must never forget that these men were not ordinary people. They were, as I said before, religious geniuses. They constituted a class all by themselves. They spoke extra-murally, outside of the Temple walls; as a matter of fact, in defiance of the ritual upheld by the fat and false priests in the face of the misery of the poor caused by the rich and the nobility.

I suppose that such men as the Prophets would not fit very well into a church or synagogue today. They were not conformists or compromisers, and any institution, even a religious one, demands compromise since it represents an aggregation of all kinds of people bound together for a common purpose and in the performance of a common task.

One thing is certain, that no board of trustees or large group of members could very well tolerate the severe independence and bold language of a prophet. As society is constituted, we need both prophets and priests. As Achad Haam pointed out so brilliantly, Moses and Aaron each had his own place in the Exodus and the wanderings in the Wilderness.

The prophet speaks with absolute authority. The priest quotes the prophets and proceeds to try to adjust his ideas to the society in which he lives.

No rabbi can be a prophet, nor would a prophet apply

for the position of rabbi in any congregation, nor would he be likely to be elected if he did.

Once, at a meeting of my colleagues, one of them, not too brilliant or clear-thinking, passed the glib remark that I have heard before, that he and the rest of us stood in the line of the prophetic tradition. In fact, he went a little further. Forgetting that he received a salary, took orders from a board of trustees, and drove about in a convertible car, he gave voice to such pompous and pious phraseology as to make himself ridiculous.

Rabbis are only human beings after all. Prophets are specially selected individuals whether because of something in their genes, because of revelation, or however one chooses to account for it. They are selected by destiny.

They speak in imagery. They are born poets. They hurl thunderbolts. They are zealots in the extreme. They live on next to nothing materially, and are willing to be tortured and killed for their principles.

To compare our position with theirs is presumptuous and utterly silly, but this does not relieve us of the obligation of endeavoring to imitate them to a degree. Without the highest ideals and some degree of courage and backbone to carry them out, we are mere nobodies unworthy of the respect of our parishioners and of our own self-respect.

How far we can go, how far we are able to go, according to our convictions, personalities, innate courage, and ability, is difficult to measure. But mere nonentities we dare not be. In the course of time, there have been some rabbis, priests, and ministers who have stood high above the level of their colleagues and have dared to defy some of the defects and weaknesses of their institutions. And they have helped to reform them from within.

One thing we must remember, however, and that is

this: that more often than not, the Prophets spoke about conditions and protested against the evils of the day, but they did not pose as authorities on every single question, and in many cases they had no specific, precise, and concrete answers to the problems of their age.

It seems to me that coupled with our zeal and ardor to follow in their spirit, there should exist a measure of humility and common sense.

We all know that injustice exists, but it is not always easy to point out the exact solutions. Nobody knows all the answers to every question, not even rabbis. But rabbis can and should point out the difference between right and wrong, and urge their congregants to seek out the right attitude and to live in accordance with the highest standards of ethics.

The Mission of Judaism

We Jews must believe that we have a part to play in the progress of civilization. We still have a mission to perform. It is part of our destiny. For this we were born. For this we have survived all the disabilities of the tragic centuries.

We may not conceive of that mission in exactly the same way as the Prophets did, but we are still the "servant of the Lord" called to bring the Light of the Torah to the nations of the earth.

True, much of what we have stood for has been taken over by Christianity and Mohammedanism, and thus has been spread over a wider area of the world than a handful of Jews could ever have succeeded in reaching. But we have our own special significance. And our very presence in the world as an entity, as a people that has defied time and all the empires of the earth, is in itself a lesson to the world, or should be.

Even Christian theologians of the more liberal type are beginning to feel that it is both foolish and wrong to attempt to convert Jews. We are the leaven of society. What I should rather like to see is that Jews shall be converted to Judaism; that the millions of our people who have wandered away from their faith shall be induced to return both for their own dignity and happiness and for what good they can do for all mankind.

You will note that I did not say for their peace of mind. Here again, the Prophets remind us of what religion means in terms of service, and not of selfishness.

Peace of Mind?

Thinking, feeling, sensitive human beings can never have peace of mind. That is for the lazy, the gross, for those who prefer to be contented cows or caterpillars crawling on a leaf.

To be alive means to be disturbed and sometimes to disturb other people; to stimulate thinking; to inject pity by means of imagination; to make the presence of God felt in the hearts of people and nations.

When God is within us, we may possess more of security, but this is not the "peace of mind" of rabbis and ministers who would make a fad of psychoanalysis or psychiatry; who would cater to the egos and the fears and pains of the frustrated.

Amos had no peace of mind. Hosea, Isaiah, Ezekiel, and Jeremiah had no peace of mind. Moses, the greatest prophet of all, certainly was not very relaxed when he knelt before the Burning Bush or when he flung the challenge into the face of Pharaoh, or even when he had to criticize his own people and was abused by them and their false leaders, Korah and his cohorts.

The religion of the Prophets was not an easy, comfortable religion. It was moving, powerful, tempestuous. It shook one to one's very bones. The Prophets were never at ease in Zion. There was too much wrong to be redressed, too many bodies and souls to be saved, to make a mockery of religion by promising everything to everybody. Prophetic religion spells sacrifice, pain, abuse, service, love, even when nothing but hatred is received in return.

God Speaks to All of Us

I now come to what I consider the most valuable contribution which the Prophets can make to us, particularly as ministers of religion, although to laymen as well, and that is the necessity for each one of us to discover God by and within ourselves and to communicate with Him.

The gist, the heart and soul of the prophetic message, lay inherent in the relationship between the Prophet and God. Greater than all the lessons which they taught us about our relationship to mankind and to the external world was what man can do with his inner world, and should do, if he is to become a fully civilized human being, more than a mere highly developed beast.

To the Prophets, God was very real, closer than their hands and feet. He was not a philosophic abstraction or a theological dogma. None of the Prophets ever theorized about God or wrote learned papers. None of them, from Moses to Malachi, ever drew up a theological treatise. None of them ever endeavored to define God by such limited media as words. God was something they knew and felt and talked with, not a concept out of a book. They never went to Sunday School or listened to the sermons of some dry preacher who indulged in useless and silly generalizations and pious pomposity and left his listeners cold and confused.

Man must know not only what to do about others, but also about himself. Each one of us like Israel, is a servant of God, a child of God. He has something of the Prophet within him and must hold communion with His Creator in his own way; otherwise, he is merely bones and flesh and blood corpuscles.

Now, East of Eden, the millennial ideal, is not just of the body or even of the mind, but of the heart. And the purpose of man's pilgrimage on earth is to develop his immortal soul. Even a world with justice and liberty for all and enough to feed everybody and a roof over everybody's head and the abolishing of arms would be far from a millennium.

Religion is an ineffable, illusive something that comes from within ourselves. Religion is emotional. While it can be checked by the head, it originates in the heart. Religion is mysticism.

I am amused when, in speaking of modern synagogue architecture, the term *functional* is used. This may go very well for the kitchen and the social hall, but religion is not functional. It is mystical. It transcends logic. It spans worlds. It blots out space and time.

The Prophets were not scholars. They were simple people, in some cases farmers and peasants. The Prophets were never ordained. They never took courses in homiletics. They were never taught how to breathe or to use gestures when they spoke. Certainly, they never used *Bartlett's Quotations*. What they had to say in their own simple, direct manner with the force of lightning from heaven became incorporated in *Bartlett's Quotations*.

I am not suggesting that all of us can reach the high pitch that they did. Of course we cannot, nor should we try to imitate them. I have intimated in this paper that we are closer to the priestly calling than to the prophetic, but I still believe that a rabbi who in his own heart does not have a deep religious feeling, who cannot commune directly with God and—may I dare to say?—hear the Voice of God, is lacking in the most important thing in the world, even though he be most scholarly, brilliant, efficient, and capable.

Recapturing the Prophetic Spirit

But we must recapture, if possible, some of the simplicity and directness of those spiritual geniuses even if we are not geniuses ourselves. Deep down within the hearts of all of us is a little lamp that burns by day and by night. It was placed there by a hidden Hand while yet we dwelt within our mother's womb. This is the light more brilliant than a myriad of suns and galaxies. He who follows that light performs miracles. He touches hearts and souls, transforms lives, brings comfort, at times, disturbs and irritates, but always he carries with himself a sense of greatness, of sweetness, and of light.

It is this sense of the knowledge of God through intuition rather than forms and formulae that alone can save this world of ours from war, revolutions, and disaster in many forms.

The Prophets speak to us out of the far distant past, and say: Formal lip service will not save us. Ritual has its place, but will not save us. Organization will not save us. Churches and synagogues laid end to end around the wide belly of the equator will not save us. Growing memberships will not save us. Sisterhoods and brotherhoods and more rabbis and ministers and priests will not save us, any more than more universities and more professors and more libraries.

Nothing will save us but our own souls. For they are

part of God Himself, and God alone is the Savior. Morality, justice, liberty, love and kindness, gentleness, confidence, reverence, respect, self-respect—these are the riches of the earth. These cannot be bought over the counter like merchandise or stocks and bonds. They are the seeds of real happiness, security, and survival. The sense of cosmic unity, One God, one universe, one mankind, one fraternity of nations, each person living his own life, but not selfishly and suspiciously, all clasping hands to create a better world for the good of all and in His Name—this is the message of the Hebrew Prophets. This is our dream. This is our hope. This is our prayer.

THE STONE WHICH THE
MODERN BUILDERS REJECTED

Levi A. Olan, D.D.
Rabbi, Temple Emanu-El
Dallas, Texas

THE GOLDENSON LECTURE OF 1960

E VERY GREAT CIVILIZATION ORIGINATES IN some supreme guiding principle around which an historical group builds its existence. This perceptive insight of Martin Buber invites us to examine our American civilization in an effort to isolate those distinguishing tenets which directed the founders of this nation. The banner of their faith held before us, for only a moment, provides an opportunity for sober reflection about the nature and destiny of our national life today It is not possible to describe a complex civilization in all its parts for, as Max Lerner suggests, after you have given an account of its people, technology, economics, politics, art, religion and cities, class and caste, mores and morals, there is still something elusive left — "an inner civilization style." Ours, then, is a more limited yet basic objective, to find the ideals and the normative principles which served as the foundation stones for the builders.

The closest parallel in history to our American civilization is that of the Hebrews in the Biblical period. Their origins were marked by the character of nomadic and shepherd life. There was a lasting effect in their devotion to blood kinship or family consciousness. Cain's question, "Am I my brother's keeper?" had a dangerously alien ring for them since they derived from one ancestor, blood brothers, living as a family. Their social structure was a simple, rudimentary democracy wherein wealth was communal without division into rich and poor. Politically, the seat of authority was vested with the head of the family, or in a council of elders, none of whom possessed despotic power. Religiously, their relationship to divinity was in the hands of the same elders who were not set apart in any ecclesiastical sense. Life being simple and uncomplicated called for a moral pattern to match, a behavior which was direct and unspoiled. In this unmediated experience with its hard and rootless existence there developed a strong sense of tribal brotherhood, and along with it a deeply rooted love of liberty, equality, and justice. It was with this nomadic people that God made a covenant, characterized by a high reach of morality, and around this desert covenant the Hebrew people built their civilization, and the memory of the covenant guided the prophets and some leaders in periods of stress and danger in later years.

The radical change from the simplicity of a shepherd's way of life to the complex urban social structure in the land of Canaan created a tension which called forth the spiritual genius of the people to resolve it. The life of farming was a new experience where success depended upon some strange customs. Private ownership was alien to the desert tradition and became more bewildering as the many became poor while a few grew rich and lived luxuriously. The despotism of rulers who conscripted the sons for war, the daughters for servants, and who taxed the poor for the lavish entertainment of a royal court, constituted a heresy against the tradition of freedom born and nurtured in the wilderness. In a childish eagerness to succeed at their new occupations the Hebrews adopted the practices of their neighbors. These worshipped their Baalim with fertility rites which blasphemed against the clean morality of the desert. The introduction of riotous feasting and drinking, and the practice of sacred prostitution as means of winning the favor of God were an impious travesty upon the memory of the people's pristine origin. The sudden arrival of a class of ecclesiastical professionals who drowned the basic moral demands of God in a sea of ritualistic pomp and ceremonial glitter shocked the sensitive spirits who remembered the purity and simplicity of the life of their fathers. The Prophets became the guardians of the guiding principles of the nation and the protagonists of its democratic tradition. The voice of their protest is heard very early in the warning of Samuel against the people's desire for a king. "He will take your sons . . . and they shall run before his chariot . . . and he will take your daughters to be perfumers, and to be cooks and bakers . . . and he will take your fields and your vineyards and olive groves, even the best of them. . . ." Elijah thundered his accusations against Ahab and Jezebel and declared that the nation must choose between the God of Moses and the gods who induced injustice, oppression, and a loose moral code in the national existence. In the eighth century there appears a body of seers who hark back to the basic precepts of Israel's origin in order to diagnose and heal the sickness of their age. Since the fruit which ripened was bad, there must be something wrong with the vine. The people had been led astray, had forgotten the moral covenant, thereby alienating themselves from God and bringing His judgment upon them. But the Prophets reminded them of the ethical standards of the earlier nomadic civilization, "The days of her youth when she came up from the land of Egypt," as Hosea described it. Jeremiah bemoaned the fact that "the artificial leaking cisterns of the cities have not the clear running water of the desert fountain."

There were some, like the Rechabites, who took literally

the call to the days of old and refused to build houses, to till the ground, and to drink wine, because these were the symbols of the new degenerate life. But such was not the intent of the Prophets, for they were progressive and in many ways outdistanced their contemporaries with their advanced ideas. The Prophets saw clearly as R. B. Y. Scott has perceived, that "She (nation) has mistaken a more complex civilization for a higher way of life and has preferred its immediate advantage to fundamental values." They held the basic ideals and moral standards which had infused the creative period of the nation's beginnings, valid enough for application to the changing circumstances of history.

Man's resistance to the demands of the spirit is normal to his nature and that resistance increases as life becomes more involved with the celebration of success and prosperity. Moreover, an exalted ideal tends to degenerate into a convention, into symbols and rituals observed in some cultic form. At the moment when a civilization reaches its highest point of achievement in satisfying man's sensuous desires and tastes, its spiritual character comes seriously into danger. It was such a historical crisis which the Prophets described in terms so specific as to arouse the condemnation of all the regnant powers including priests and kings. The Prophets warned that the God of the covenant will judge the conduct of the people, individually and socially, in the market place and in the home. They called upon the nation to turn from its reliance upon the magic of cultic practices to the demands of a God of justice and righteousness, of love and mercy.

The events of violent history were the anvil upon which the Prophet hammered out the Ethical Monotheistic faith destined to become the foundation of Western Civilization. He was, in his age, a social revolutionary because he was a religious conservative calling the nation back to the essential

ethical nature of the covenant with God. With the genius of
the creative artist he broadened the horizons from those of a
tribal experience into a universal vision of one God for all
humanity. The God of Moses who demanded of the Israelites that they obey His commandments became in the days
of Deutero-Isaiah the God who judged all the nations by the
standards of justice and love. Not only was *He* the Creator
of the physical world which was the arena of human history,
but He himself was an active participant in its events.
The Exodus from Egypt, the revelation at Sinai, the conquest of the land, and the exile from it were all part of God's
plan for a humanity on earth which shall be just, righteous,
and merciful. It was He who brought Assyria against His
own people as the rod of His anger, just as He later brought
Babylonia and Persia as instruments of His moral purpose
in history. The Prophet's God set a plumb line in the midst
of Israel as well as in Ethiopia, and His eyes are on the sinful people to destroy it from the face of the earth.

The capstone of the Prophetic faith is the kingdom of God
wherein men "shall beat their swords into plowshares . . .
and none shall make them afraid," which will come to pass
in the end of days. In prophetic thought time is linear, moving always in one direction from a beginning which was
God's creation to a final victory, and there extends into the
amoral physical nature of the universe a Power that is not
of it, but something apart and different. God is involved in
the experience of the people as at the Red Sea and at Sinai,
and is not dependent upon the cycle of nature. He is covenanted to act with man as a partner in order that beyond
the darkness there will arise a new dawn. Though the
Prophets announced doom and destruction upon the nations
because of their failure to seek God, to know His commandments and to do them, they regarded such failure as tempo-

rary. There will be, they believed, a triumphant end when God's purpose will be fulfilled, not for man's sake, but for "His sake." The certainty of ultimate victory was an integral part of this moral interpretation of history. It was in the deepest sense a hopeful and optimistic faith which envisioned the salvation of man within history. First, man would have to learn that it is the righteous who shall live by his faith. There can be no unearned victory and the road is not an easy one. The kingdom of God is for hardy men who are committed to call good, good, and evil, evil, and not to confuse them or compromise them for some immediate gain.

That the course of American civilization closely parallels that of the Biblical people of Israel was acutely observed in 1783 by the Rev. Dr. Ezra Stiles preaching to the General Assembly at Hartford, Connecticut. He took as his text: "And to make thee high above all nations which He has made in praise, and in name, and in honor." The title of this sermon running 120 closely printed pages was, "The United States Elevated to Glory and Honor." He envisioned the new nation as "God's American Israel." Later, Thomas Jefferson believed and publicly said that God had a special purpose in founding this new community, to make a new beginning in a corrupt world. Here the power of tyrants could be broken, and in a wide new continent opportunities could be provided for all men so that the vices which characterized the social life of the overcrowded continent of Europe may be avoided. Indeed, the poet Freneau sang, "A new Jerusalem sent down from heaven shall grace our happy earth."

The sense of a divine purpose comparable to the Biblical pattern pervaded the writings of the founders. John Adams in 1765 declared that he always considered the settlement of America "with reverence and wonder, as the opening of a grand scheme and design in Providence for the illumination of the ignorant and the emancipation of the slavish part of mankind all over the earth." Herman Melville later wrote: "We Americans are a peculiar, chosen people, the Israel of our time; we bear the ark of liberties of the world." In his flowery oratory Albert J. Beveridge exclaimed: "He has made the American people as His chosen nation finally to lead the regeneration of the world. This is the divine mission of America, and it holds for us all profit, glory, happiness possible to man. We are trustees of the world's progress, guardians of its righteous peace. The judgment of the Master is upon us! 'Ye have been faithful over a few things, I will make you master over many things.'" Similarly Hegel, writing in his *Philosophy of History,* was moved to announce that America was "the land of the future, where, in the ages that lie before us, the burdens of the world's history shall reveal itself." Thus, there was a pervasive feeling in the early days of our national history that America is an original thing in the political history of the world for many an age. De Tocqueville found in America a "troublesome and garrulous patriotism because Americans just could not stop talking about the freedom and morality of their new nation as distinguished from the old, sick, tyrant-ridden, and corrupt world of Europe."

It is significant that the spokesman of religion played a vital role in the revolution and in the formation of the national character. The sermons preached in the eminent pulpits of the prerevolutionary period are not only learned, but they are also characterized by political wisdom. They contributed notably to the moral force that brought about independence. Some of them were officially published by the legislatures, and thereby became the text books of human rights, and in many a parish they were regarded as the political pamphlets of the day. Ministers then, it seems, preached politics as part of religion, even as did the Prophets of Israel. In 1766 the Rev. James Otis delivered a sermon called "Repeal the Stamp Act" in which he said, "Where the spirit of the Lord is, there is liberty, and if any miserable people on the continent or isles of Europe be driven in their extremity to seek a safe retreat from slavery in some far distant clime, O let them find one in America." Liberty, in the rationale of the founders, had been established by deity in an empty western continent so that, freed from the burden of European tradition, it could flourish and become an inspiration to the world. Thus they could feelingly sing a hymn which began:

> "O God beneath Thy guiding hand
> Our exiled fathers crossed the sea."

It is not fashionable in academic circles today to attribute movements of history to the ideas of men or to the universal ideals of mankind. Ideas and ideals are generally regarded as a mythology which conceals the real forces, which are a struggle for material things or a psychological urge to satisfy the demands of self-interest. Marx and Freud have conditioned the modern mind to hold suspect any body of moral or spiritual guiding principles. Accordingly, the high idealism which informed those who framed the documents of our national establishment is today a subject for examination as to the economic motivation and the psychic origin.

It is one of the characteristics of modern thought that it must accept an either/or interpretation of the course of events. Yet, social, economic and psychological forces play a role along with ideas and ideals. It was the violent upheaval of the nations in the time of the Prophets which led them to the vision of an ethical monotheistic faith. It was the experience with the tyranny and immorality of an old world which led the American heirs of the Prophets to fashion a foundation stone of moral and spiritual idealism. The nation came into being because some men held that there are basic moral truths.

There are two main currents of thought which fed the minds of the founding fathers of America—the God of the Hebrew Prophets and the moral idealism of the Enlightenment. In the strange merging of natural law and theological doctrine, in some instances God was reduced to a mere author of nature in a mechanistic cosmos governed by natural law. This is illustrated in Isaac Newton's principles of motion which provided the inspiration for the 18th century philosophers who proposed the thesis that human society is governed by natural moral laws. Yet the unique contribution of these creators of the moral philosophy of the Enlightenment is that they did not fall into the trap of social determinism. Rather, they transformed natural laws into natural rights which endowed human nature with moral freedom. The Deism of the time soon disappeared, but the concept of natural rights and moral law became a feature of American thought, and gave birth to the basic concept of our national character that we are a society guided by laws and not by men. The Declaration of Independence is the fruit of this philosophy of human rights and is valid, therefore, not only for America, but for men everywhere.

The voices of our past ring mightily with the affirmation that there is an eternal law which must guide the affairs of men. John Marshall expressed it without reservation: "There are principles of abstract justice which the Creator of all things has impressed upon the mind of His creature, man, and which are admitted to regulate, in a great degree, the rights of civilized nations." Justice Joseph Story declared that there are some great principles upon which society rests that are of "eternal obligation, and arise from our common dependence upon our Creator. Among these is the duty to do justice, to love mercy, and to walk humbly before God." In a remarkable commentary on the Constitution, Justice Story said, "The rights of conscience are indeed beyond the just reach of human powers. They are given by God, and cannot be encroached upon by human authority without criminal disobedience of the precepts of natural as well as of revealed religion." The builders who laid the foundation stone of American civilization believed with Emerson that the moral law lies at the center of nature and radiates to the circumference.

There are three main world views which may inform a civilization. There is the pessimistic outlook which renounces the world as senseless and crude, a view which appears in some oriental cults or in western thought systems like Schopenhauer's. There is, on the other hand, an affirming life view which is built on the will to power, and holds the mass of humanity in low estate. Nietzsche is the modern source book for this outlook, and our age has had some sad experiences with exponents who attempted to realize it in practice. There is a third philosophy of life which is basically optimistic and life-affirming, believing that the ethical will of men can overcome evil and suffering and cause the good or better to prevail. This is the Biblical view and it was this third view which was adopted as the guiding principle for the nation. This philosophy was the soil in which the ideas of liberty, equality, and democracy were planted and took root. There is a robustness in this belief because it is directed to a conscious purpose in the unfolding of history. The unflagging efforts of men toward a better way of life makes sense and have meaning because they are integral to the moral nature and purpose of life.

Man, in this view, is a creature of worth because he is a

creature of God. He derives his significance and his place in the scheme of history from his Creator and not from men or governments. His liberty is an endowment of his birth and inviolable by any human power. There is only one condition to his freedom—he must use it to serve the goals which the author of life has set for all men. Liberty is not the license to do as the lowest in human nature desires, but to obey the highest law which is the will of the law-giver. Any moral system must posit a free human being who may choose and take the consequences. Life sets before him the good and the evil, and the freedom to choose between them is a responsibility by the very essence of his nature. Such freedom makes sense only in a moral order and is at home in a philosophy of progress. The forward look of civilization depends upon man's ability to apprehend and to translate into individual and social action the eternal principles which comprise the moral law. This is to say that the advance of civilization rests upon the progress of human virtue.

The assertion that all men are created equal is sadly negated by the inequities and injustices of life. Some come forth strong and healthy, others weak and crippled; some are born to wealth and others to poverty, some are endowed with great talent, and others without it. Then, were the men who wrote the Declaration naive, or blind to reality? Far from it! They affirmed the basic truth that in a moral order all men have a common origin, the image of the divine, and in this no man is better than another. In contrast to an old world which recognized caste and birth as distinguishing characteristics, they affirmed the essential common nature of all humankind. Their declaration had the ring of the Prophetic conviction that the society which is moral permits to every person, regardless of color, class, national origin, or heredity, the opportunity to fulfill the richest and deepest of his nature. A nation is to be judged not by its productive capacity, its standard of living, or its might. There is only one test for any social system—does it foster and encourage the moral and spiritual development of every individual without any discrimination invented by men?

One of the distinctive ideas which pervaded the thought of the Enlightenment was the belief that man is a rational creature whose mind can discover the laws of the physical and moral order. The universe revealed itself as one pervaded by a universal intelligence, and essentially benevolent in nature. The individual is endowed with a bit of universal intelligence with which he may discover and make manifest the universal reason implicit in things and events. A man who is properly informed and in his right mind should be able to distinguish between the highest interest and his selfish desires. He should be able to recognize the truth and submit to it. Law, in this view, is but another name for universal intelligence and is called "natural law." Reason must discover the particulars of this law so that men may conduct themselves ethically. God has provided the Bible, his prophets and teachers to guide men by the experiences of the past in order that they shall not stray from the right path. "We believed," said Jefferson, "that man is a rational animal, endowed by nature with rights and with an innate sense of justice."

Such was the climate of ideas in which the new experiment in democracy had its birth. The universe is a cosmos, both physically and morally, and man is a creature of God endowed with a natural freedom and ready opportunity to use his God-given mind and spirit to make known the will of the Creator and to guide himself by it. These truths were widely accepted by the founding fathers as self-evident, meaning that the society which men fashioned ought to conform to God's purpose as revealed in the essential nature of man.

It was this body of ideas which differentiated the revolution of the American colonists from the one in England in 1688. The English had stopped when constitutional prerogatives were placed around the crown. America however, moved from the crown to the people. "The people" said Roger Williams, "were the origin of all free power in government." The people endowed with liberty, equality, and rationality could be trusted because it is the nature of man to strive after the natural law of the universe. Here in America, said Theodore Parker, "a new nation could develop the idea into institutions, and ultimately found an empire on the proposition that all men are created equal and endowed by their Creator with certain inalienable rights." Thus, too, did Lincoln in 1861 as the nation headed for Civil War stand at the cradle of liberty in Philadelphia and say, "I have never had a feeling politically that did not spring from the Declaration of Independence . . . I have often inquired of myself what kept this Confederacy together. It was not the mere matter of the separation of the colonies from the motherland, but something in the Declaration giving liberty, not alone to the people of this country, but hope for the world for all future time. It was that which gave promise that in due time the weight would be lifted from the shoulders of all men and that all shall have an equal chance . . . I would rather be assassinated on the spot than surrender it."

Two centuries have passed since the days when the founders set the foundation stone for a new society of man. The splendor and glory of modern day America would certainly astound them just as the generation of the wilderness would have gazed in unbelievable wonder at the pomp and riches of Solomon's kingdom. Who would have believed in the 18th century that these lowly, struggling colonists would some day create a nation to be praised for its supreme power and fabulous wealth? Its people today enjoy a standard of living which the rest of the nations do not even dream of achieving in their lifetimes. The arts, sciences, and letters are flourishing amidst a plethora of popular entertainment and recreation. On the drawing boards there are blueprints for ever more and more of the goods which will bring comfort, pleasure and relaxation in an unending procession. The Day of the Lord is either here now or it is just around the corner.

And yet there is uneasiness and a subtle premonition that all is not well in America. An almost forgotten voice of a distant past seems to be warning us about the future. The ghosts of the days when the Roman Empire fell haunt us, and some historians are trying to draw a frightful parallel. Prophets of doom, now called philosophers of history, following either Spengler's cyclical theory of history, or Toynbee's Watsonian stimulus-response psychological measuring rod are agreed that our way of life is coming to an end. More to the point is a suggestion from the English historian and essayist, Gilbert Murray. He reminds us that in the history of Greece the classical writers, Sophocles and Aristotle, were followed by the Gnostics and Mithras worshippers, for there had developed a loss of confidence in normal human effort, a despair of man's capacity to inquire and to learn. The cry now was for an infallible revelation to free man from his immeasurable sins and pardon him for his unspeakable unworthiness. The purpose of life was no longer the achievement of the true, the good, and the beautiful, but rather, by means of a burning faith and contempt for the world, to be led through suffering, ecstacy, and martyrdom to the bliss of a heavenly utopia. In this second period, says Murray, certain spiritual emotions were highly intensified, when in the face of the challenge of the world men were taken by a "failure of nerve."

Whatever parallel in past history we may find for it, it would appear that our era closely resembles that of the beginning of the fall of the great Athenian civilization when its writers and spokesmen were in the throes of a cry of despair. At the present our culture reveals nothing so much as it does a "failure of nerve."

The cultural environment in which modern man suffers his unrelieved anxiety tends, in large measure, to undermine his self-confidence. Wherever he turns in the cultural market place he is confronted with a portrayal of frustration and hopelessness. If he enters a theater today in the hope of relief and recreation, he is apt to view a play by Tennessee Williams, *Cat On a Hot Tin Roof,* let us say. He will experience for a few hours a powerfully written drama of uninterrupted vileness, corruption, and deceit, and this by one of our leading and successful authors. There is neither comedy nor tragedy here, just a sense of futility and degeneration. In greater or lesser intensity, this mood of defeatism is characteristic of a good deal of the literature he reads, the art to which he is exposed, and the music he hears. In the popular arts, in radio and television, newspapers, magazines, and comic books he feeds upon immature romanticism, cruelty, violence and insidious sexuality. This cultural climate of despair, often unrecognizable because it is pervasive, operates on the subconscious level to intensify his fears. The dominant note for our age was sounded by Joseph Conrad, who counselled creative artists, "In the destructive element immerse. That is the way." The immersion is almost total. A dark cloud of despair hangs over the race of men and their moral will seems to be in a state of shock.

Popularly, and somewhat superficially, the mood of disillusionment is ascribed to the failure of the First World War to fulfill the promise of ending all wars and "making the world safe for democracy." The horror of the Second World War was matched only by the dismal futility of the victory. International chaos linked to business cycles of depression and boom seemed to tear the gyroscope from the center and send life whirling in all directions. More subtle and more basic have been those movements of our century which have unconsciously conspired to root out man's confidence in the business of living. It is obvious that technology has wrought vast changes in our way of life, but what is not even dimly understood is the revolution it has brought into our civilization. We seem to be in the presence of an impersonal power which controls a highly sensitized productive machine whose decisions affect our daily well-being. We are filled with the feeling that something is going on behind our backs. There is a temporary quality to most of our lives, with people always on the move, and ever joining new groups though belonging really to none. The family which ever nurtured us and gave us a center of gravity is steadily losing its influence.

Behind the changes in our pattern of living there are revolutionary discoveries about the universe and man which emphasize the sense of loneliness. The new cosmology has snatched away the comfortable firmament and substituted for it a universe with no center, where everything is in motion, all positions are relative, and where distance is measured by light years. At the same time, the globe we inhabit is growing very small and we are running out of room. We are confronted with a vast emptiness which staggers our imagination and makes of human life a tiny affair, but along with it we feel the effect of the finite size of the earth where technological progress must occur. Psychology since Freud reveals man as a creature of conflicts in the depths of his unconscious, and his conscious behavior as well as his life of reason, it seems, are really at the mercy of these submerged forces. The slogan today is "adjustment," hardly ever a matter of right. Anthropology and sociology unveil a variety of moral patterns and raise in our minds the disturbing question of whether there is, or ever can be, a moral law amidst social relativism. The climate of our culture steadily lowers man's spiritual resistance and weakens the confidence which he needs to handle a changing world and his own growing fears. Today, these lines of the poet of yesterday sound terribly naive:

> "Do your best, whether winning or losing it,
> If you choose to play!—is my principle.
> Let a man contend to the uttermost
> For his life's prize, be it what it will."

In our day we feel more at home with the lines from Yeats:

> "Things fall apart; the center cannot hold;
> Mere anarchy is loosed upon the world,
> The blood dimmed tide is loosed, and everywhere
> The ceremony of innocence is drowned."

There are some telltale signs suggesting that the foundation stone which the builders established is beginning to crumble and disintegrate. The concept of a moral order which is integral to the universe is now out of fashion. The eternal character of right and wrong has been displaced by expediency. This is a time when the end justifies the means, and the end is the man-made ideal we call success. This is the new god, and all that serves him has become right. The important thing is to deliver the goods and if men must rig televison programs, have recourse to prostitution, pour out violence, sex, and crime, the cynical answer as Carl Becker said is "so what." The only goal of life is success, and nothing succeeds like it. An entirely new class has arisen in our society whose business it is to fashion the desires and tastes of men. It is the age of the public relations priest whose dedication is to make men want things they do not need, from deodorants to swimming pools. In dramatic fashion we are confronted with the tragic fate of the girl who fails to buy a brand name hair shampoo. All of this would be trivial and infantile if it were not that these supersalesmen have at their disposal the powerful instruments of communication—television, radio, newspapers and magazines. They are in a position to influence and direct our very way of life. The public relations man is today the spokesman for politicians and businessmen, for schools and labor unions, for hospitals and charities. Indeed, we are in a period when the heads of the two most powerful nations in the world have become global salesmen, using all the paraphernalia of the new craft, smiles, parades, cheers, and glittering words, in order to sell a parochial national image to the world. The basic problems of terror and tyranny, of poverty amidst wealth, of tensions of race and class, are hidden by a barrage of glamorous salesmanship, which is essentially the art of make-believe.

The universe for us is no longer something constructed by a benevolent intelligence—it is not a creation—but rather a self-conditioned becoming. Man, too, is a part of that becoming, an animal organism who has arrived upon the scene without invitation and into a universe which is as unaware of him as of itself, and as indifferent to his fate as to its own. Having no place in the scheme of an undirected evolutionary process, man is what he alone makes himself. He is truly the measure of all values, and since he is the product of biological and cultural forces which are conditioned by time and place, the moral code he professes is entirely dependent upon these given factors. It is, today, less important to know what the truth is than to study its history, its place of origin, and its social conditioning. Good and evil, right and wrong are no longer either the will of God or of natural laws. Instead we celebrate a moral neutrality wherein everything depends upon the circumstances, it is on the one hand and on the other, yea and nay. The idea that man was created by his Creator with certain inalienable rights is, for our time, what Carl Becker calls, "the glittering generalities" of a bygone revolutionary age.

The image of man's nature has been radically altered from the days when Jefferson relied upon him to use his reason and his freedom to know and to choose the good and the true. Man is today conceived to be a creature of deep unconscious drives whose mind is adequate to measure time and space, but who is disqualified, however, to seek and find truth and virtue. The attack upon man as a rational creature comes from the disciples of Freud, Marx, Schopenhauer, and Kierkegaard. Psychologists and theologians have joined forces against the important role of reason in human nature so that we find ourselves confronting an unintelligent universe inhabited by a creature with a very fallible mind. In such an atmosphere law cannot possibly be the expression of enduring principles, and in place of natural law we must rely upon temporary hypotheses. Here man uses his reason as a front for his subconscious desires, and creates "good reasons" for doing what he wants to do. Government by law has become government by men pressuring for their own interests.

Liberty was a natural human endowment for the founders because they conceived of man as a creature with a capacity to make choices and take consequences. They were not unmindful of the Mosaic declaration, "I place before thee the good and the evil, life and death, choose thou the good, choose thou life." Man may be conditioned by many physical elements—but in the moral realm he is a free agent who can use his mind to find the will of God and of nature and obey them. In our day the climate is not hospitable for human liberty. Man is propelled either by environmental forces as defined by Marx, by a repressed storehouse of animal desires as pictured by Freud, or by a mark of ineradicable sin as revived by Niebuhr. To proclaim liberty throughout the land when the inhabitants are conditioned instead of free has a hollow ring. It was believed in an earlier day that man can learn to know what is good and what is required of him, and there was a strong faith in education as a preparation for the good life. Today, in large measure, our schools aim at success in terms of the standards of this material civilization. If democracy is government by men who may be trusted to analyze, to understand, to judge, and to choose the right path, the climate of our culture does not encourage it.

It is currently fashionable to point with supercilious disdain at the naivete of the fathers of the American Revolution for their supposedly childish belief in the easy triumph of right thinking men. Let it be recorded, then, that they knew the ugly facts of life as well as any so-called modern realist. John Adams once said: "The first want of man is his dinner, and the second want his girl." In a letter to John Taylor he said that men are by nature, "indolent, jealous, selfish, cruel, craving of luxury, and addicted to intrigue." "The masses," he said "kiss the feet of those above them and trample on the fingers of those beneath." Hamilton warned that indolence, vicious luxury, and licentiousness of morals stemming from commerce and riches would corrupt the government, enslave the people, and precipitate the ruin of the nation. In 1832 John Calhoun saw, "growing symptoms of disorder and decay discernible on every hand." These men knew the nature of man as well as any modern Freudian, Marxist, or Niebuhrian. They were aware of the limitations of man, both as a creature of reason, and as a child of his sensuous desires. They believed, nevertheless, that with the help of God and His Prophets and teachers, man can move forward toward the triumph of his ideals. If the truth is in some sense relative it does not follow that men cannot distinguish it from error, or that the margin of error cannot be reduced. Man has lifted himself by his reason and his will from the stone age to a position above the level of the brute. He has slowly learned to know the difference between fact and illusion, and the founders chose to encourage his humane and rational qualities, and to fight against those forces which deny and degrade them. The dignity of man and his intrinsic worth, the possibility of an ultimate victory for justice and truth, these were the pillars upon which our American civilization was founded. But these are in our time often rejected and more often neglected by a new generation which has adopted new gods and has fashioned corresponding new rites and ceremonies. It is time for the voice of the Prophet to remind us of the faith of our fathers.

There is a noticeable renewal of interest in the power of spiritual salvation, and the theological market place is alive with both popular and esoteric merchandise. Books on how to achieve peace of mind and how to find happiness outsell any other kind of literature. Television has made priests and ministers as popular as idols of the screen. Popular magazines, and even the more intellectual "small" ones, feature articles on religion. More people crowd into a ball park to hear a famous revivalist than come to watch a home run king hit the ball over the fence. All of this preoccupation ought to thrust a ray of hope and confidence into a cultural era which is dark with despair and defeat. The sad and disillusioning truth is that man, in the sacred portals of the cloister, is feeding on food which helps to intensify his sense of frustration and futility.

The wide appeal of the litany which accentuates the positive is understandable in terms of a way of ridding ourselves of all our problems without the need of doing anything about them. By the power of positive thinking we can be saved without being called upon to tamper with the complex social machinery, without suffering the confrontation of evil, and without devising plans to save ourselves from a final war of annihilation. The ecclesiastical busyness of our time is not only futile, it is harmful since in the face of grim reality it only intensifies man's helplessness and hopelessness. Its cheery optimism is that of a sick mind from which the anxious presence has not been released. It will take more than happy thoughts, or dramatic television conversions, or pleasantly simplified mysteries, to steady our lives and give us the strength to do something about our plight. We will not revive by appealing to the "man upstairs," or by refurbishing some old ceremonies. These "cures" are for people who are not really troubled and who have no basic problems. The danger lies in the illusion given to millions of people who are desperate and who only become more desperate under the anaesthesia. It was this kind of danger which the Prophets of Israel recognized and against which they warned the people. It was likewise, the same "failure of nerve" which corroded a great Hellenic civilization.

A long time ago Lucretius wrote: "When a whole world trembles beneath our feet, when cities are shaken and fall, what wonder if the sons of man feel contempt for themselves, and acknowledge the great potency and wondrous might of the Gods in the world to govern all things." Our day is characterized by an increasing emphasis upon the irrational, an abnormal concern with man's incurable sinfulness, and a pious hope of an easy and quick redemption from all suffering and evil. This strange and alien fruit hides from our sight the crumbling of the foundations of moral faith and human liberty upon which the founders established the nation. This stone which the modern builders reject must again become the chief cornerstone if the nation is to regain its sense of purpose and mission.

SAMUEL AND THE
BEGINNINGS OF THE
PROPHETIC MOVEMENT

William F. Albright, Ph.D., Litt.D., D.H.L., Th.D., LL.D., etc.
*The Gustave A. and Mamie W. Efroymson Memorial
Visiting Professor of Biblical Archaeology, 1961*

THE GOLDENSON LECTURE OF 1961

D URING THE PAST CENTURY HISTORIANS
and theologians have come to agree that the Prophetic movement was the culmination of Israel's history. The better we understand the Prophets the more we marvel at their insight into the nature of man. The Prophets saw man from the standpoint of implicit faith in Israel's God and His purposes. Prophetic literature is quite devoid of anything that can properly be called "mythology"; it is equally free from the sophistication of Greek postulational reasoning. Through simple fusion of implicit faith in the power of Yahweh with consistent realism in judging human nature, the Prophets developed a devastatingly true empirical logic. Without the Prophets we could not possibly have Judaism, Christianity or Islam.

Every serious student encounters two fundamental questions when he begins to occupy himself with Israelite religion. What was the source of Hebrew monotheism? How did the Prophetic movement come into being? The first question was long subordinated to the second, since it was formerly held by nearly all critical scholars that monotheism originated within the Prophetic movement—in short that Amos and his successors created monotheism. This point of view made it quite impossible to understand a movement which itself presupposes monotheism in all extant biblical tradition.

Today the critical views associated with the name of Julius Wellhausen no longer hold the field undisputed, and the number of scholars who follow either Yehezkel Kaufmann or the so-called American archaeological school increases rapidly. (This evening we have here two of the men who have contributed most notably to enlarge the horizon of biblical archaeology, Nelson Glueck and George Ernest Wright.) The two schools agree on the important proposition that we cannot understand either Israel's religious or its political history—even less its literature—unless we begin by recognizing the monotheism of Moses. During the past thirty years Kaufmann and I have modified some of our views, without influencing one another directly. Kaufmann started with a somewhat indefinite position, insisting that monotheism was the creation of Israelite spiritual genius, just as Greek philosophy was the product of Hellenic genius. He did not at first stress the role of Moses, but considered him rather as the embodiment of Israelite spiritual genius than as a clear-cut historical figure. He subsequently laid greater and greater emphasis on Moses as the Israelite founder of the nation Israel and its monotheistic faith. This monotheism he distinguishes in the sharpest way from precursors and contemporary pagan faiths.[1]

I have also modified my own original point of view during the past four years. I still hold that the faith of Moses was true monotheism, now explicit and now implicit, exclusive but always empirical in its logic. But I maintain today that the religious traditions of Genesis were just as tenacious as its customary law and its traditional geography. The religion of the Patriarchs was thus composed of both monotheistic and polytheistic strands. In short, Moses was a reformer, not an innovator; he would presumably have been just as shocked as any later Prophet at being considered as an innovator. (Of course, like every great reformer Moses undoubtedly introduced extremely significant innovations.)[2]

The Prophetic movement struck deep roots into the ancient East, but we cannot even begin to understand it without taking the Hebrew background into consideration and drawing on all the resources of contemporary psychology. The names applied to the prophets are significant: *rô'êh*, *hôzêh*, and especially *nāvî'*. The first two mean "seer," that is, a diviner who sees what is invisible to the ordinary eye by some kind of clairvoyance or organized divination. In practice it would seem that the early seers were mostly diviners who had learned indirectly from the elaborate divinatory techniques of Mesopotamian and other pagan origin, but who were uneducated quacks from the standpoint of a graduate diviner, a *qôsēm*. There are many other expressions which refer with greater or less probability to different kinds of "diviner"; curiously enough, few of them have any etymological relation to a host of terms in Accadian, Ugaritic, Phoenician and other Semitic languages. Our best material, from a comparative point of view, comes from Mari on the Middle Euphrates, whose archives have so illuminated Hebrew Patriarchal tradition. We learn about the activities of the diviner *(bārûm)*, of the oracle-priest *(āpilum)*, of the ecstatic *(maḫḫûm)*, all of whom flourished in the 18th century B.C. and all of whom continued to prosper in the pagan world around Israel.

One moot point may now be considered as settled: the original meaning of Hebrew *nāvî'*, "prophet." All Hebrew verbal forms from the stem *NB'* are derived from the noun *nāvî'*. There is not the slightest real basis for the usual explanation of the original meaning of the word as "speaker."

For instance, Moses was traditionally not a "speaker"; his spokesman was Aaron. When Abraham is called a *nāvî'* (Gen. 20:7), it is clear from the context that the Patriarch receives this appellation because he can intercede with God for the health of Abimelech. In other words, he is a special favorite of God. Many years ago Harry Torcyzner (Tur-Sinai) pointed out that the Accadian word *nabā'um,* with the same consonants, is used constantly in Old Babylonian times in the sense "to call," nearly always of a god's special creation or designation of a man to hold an important post, such as kingship. Derivatives of the verb often mean "favorite (of a god)." I have held this view, which I appear to have reached independently, since the thirties.[3] That it has not made much headway is perhaps due to the absence of the word in its original sense from Hebrew and the directly cognate Northwest-Semitic dialects. In recent years the same verb *nabā'um* has turned up repeatedly, in the same meaning, as an element in Northwest-Semitic personal names at Mari (18th century B.C.), so there can no longer be any doubt as to the basic meaning "call" in Hebrew. Nor does the alleged active meaning for the form *qātîl* have any real basis; for instance Heb. *pāqîd,* "official," is etymologically passive, "one who has been charged with an office," and Arabic *'amîr,* "leader, commander," meant originally "one who has been given a command," from *'ámara,* "to command."

The *nāvî'* was thus one who had been specially called by God for a purpose, one who had a call or vocation from God. The word was limited to non-political and non-administrative use, and designated a charismatic religious figure, a person without hereditary right or political appointment who was authorized to speak or act for Yahweh. Of course, in later practice, prophets tended to form a guild, whose members were the "sons of the prophets" *(bnê nevî'îm).* It is significant that we have scarcely any reference to *nāvî'*, in the later sense of the word, before the active career of Samuel; instead we generally find "man of God" *(îsh hā-'Elôhîm)* or even simply "messenger of God," an expression which seems at first to have referred to human agents as well as to angelic beings. In the early Monarchy "man of God" was apparently a synonym of *nāvî'*.

The sudden appearance of the ecstatic movement in the time of Samuel has long interested biblical scholars, and many explanations have been advanced for it. After many failures it is clear that we must approach this phenomenon from a functional rather than from a genetic point of view. In other words, there is simply not enough evidence to indicate that this particular outburst of ecstaticism came into Israel from abroad, though there is plenty of evidence for ecstatics in earlier, contemporary and later times. Recent psychological research has enormously deepened our understanding of the physiological as well as of the emotional stresses which precede or accompany the radical change of behavior patterns which we call "conversion." Comparative study of the technique employed by Quaker and Methodist revivalists as well as in Communist brain washing has been reinforced by experimental analysis of patterns of behavior in dogs and other animals. Thanks to the work of Pavlov and his disciples on canine behavior, as well as to the intensive work of recent years on the neurophysiology of the brain, much of the fog that formerly shrouded mass movements of religious or quasi-religious nature has been dispelled, and we can see much more clearly. I should like to refer particularly to the brilliant presentation of the subject by a distinguished British neuropsychiatrist, Dr. William Sargant, in *Battle for the Mind* (1958 with a 1961 revision). The case of Saul among the prophets (I Sam. 10 and 19) is typical. After being thrown into a state of intense excitement by Samuel's formal announcement of his consecration as military leader (*nāgîd*) of his people, he meets a band of ecstatic prophets, singing and dancing to the accompaniment of a whole orchestra of musical instruments. We are told that Saul was seized by the ecstatic frenzy of the prophets and joined them in their activity. Another tradition says that he joined the ecstatic prophets, stripping off his clothes and going into a prolonged trance. That he was the last man of whom this might then be expected, is suggested by the proverb quoted in both stories: "Is Saul also among the prophets?" All these phenomena are completely typical. First comes intense emotional stress and then wild dancing and singing to musical accompaniment; the subject discards encumbrances and goes into prolonged trance. The biblical tradition states expressly that "the spirit of God came upon him," and that "God gave him another heart"—that is, his behavior patterns were radically changed.

After what we have learned from neuropsychologists during the past decade there can no longer be any doubt that these traditions reflect a substantially correct idea of what actually happened. Of course, the ancient Israelites had no more notion of just what such profound physiological and emotional experiences meant for the spiritual future of Israel than the orthodox Rabbis of the 18th century had of the significance of Hasidism for the future spiritual vitality of Judaism. Despite the excesses of the movement, we should not have Martin Buber and Abraham Heschel today unless the Ḥasidim had led the way. Gershom Scholem's emphasis on the permanent value of the movement is based on severely intellectual appraisal, with full recognition of its affective sources. In the same way there could have been no Christianity without Pentecost, no Society of Friends without the wild scenes at early Quaker meetings, no world Methodism or its offshoots without John Wesley and subsequent revivalists.

It is to be noted that all of these stories bring Samuel into the closest possible relation to the ecstatic prophets, and that Samuel not only encourages them but actually presides over their meetings (I Sam. 19:20). There is obviously an organic connection between the activity of Samuel and nascent Israelite prophetism. We can now begin to appreciate why Jeremiah ranks Samuel with Moses (Jer. 15:1): "And the Lord said to me, '(Even) if Moses and Samuel stood before me, I should not have sympathy for this people.'" We may also grasp the meaning of the words attributed to Hosea, but probably earlier (to judge from stylistic evidence):

And Israel served for a woman,
    And through a woman was it preserved . . .
And through a prophet did Yahweh bring Israel up
    from Egypt,
    And through a prophet did he preserve . . .
                    (HOS. 12:13f.).

The first verse contains a reference to two women, the first of whom was Rachel, the second possibly Deborah or Jael; the second verse refers to two prophets, the first of whom is obviously Moses and the second probably Samuel. The repetition of words in perfect balance (after a few explanatory words have been omitted) points to the eleventh century B.C., as will be shown elsewhere.

We shall now consider the state of the traditions about Samuel which are found in I Samuel. There can be no doubt that they appear to conflict drastically—to such an extent that scarcely any recent historian of Israel has ventured to reconstruct the historical background of Samuel.[4] Albrecht Alt, who was usually so penetrating in his grasp of underlying political and institutional tendencies in ancient Israel, seemed totally at a loss — a situation reflected in Martin Noth's *History of Israel* (1958). John Bright is also cautious in his own *History of Israel* (1959), and until recently I felt equally helpless. Kaufmann treats the Samuel tradition with respect, but also fails to place him in the development of Israelite religion and society. Aside from daring excursions into the unknown on the part of various scholars, the only serious student who has really tried to place Samuel in the history of Israel is Edward Robertson of Manchester.[5] In my opinion he goes too far in attributing the best part of Deuteronomy to Samuel, but he seems to have been on the right track and to have just missed salient points elsewhere.

After plodding through many efforts to analyze the sources of the Samuel tradition I have given up literary analysis; we simply do not possess the necessary data for such analysis. In the first place, it is clear that the Deuteronomic editor and his precursors were unusually careful not to omit conflicting traditions in order to produce a uniform narrative. Since some editor of Joshua has succeeded pretty well in producing a uniform picture, we can scarcely doubt that the editor or editors of Samuel could have done the same if they had possessed anything like a canonical interpretation of Samuel's career. There was apparently no such interpretation, so they treated the discrepant traditions with respect, though they must sometimes have been just as puzzled as we are.

We have four classes of real or apparent discrepancies. Samuel was an Ephraimite layman of the Zuphite clan (I Sam. 1:1), but he appears elsewhere (I Chron. 6:16-43) as a member of a family of Levitic singers. Again, Samuel was judge over all Israel and left his power to his two sons when he retired (I Sam. 7:15 ff.; 8:1 ff.), but he appears in the

Saul story (I Sam. 9:6 ff.) as a little known diviner. Samuel is said to have roundly defeated the Philistines and to have freed Israel from their yoke "all his days" (I Sam. 7:3-14), but elsewhere Israel is said to have been under Philistine domination during Samuel's time (I Sam. 10:5; 13:3, etc.). Finally we hear that Samuel was strongly opposed to the establishment of the monarchy (I Sam. 8:6 ff., etc.) and also that he favored it (I Sam. 9:17 ff., etc.). What *is* the truth? Obviously we cannot simply distribute these discordant points of view among artificial "sources," or flatter ourselves that we can select among them to suit our own notion of historical probability.

Nor do we have stylistic criteria to help us. For one thing, Cave IV at Qumran has yielded fragmentary manuscripts of Samuel to be published by Frank M. Cross, Jr. They range from a textual type akin to that of all later Hebrew manuscripts and printed Bibles (the Massoretic text), through a text which stands between our Bible and the Greek translation of the third or second century B.C. (the Septuagint), to a text which comes quite close to an archetypal recension from which both the Hebrew Bible and the Greek translation are clearly derived. This means that the text of Samuel which circulated before our extant recensions was considerably longer than either of the latter and that it differed in some important respects from both of them. In the absence of a fixed Hebrew text it is simply impossible to analyze the literary composition of Samuel with any hope of success. The situation is thus even more complex in Samuel than in the earlier books, where the foundations of detailed literary criticism are also being undermined by Cave IV at Qumran.

But in spite of these stubborn facts, the situation of the scholar is actually much better than it was a few years ago. For one thing, we can rely on the relative antiquity of most

Samuel traditions and can treat them as true reflections of
different early Israelite attitudes toward Samuel. For another
thing, we have new evidence from Qumran and other
sources bearing directly on the meaning of common elements in the tradition. We shall see that the care with which
later editors preserved different points of view actually gives
us an unusually wide perspective in reconstructing the data
of Samuel's life. In this respect the Samuel tradition is un-
equalled elsewhere in Israelite literature. What seemed to be
our loss is actually our gain! And the historical picture which
emerges, can be made vivid and intelligible by systematic
use of directly pertinent historical analogies.

Returning to the four outstanding discrepancies which we
noted in the Samuel tradition, the first is not difficult to understand. (Observe that we are trying to understand, not to
harmonize in the old sense.) Samuel was not a member of
the tribe of Levi by birth, but he became attached as a lay
Nazirite to the Tabernacle. The Mishnah states this tradition
categorically in the tractate Nazir: "Samuel was a *nāzîr*."
Modern scholars, following the absurd principle of rejecting
what is not expressly affirmed in all our recensions of the
Bible and disregarding rabbinic tradition entirely, have denied that Samuel was a Nazirite. But the Massoretic Hebrew
text says that Samuel was never to cut his hair or beard, and
the Greek translation not only repeats this prohibition but
adds that he was not to drink alcoholic beverages. Were there
any remaining doubt, it should be removed by the words
preserved in a fragmentary Hebrew manuscript of Samuel
found in Cave IV at Qumran and published by Frank M.
Cross: "he shall become a *nāzîr* for ever," (I Sam. 1:22).[6]
Both Hebrew and Greek have lost this clause by a common
form of scribal omission. The haplography is characteristic
of the Hebrew Samuel and also appears frequently in the

Greek translation. In fact, as stated above, it is now certain that the text of Samuel underlying the Hebrew recensions from which the Septuagint and the Massoretic text are derived, was considerably longer than either. In such cases we must consider the possibility of textual *losses* before we assume that the preserved text contains *glosses*. Once granted the correctness of the tradition that Samuel was a *nāzîr*, it becomes easy to see approximately what happened: Samuel was almost automatically drawn by Levitic tradition into family attachment to the tribe of Levi.

Incidentally, the word *nāzîr* is exactly parallel in formation to *nāvî* "prophet"; it is a pre-Israelite word from the West-Semitic verb *NZR*, "to vow," identical with Ugaritic, Aramaic and Hebrew *NDR* (originally *NDR*, as in Arabic). The meaning of *nāzîr* was therefore originally "one who is vowed (to divine service)"; etymology and place in life fully coincide in the case of Samuel.

Our second discrepancy is the public role attributed to Samuel. As charismatic leader of Israel he was automatically also a "judge," that is, a recognized arbitrator because of his inter-tribal role in the amphictyonic confederation of Israel. But as leader and patron of the ecstatic prophets, who had carried on their ancient function as oracular diviners, he was also a *rô'êh*, a "seer." Furthermore, continuing ancient West-Semitic and specifically Hebrew custom, he was a *nāvî*, one called directly by God to his service, outside hereditary office and royal appointment. In Israelite usage both words had probably received meanings quite different from their original connotations. The Israelite seer was essentially limited to non-Mesopotamian practices, especially to visions and oracles delivered in a state of trance. Similarly, the self-mutilation characteristic of the Phoenician and Syrian *nevi'îm* (I Kings 18:19-40) must have disappeared early in Israel, where castration and other forms of mutilation were an abomination. In short, all the public roles ascribed to Samuel were probably correct—each in its proper time and place.

A third discordancy in the tradition about Samuel is his role in political and military history. Was he successful in whipping up patriotic and religious fervor to the point of successful rebellion against the Philistines? Obviously, not all the traditional accounts can be correct. Personally I see no reason to doubt that the Israelites did win one or more victories over the Philistines, enough to win important concessions from their hereditary foes, who were presumably interested mainly in keeping the trade-routes open. (We must remember that the wholesale use of camels in large-scale trade with Arabia had just begun, and that this revolution in commercial relations made it vitally important to keep Palestinian trade-routes open.) The Assyrian records offer instructive parallels. In the immediately following centuries we often hear that the great king restored a defeated rebel to his throne under suitable conditions. After all, it was much easier to control a subjugated nation through its recognized leader than by imposing an unpopular regime. Once Philistine punitive expeditions had ended, Israelite tradition could easily transform a calculated truce into a military triumph. If Samuel remained as a highly respected arbitrator and religious head of the Israelite tribes, the Philistines had less to fear than if the unruly tribesmen were deprived of all leadership.

The last and most striking discrepancy in the Samuel tradition has to do with his attitude toward kingship in Israel. Before the time of Wellhausen most scholars were intent on harmonizing apparent contradictions, which they achieved by questionable methods. Basically, the inconsistencies were eliminated by assuming that Samuel changed his mind repeatedly because of direct divine intervention. (I fully recognize that Providence intervenes in human affairs, but I object to use of this principle in order to rule out efforts to explain human phenomena by applying historical and psychological principles.) Acute tension doubtless existed in Samuel's mind, with resulting shifts in policy and action, but there is a simple, objective explanation of the origin of this particular discrepancy in our oral sources.

In three passages referring to Saul's rise to power and in four more which similarly refer to David, we note that the new ruler was anointed as *nāgîd* over his people; he is not said in any of these passages to have been anointed king, though the word *melekh,* "king," is often applied to him in other contexts. Solomon, Jeroboam and Baasha are also said to have been anointed as *nāgîd,* but by their time the title may have become otiose. In view of the great significance attached to titularies in the ancient East we may be quite certain that the appearance of *nāgîd* instead of *melekh* in the formula of installation was intentional. In other words, Saul and David were not meant by Samuel or the tribal heads of Israel to be enthroned as kings but only to be anointed as military leaders of the tribal confederation. Of course in practice a distinction became rapidly impossible, and the appellation *melekh* may well have been used by admirers and sycophants from the very beginning. In Judah the establishment of a hereditary monarchy made the term *nāgîd* meaningless, but in the Northern Kingdom the principle of elective leadership was never completely forgotten.

A number of scholars have recently seen that the use of the term *nāgîd* must somehow fit in with the transition from charismatic leadership to monarchy, but preconceived ideas and fanciful etymologies of the word *nāgîd* have invariably spoiled their efforts. Actually we can trace the Aramaic

words *negîdâ* and *nâgôdâ,* "leader, commander," back
through several dialects to the word *ngd* in the Sefireh
treaties of the mid-eighth century B.C. Here, as first seen by
Father Joseph Fitzmyer,[7] the word occurs in the plural between words for "royal princes" and "officials"; the only possible translation is "military commanders." We now see that
the office held by Saul and David was intended by Samuel
to be military leadership over the tribal confederation, stabi-
lized by formal election and religious sanction. That the
nāgîd remained a charismatic figure is proved by the traditions with respect to the elevation of a *nāgîd* from humble
origin to command of Israel. Whether Samuel intended Saul
and David to hold office for life or only for a term, to become
founders of dynasties or not, we shall probably never know.
That his opposition to kingship, as such, remained completely intransigeant is clear enough from the traditions preserved in I Samuel.

One of the most striking features of our Samuel tradition
is the absence of any references in it to Tabernacle, Ark or
priesthood after the death of Eli. The Shiloh Tabernacle had
been destroyed by the Philistines (Psalm 78:60 ff.) and Shiloh lay in ruins for centuries, as stated repeatedly by Jeremiah and confirmed by the Danish excavations on the site.
Its priests were slaughtered (Psalm 78:64). In fact, it was not
until Samuel's protégé, Saul, had become his arch-enemy
that the surviving priests were installed at Nob, only an
hour's walk from Saul's residence at Gibeah. The Ark is said
to have remained on the Philistine frontier at Beth-shemesh
and Kirjath-jearim during the whole of Samuel's career and
well into the reign of David. (A supposed allusion to the
Ark in the time of Saul [I Sam. 14:18] certainly refers to the
ephod, as demonstrated by the Greek translation and by the
use of the verb *higgîsh.*)

Samuel is said to have offered sacrifices himself on several occasions, without any suggestion that this was not normal practice. The assumption of modern critical scholars that cultic sacrifice had not yet been limited to Levites, is just as arbitrary as the position of the Chronicler that Samuel was actually a Levite himself. Samuel's attitude toward cultic ritual is well illustrated by tradition, according to which his view of the efficacy of sacrifice was substantially identical with that of Hosea, Isaiah, Micah and Jeremiah:

> Behold, to obey is better than sacrifice,
> To listen than the fat of young rams!

Samuel's attitude toward sacrificial ritual seems to have extended toward the whole institutionalized system. It is made perfectly clear by tradition that he was quite ready to replace the official sanctuary by local high places. We must remember that our evidence now points overwhelmingly to an original memorial function of the high places, which corresponded quite closely to the hero shrines of the Greek world.[8] Even rabbinic tradition recognized that the *bâmôt* of Samuel's time were not so objectionable as they later became. We may suppose that Samuel and his band of prophets cleared away the more obviously pagan symbols and practices, much as the Christian missionaries of the Middle Ages did in the case of Germanic and Slavic shrines.

It is not hard to see why Samuel rejected the priestly ritual of Shiloh. As a youth he had been an intimate spectator of the corruption which made the Elide family a byword in Israel, leading ultimately to its exclusion from the Levitic genealogies in Chronicles. (This is presumably also the reason for its attribution to the family of Ithamar instead of to that of Eleazar, ancestor of the Zadokites [I Chron. 24:3].) The destruction of Shiloh and the decimation of its priests were the most convincing possible proof to men of Samuel's time that God was angry at the religious leaders of Israel and their ritualized form of Mosaic tradition. There may also have been a very human element in Samuel's reform movement. As a youth he presumably suffered from the persecution of other boys at Shiloh who belonged to priestly and Levite families. Our own experience of the cruelty of the young is here reinforced by many systematic studies, ranging from phenomena of gang psychology to social parallels with the so-called "peck hierarchy" of barnyard fowls. We need have little doubt that Samuel's recorded harshness and refusal to compromise received part of its impetus from unhappy experiences as a boy in Shiloh.

Our contention that Samuel was the first great religious reformer after Moses and that he rejected—or diminished—the spiritual role of priests and Levites at the same time that he turned to ecstatic prophets and local sanctuaries to replace the Shilonic system is actually not hard to defend. For close analogies we have only to turn to the later history of the Judeo-Christian religious continuum. Analogy is a method of proof which must be used with the greatest caution. During the past few years I have been trying to analyze its use in different fields of knowledge, with interesting results. It is used and abused in all fields, even in such austere disciplines as mathematics and physical science. The historian must be doubly careful, in view of the tendency among research scholars to neglect essential precautions and to forget the relative absence of experimental checks. However, if one stays within a given continuum and limits historical analogy to the areas which are functionally involved in the continuum, one has at least a good heuristic base of operations. If, moreover, there is enough illustration and confirmation within the tradition itself, good analogy may become demonstration—though the historian must always welcome additional evidence.

The Judeo-Christian religious continuum is historically a synthesis of two main factors. First we have a developing pattern of covenants between God and early Israel, governing faith, ethics and cult. Second we see the interaction of two distinct elements in periodic tension: an institutionalized hierarchy of religious functionaries and an upsurge of charismatic spiritual leaders. Because of this ever-renewed tension between hierarchy and charism, the Judeo-Christian continuum has always been capable of periodic self-criticism —a process to which Western conscience owes its persistent revivals of sensitivity.

We must limit ourselves to a few striking examples of the replacement of priests by prophets in post-Israelite times. First may be mentioned the emergence of the Essenes in the second century B.C. During the last two centuries of the Second Temple, the Essenes turned their backs on the Jerusalem priesthood, disapproving of its impure blood and its corruption. Priests of Zadokite descent enjoyed high prestige value among the Essenes, but very little power; they were held in reserve for the purified Temple of the future. The early Christians went still farther. While the Essenes included three priests with twelve laymen in their governing body, the apostolic Church kept only the twelve laymen. All believers became spiritually priests. Meanwhile the Pharisees had been encouraging teachers, called *rabbânîm,* who began to replace priests as leaders of the community before the end of the Second Temple. Afterwards the priests retained only modest prestige value and for all practical purposes were replaced by ordained rabbis. Meanwhile Christians were ordaining laymen as spiritual leaders of the community until they became in turn an organized priestly hierarchy. In the fourth and subsequent centuries the secular clergy began to be supplemented—and often bitterly opposed—by solitary desert monks (hermits) and monastic communities, most famous of which were the Benedictines, founded in the sixth century. It was not, however, until the thirteenth and fourteenth centuries that the mendicant friars ("brothers") began their phenomenal rise, in constant protest against corruption among the secular clergy. From this long-continued tension arose the accepted system of checks and balances between the secular hierarchy and the religious bodies (orders and congregations, etc.) which has kept the Roman Church on such an even keel during the past few centuries.

The Reformation brought much more violent revolution. Lutherans and Calvinists replaced ordained priests by pastors ("shepherds"), of both priestly and lay origin. Even Sweden and England, which nominally kept the old hierarchy, accepted some Protestant innovations with respect to the nature of the priesthood. In the 18th century John Wesley, though an Anglican priest all his life, introduced a system of lay preachers which soon turned again into an ordained ministry. In America this system has become the most tightly organized hierarchy known in any large Protestant church in the world.

At the same time similar processes were at work in Jewish religious circles. In the eighteenth century the Hasidic movement replaced the orthodox rabbinate by saints and miracle-workers (tsadikim and rebs), who in turn became regularized among their sectarian followers. Today the same process is visible in younger movements within Judaism, while among Christian sects illustrations might easily be multiplied. All these phenomena are characteristic of the self-critical continuum of Judeo-Christianity. It is interesting to note that the only really effective checks and balances which arose as a result of these periodical reform movements are to be found in the pre-Exilic Monarchy and in the Catholic Church today. The constant tension between priests and prophets in Israel, under the vacillating control of the kings of Judah and Israel, gave rise to the Age of the Prophets, from which emerged both Judaism and Christianity.

For lack of time we shall limit ourselves to a concise analysis of a final problem: Have we any literary monuments of the Prophetic movement of Samuel's time? In my opinion we do have at least one such monument—the wonderful poem in Deuteronomy 32 which was subsequently credited to Moses and which is known in Jewish tradition by its first word, *Ha'azînû*. The first recent scholar to defend a date as early as the middle of the eleventh century is Otto Eissfeldt, who proposed this early dating in 1956 and defended it in detail two years later.[9] The following year I accepted his early date, attributing the composition of *Ha'azînû* to about the third quarter of the eleventh century, between ca. 1050 and 1020 B.C.[10] Eissfeldt first drew Samuel into the picture; it has only been since 1959 that I have recognized that there was a close relation between *Ha'azînû* and the reformation of Samuel.

During the past twenty years I have become increasingly confident that the minimal dating of Israelite poetry by the Wellhausen school is generally quite erroneous. This is particularly true of the earliest Hebrew verse. (In this research I have been ably assisted by former students, notably by Frank M. Cross, Father Mitchell Dahood, and David Noel Freedman.) Thanks to the discovery and decipherment since 1929 of early Northwest-Semitic epics at Ugarit in northern Canaan, it is now possible to place the Song of Miriam (Exodus 15) at the beginning of Israelite verse, since it is consistently closer to Ugaritic style than any other poem of any

length in the Bible. The Song of Miriam is followed in stylistic sequence dating by the Song of Deborah and the Oracles
of Balaam, both from the twelfth century. The latter two replace the types of repetitive parallelism characteristic of Ugarit and the Song of Miriam by repeating single words in
parallel verse units. They are followed by the Blessing of
Moses (Deut. 33), *Ha'azînû,* and the Blessing of Jacob (Gen.
49) in an order which is supported both by stylistic sequence
dating and by indications from the content. For instance,
Levi is still highly praised in the Blessing of Moses, *before*
the fall of Shiloh, but is bitterly condemned in the Blessing
of Jacob, *after* the fall of Shiloh. With the Blessing of Jacob
we enter the period of elaborate play on words (paronomasia), which continued for several centuries. Stylistic sequence alone would place the Song of Moses in the eleventh
century. There are numerous other indications of genuine
archaism, and the author's rugged and often intemperate
monotheism best suits the time of Samuel, as we shall presently see.

My uncompromising insistence on the high antiquity of
these poems—and of others in the Psalter and elsewhere—
may sound like a return to pre-critical methods of biblical
research. Actually it is nothing of the kind. Here again we
have complete agreement between internal evidence—both
of content and style—and the evidence of historical analogy.
It would be passing strange if the Hebrew Bible were the
only extant national literature of the Old World which began with prose and did not compose poetry until later. (I
am not referring to tiny snatches of verse like the Song of
the Well, which are commonly included among early compositions, but to whole poems.) In Greek and Latin, Germanic and Slavic, Romance and Ugro-Finnic literatures, men
began to compose songs and epics in verse; prose always

came later and the few apparent exceptions disappear on closer inspection. The same is true of Indian and Iranian, Chinese and other East-Asiatic literatures. It is also true of the literatures (as distinct from formal inscriptions and economic texts, etc.) of Egypt and Babylonia, Canaan and Arabia. The overwhelming list of parallels for the priority of poetry to prose does not prove that Israel followed the same rule; this is demonstrated by the chronological study of linguistic and stylistic elements, after the burden of proof has been completely shifted by analogy from followers of Wellhausen to his opponents.

Fortunately the text of *Ha'azînû* is, like the older Song of Miriam, in a good state of preservation; Qumran fragments published by Patrick W. Skehan, have shown that the fuller Greek translation is older than the shorter Massoretic recension. The good state of the text is naturally due to the fact that these two poems were the most popular verse compositions in the Hebrew Bible, as might be inferred from the fact that the stichometric form which was doubtless characteristic of most early copies of Hebrew poetic texts, has been preserved in the Massorah.

It is now widely recognized that a pattern of controversy appears clearly in *Ha'azînû,* even though the word *rîv* itself is missing. The *mise en scène* is the same as in Micah 6:1 ff., where the mountains and the foundations of the earth appear as judges between God and his people, and we have similar scenes of divine controversy elsewhere in the Prophetic books. There is nothing late, as often assumed, in the opening verse of *Ha'azînû* (Deut. 32:1):

> Listen, O heaven, to what I say,
> And hear, O earth, the words of my mouth!

We have Old Accadian and Middle Babylonian parallels, dating from the late third and early second millennium, and

preserved in Old Babylonian and Assyrian copies. An Old
Accadian hymn begins:

      Listen, O comrades,   Hear, O warriors!

The Song of Deborah continues this tradition, about a century before the probable date of *Ha'azînû*.

Heaven and earth appear as guarantors of incantatory
oaths by which the Mesopotamian magician expelled de-
mons, just as the gods of heaven and earth guarantee the
oaths which bind the contracting parties in Hittite treaties of
the fourteenth-thirteenth centuries B.C. Similarly, the mountains in Micah are surrogates for the mountain gods of ancient Syria and Anatolia which also appear prominently in
the same treaties. Many of the most important Anatolian and
Northwest-Semitic deities of the second millennium B.C.
were deified mountains—a fact which incidentally explains
why *ṣûr* "mountain" (Aramaic *ṭûrâ*, Ugaritic *ghûru*) appears so often in such an archaic poem as *Ha'azînû* in the
meaning "god, God," as well as why it has the same sense in
several Hebrew personal names of the Mosaic period.

It now becomes obvious that *Ha'azînû* presupposes the
covenant pattern of early Israel which, as George E. Mendenhall has pointed out, reflects with astonishing fidelity the
structure of Hittite suzerainty treaties of the Mosaic age.[11]
(These treaties probably follow Northwest-Semitic or Hur-
rian [Horite] models from Syria and Northern Mesopotamia.) The stipulations of the covenant preserved the civic
morality and religious teaching of early Mosaic faith for
later generations; the Prophets saved them from submerg-
ence under the rising tide of cultic and administrative practice, both priestly and royal.

The theodicy of *Ha'azînû* is particularly instructive. It is
remarkably archaic when compared with such later recitals
of the acts of God (to use George Ernest Wright's felicitous

term) as Hosea 2, Jeremiah 2 and Ezekiel 20. Starting with
the pre-Israelite myth of the distribution of nations among
members of the divine assembly, it alludes only in the vagu-
est terms to specific historical events which were, of course,
perfectly clear to the audience for which the poem was composed. Since the Greek reading of verse 8, "according to the
number of the sons of God," has been corroborated by the
reading of the Qumran recension published by Patrick W.
Skehan, *"bnê 'Elôhîm,"*[12] there can be no doubt as to the
meaning of this ethnogonic myth nor, in my opinion, that
the Most High (*'Elyôn*), who supervised the distribution of
nations is identical with Yahweh, to whom Israel fell as His
lot. The ancient myth has thus been demythologized, yet it
remains more archaic than anything comparable in later biblical literature.

In a paper published in 1959 I called attention to numerous
archaic elements of style, vocabulary and imagery which are
characteristic of *Ha'azînû*: there are many other examples
which I did not quote. In my opinion there cannot be the
slightest doubt that the poem is pre-monarchic. Eissfeldt has
further demonstrated the close relation between it and Psalm
78, which he correctly attributes to the time of David. (It
may actually date from the time of Solomon or a little later,
when the figure of David was still recent and romantic.)
Psalm 78 contains the earliest detailed recital of the acts of
God, ending with the destruction of Shiloh and the replacement of Ephraim by Judah as political and cultic center. It
contains important traditional data not found in any other
source, and includes direct quotations and reminiscences of
both *Ha'azînû* and the Song of Miriam.

Two main streams of later Israelite religious literature may
both be traced through direct borrowing and adaptation back
to *Ha'azînû* and the genre of which it is the chief exemplar;

they are Deuteronomic theology and Prophetic theodicy. In
Ha'azînû and Psalm 78 the conquest of Israel by the Philistines and the dramatic fall of Shiloh represent the final and
bitterest phase of divine punishment of rebellious Israel. This
phase is followed in *Ha'azînû* by divine punishment of Israel's foes, and in Psalm 78 by the messianic rise of David.
The later Prophets learned by bitter experience that the pattern is not so simple, that renewed rebellion would be followed by more punishment, that the "day of the Lord" is
"darkness, not light." The burden of the Prophets from Elijah to Micah is then formulated into the sober warnings
from generalized experience which we find in the Book of
Deuteronomy. The incorporation of *Ha'azînû* into the final
edition of Deuteronomy is a recognition that the message of
the Book is prefigured in the magnificent cadences of the
poem.

It is interesting to note that later Levitic tradition (I Chron.
6:18, etc.) made Heman, one of the founders of the musical
guilds of David's time, a grandson of Samuel. Since this
tradition conflicts directly with other, older, evidence,[13] it
cannot be correct as it stands, but it suggests an early association of Samuel with the beginnings of Israelite hymnology.
We can, at all events, use *Ha'azînû* to illustrate the great religious reform which Samuel brought about and without
which Elijah and Jeremiah could not have filled their place
in history. A *Leitmotif* appears in the stern, but healing
words of Deut. 32:39:

Behold now, I am I[14] And there is no other God than I;
I kill and restore to life,[15]
    After I have smitten I heal,
        and none can save from my hand!

NOTES

[1]See now the English abridgement of Kaufmann's great work, under the title of *The Religion of Israel*, by Moshe Greenberg (University of Chicago Press, 1960), especially pp. 212 ff.

[2]Besides my concise treatment in the latest edition of *From the Stone Age to Christianity* (1957), pp. 257-272, see my forthcoming detailed discussion in the first volume of Louis Finkelstein's projected "History of the Jewish Faith" (approximate title).

[3]See *From the Stone Age to Christianity* (1957 edition), pp. 17, 303-305.

[4]A curiously thorough attempt to reconstruct the situation reflected in the Samuel tradition, written against the point of view of Robertson Smith, S. R. Driver and H. P. Smith (who introduced modern German criticism into the Anglo-Saxon world) was a book by George C. M. Douglas, *Samuel and His Age: A Study in the Constitutional History of Israel* (London, 1901). Here we have a painstaking attempt to harmonize, running to 300 pages, which utilizes nothing except the Hebrew-English Old Testament, refusing even to consult the versions! It is worth reading if only in order to realize the ground we have covered—and are having not infrequently to retrace—since the late Victorian age.

[5]Cf. his articles in the *Bulletin of the John Rylands Library* and especially his book, *The Old Testament Problem: A Reinvestigation* (Manchester, 1950).

[6]See *Bulletin of the American Schools of Oriental Research*, No. 132 (1953), pp. 15-26.

[7]*Catholic Biblical Quarterly*, 20 (1958), pp. 444-476.

[8]See my essay, "The High Place in Ancient Palestine" (*Vetus Testamentum, Supplement* IV, 1957, 242-258).

[9]See his *Einleitung in das Alte Testament* (1956), pp. 271 f., and *Das Lied Moses Deuteronomium 32 1-43 und das Lehrgedicht Asaphs Psalm 78 samt einer Analyse der Umgebung des Mose-Liedes* (Berlin, 1958).

[10]See my paper "Some Remarks on the Song of Moses in Deuteronomy XXXII" *Vetus Testamentum*, IX (1959), pp. 339-346.

[11]See Mendenhall, *Law and Covenant in Israel and the Ancient Near East* (Pittsburgh, The Biblical Colloquium, 1955).

[12]See *Journal of Biblical Literature*, 78 (1959), p. 22.

[13]See provisionally my discussion of the origin of the guilds of singers, *Archaeology and the Religion of Israel* (1956 edi-tion), pp. 125-129, 209-211, 227 f., 230, n. 70.

[14]For this translation see my remarks in *Vetus Testamentum*, IX, pp. 342 f.

[15]It is no accident that this colon recurs in almost identical wording I Sam. 2:6, probably from the time of David (as pointed out by D. N. Freedman).

ADDITIONAL NOTE TO GOLDENSON LECTURE

For a connected historical survey of the age of Samuel see my Harper Torch Book, *The Biblical Period from Abraham to Ezra* (New York, 1963), pp. 36 ff.

On the use of historical analogy and models in connection with the role of Samuel, see my *Archaeology, Historical Analogy and Early Biblical Tradition* (Rockwell Lectures at Rice University), Baton Rouge, 1966, especially pp. 42 ff.

On various topics see also my book *Yahweh and the Gods of Canaan,* London, March, 1968, and New York, September, 1968 (with different paging and more fully corrected text). For a detailed account of the stylistic evolution of early Hebrew verse, see pp. 1 ff.; for the Prophetic movement in Israel see the London edition, pp. 181 ff., 212 ff., and the New York edition, pp. 208 ff., 244 ff.

PROPHETIC RELIGION
IN AN AGE
OF REVOLUTION

Leon I. Feuer
Rabbi, Collingwood Avenue Temple
Toledo, Ohio

THE GOLDENSON LECTURE OF 1962

WE HAVE REACHED THE GREAT DIVIDE OF history. The alternatives before us are universal destruction, or the great surge forward toward plenty and the opportunity of fulfillment for the entire race. The crisis and tension involved in such a choice demand an urgent spiritual response which will help men to choose the right way. The guidance required can best be provided by prophetic religion. This will be the thesis of this paper, dedicated to the labors of one of the preeminent prophetic spirits of our time, Samuel H. Goldenson. Inadequate though I feel to the challenge, I am deeply grateful to President Glueck for the opportunity.

As we review the meaning and purpose of prophecy in ancient Israel, we shall not be surprised to discern intimations of our own time, for inherent in prophecy has always been the quality of immortality, of relevance to any age and circumstance. Three functions of prophecy seem to have been paramount. First, to remind the people of and to demand their return to the basic principles of pure religion, in their case to the ethical mandates of the Torah as revealed to and lived by their ancestors in the desert. In the desert there were no elaborate rituals and no mounds of sacrifices, so the prophet declared. It was an ideal time of simple but rigorously moral living by the members of the tribes, and of the practice toward each other of brotherly democracy. It is of course probable that nostalgia had somewhat transfigured the reality, but the conception of religion implied in this looking backward is crystal clear. "Thus saieth the Lord: Stand ye in the ways and see, and ask for the old paths, where is the good way and walk therein, and ye shall find rest for your souls." (Jeremiah 6.16).

The second function of prophecy was to examine critically the personal, political, and social morality of the contemporary age, especially the equation of cultic with ethical religion. "But I truly am full of power by the spirit of the Lord, and of justice and of might, to declare unto Jacob his transgression, and to Israel his sin." (Micah 3.8). The prophet insisted that personal conduct and social righteousness are inseparable. Therefore he was deeply concerned with the social consequences of men's actions. "Seek justice, relieve the oppressed." (Isaiah 1.17). The wrongs of Society—exacting interest and pledges from those too poor to afford them, the foreclosure of mortgages, enslavement for debt, profiteering, sharecropping, judical venality, and so on— all were roundly denounced. "What mean ye that ye crush my people and grind the face of the poor?" (Isaiah 5.8). It must be emphasized, however, that the prophets were not class revolutionaries. They tried to ferret out evil wherever it was to be found, among the poor as well as among the powerful and the wealthy. "Cease to do evil, learn to do well." (Isaiah 1.16). But they certainly did not hesitate to direct their verbal shafts at the seats of authority and power. Samuel, Elijah, and Nathan addressed their blazing admonitions to kings, Amos to the rich and privileged classes, and Jeremiah the priest attacked in the very court of the Temple the substitution of placatory rites for personal morality and social righteousness. They refused to speak "smooth things," to "prophesy delusions." Like Amos, they spoke up in times of apparent national prosperity and well-being, warning that behind the good times was the spectre of corruption. More important, however, they did not hesitate to prophesy in times of national crisis and danger, addressing their words to their own nation and to all nations, predicting defeat, disaster, and desolation, especially in the absence of repentance and reform, and in terms which could well seem to the imaginative a startling preview of megatonic firestorm:

> "Then said I: 'Lord, how long?'
> And He answered:
> Until cities be laid waste without inhabitant,
> And houses without man
> And the land became utterly waste." (Isaiah 6.11)

The third function of prophecy, particularly in a "time of trouble," was to extend comfort to the people and to project a vision of hope for their future. In a besieged Jerusalem about to fall, Jeremiah purchased land, and in the midst of destruction he foresaw restoration. The prophet was the emissary of hope, even when it had to be of hope deferred. Like the author of Jonah, he sometimes reckoned with the possibility that doom might be averted by moral regeneration. Or a saving remnant might heed the challenge and the nation be redeemed under its leadership. If disaster did come then ultimately there would be redemption, return from exile, and rebuilding. In one form or another, hope for the future had to be kept alive, and the prophets were all of them very much concerned with the form and shape of that future. They hoped for it in terms of justice and peace for all men and nations, in exalted forecasts of freedom for the oppressed, of opportunity for the downtrodden, of individual aspiration for moral integrity, of collective striving for the better life. "And it shall come to pass in the end of days—." (Isaiah 2.2ff.). In discussing the element of hope in prophetic faith, Dr. Sheldon Blank reminds us: "To the writers collectively known as Trito-Isaiah it was obvious. Hope was not so much a heavenly gift as a divine requirement. God commanded the prophets to clear the way and they, faithful to their charge, decried despair, demanded hope. And their hope was half determination. They and their people were frontiersmen of the spirit looking to the future with creative expectancy."

In view of the role we shall later attempt to ascribe to prophetic religion in our own time, we need to recall one or two more of its characteristics. Most significant was the prophet's claim, and therefore, his confidence that he was "called by God" to speak. He was as certain of this as he was of God's and of his own existence. God is and therefore I prophesy, might have been his credo. God was his authority, and the only one he needed. God was the criterion, the pattern, the "plumbline" for man. Man must do justly, love mercy and walk humbly because God requires it of him. No other guide is to be so implicitly trusted—neither ruler, priest, prophet, and we may add, leader or party. The prophet's only weapon was speech, speech flowing out of his conviction that God was speaking through him. "The Lord God hath spoken, Who can but prophesy?" (Amos 3.8). He possessed no other weapon. He did not have at his disposal either the power of the state or the prestige of the official cult. He spoke whenever and wherever the spirit moved him or the opportunity presented itself—in the royal

court, in the shrine, in the market place, at any assembly
of the people. Therefore his speech had to be authoritative,
urgent, challenging, and compelling.

The prophetic response is by no means the only one possible in a "time of trouble," or for that matter under normal
conditions. William James defined religion as the total reaction to reality. As such it manifests itself in varying moods
and on different levels of human awareness, answering as it
is required to, many types of intellectual and emotional
needs. There are, again to refer to James, "varieties of religious experience." There is the ritual-magic response. Man
tries to appease, to divert the anger of, to extort mercy from
the Deity through the tendering of gifts and sacrifices. Or
in a more mature approach, he endeavors to fortfy himself
in periods of difficulty by drawing the divine strength into
himself through supplication and prayer. Job incidentally
was refused such sustenance and had to accept God and
Nature as they were, as impenetrable riddles. Then there is
the mystical strategy. By the leap of faith to identification
with God, man soars above his predicament and in the
ecstasy of the consummation of the unity between the
human and the divine transmutes his pain into joy, or at
least into understanding. Mysticism has been one of the
most popular methods by which man sought the help of
God. There is, of course, considerable of it in the work of
the literary prophets. Certainly, in the Psalms. Illustrative
too are the mystery cults in the religions and philosophies
of the Greco-Roman world, the confessions of the medieval
Christian saints, and Jewish Chassidism. Finally, there is
the apocalyptic response which involves a flight through
dreams, trance, projection from present reality to another
life or realm of being. "God's kingdom is not of this world."

The individual seeks his salvation by regarding the pain and misery of this life as incidental, or bearable, or indigenous to mortal existence, because he looks forward to the prospect of another, a more real and significant, an eternal life in which there will be no suffering or disquietude except for the damned. There is a considerable admixture of this view in Hellenistic Judaism. It is of the essence of some forms of Buddhism. The best example, however, is early Christianity. Walter Kauffman and others have observed that although the Church has been compelled in its historic career to come to terms with the world, Christianity has never altogether left behind its original apocalyptic orientation. The evidence for this we find not only in Catholicism, but in some of the currently popular systems of Protestant theology.

When men react to their circumstances religiously, they generally react in one or the other of these modes of expression—the prophetic, the ritualistic, the mystical, and the apocalyptic. The matter is not, of course, so clear cut. Sometimes we oscillate from one mood to another. We know that the prophets did so. We find these forms of expression in all the religions. No one faith has a monopoly on any of them. As moods they fade into and out of each other in the various circumstantial phases of a religion's history. The various religions, however, as we have already indicated, do exhibit tendencies to favor one type of response over the other, and thus to some extent at least to condition the spiritual reactions of their followers. All of these moods are present in Judaism and find expression in Jewish thought and literature. Under varied and especially under more rigorous conditions, Judaism utilized one or the other to enable Jews to withstand abnormal strains and pressures. We have already adverted to the examples of Hellenistic Judaism and of Chassidism. The influence of popular schools of philosophy—we shall see how this operates today—and of contacts with new types of religion also played their role.

Nevertheless, it is undeniable that the prophetic response was and remained the most characteristic and persistent. Basically, Jews felt that man's destiny in the meaningful sense was to be played out on this earth, and that if his lot was to be improved, it had to be done here. As Dr. Abba Hillel Silver has written: "The kingdom of God—which mankind with the help of God is to build—is in Judaism's view definitely of this world, and all of man's tasks are centered here. In Judaism, the kingdom of God means the Good Society." This is the core of prophetic religion, and there can be no doubt that it is the predominant motif of Jewish thought, and certainly at the root of the Messianic impulse in Jewish history. Moreover—this is the thesis which Dr. Jacob Agus developed in a previous Goldenson lecture— the prophetic image of itself was the characteristic one which the Jewish people cherished in its tradition, and which it has exhibited most conspicuously in its literature, from the earliest to the contemporary period. It is undebatable that in Judaism a sensitized social consciousness is considered preferable to individual salvationism—in any form, temporal or eschatological. The very emphasis, continuous in Jewish thinking, upon the peoplehood of Israel is conclusive evidence. From Moses onward, Judaism has been *the* prophetic faith of mankind. Moses is depicted as the first and the foremost of the prophets. The prophets hold an honored place in the Canon, and regardless of difference of opinion between biblical critics about chronological sequence, their influence upon Torah and tradition is clear. While there has always been some ambivalence among Jews as between their roles as a priest-people and prophet-people, the ambition to become a prophet-people has been insistent. "And your sons and daughters shall prophesy." (Joel 3.1). Judah Halevi said that upon Israel was bestowed the highest of the divine gifts, prophecy.

The present Age of Revolution is more severe in the various aspects of its crisis, and more universal in its involvement than any previous in man's experience. Like an irresistible tide, social upheaval is sweeping the earth. The revolutionary ideology of Communism or Marxism-Leninism, as its followers now prefer to call it, has installed its rule in vast territories and over hundreds of millions of people. The several deviants of it have become the modi operandi of smaller nations struggling for political independence and for economic sufficiency. To many peoples the lure which it dangles of material plenty quickly achieved has become irresistible bait. In the name of the submerged and miserable masses it trumpets the end of inequality, class distinction, and poverty, and the demise of imperialism and colonialism. Wherever revolutions have not already taken place, they are seething not far beneath the surface. In such countries, only the armed forces and military dictatorship are temporarily preventing revolts from erupting, and with the demonstrated success of guerrilla tactics, they will probably not be able to do so for long. No people anywhere today is willing to resign itself to the chronic condition of want. Peoples wrenching themselves away from colonial empires are struggling on two fronts, first to make good their political liberty and then to raise their standards of living. The end of colonialism is simply the dawning awareness that some groups of men need not be at the mercy of others for their freedom and livelihood. Involved in this revolutionary situation, but crossing national boundaries and continents, is the drive of the colored peoples, not only for their civil rights and for economic opportunity, but for the recognition of equality and of their dignity as human beings.

The nations of the West, economically advanced, having passed through their own revolutionary phases, seeing their economic and political hegemony over large areas of the earth dissipated, feel threatened by the current cycle of revolutions and are arming to the teeth to resist them. Russia and China, basing themselves upon the Marxist-Leninist doctrine that the end of the age of Capitalism-Imperialism is at hand, are exploiting every area of dissatisfaction, and transforming themselves into military states which challenge the West at every point. Thus universal war has become an imminent threat. What makes the situation so serious, of course, is not only the extent but the depth of the revolutionary ferment. It is radically different from any crisis in the past. The advance of technology has been so rapid and so remarkable that it holds implicit, paradoxically, both the threat of doom and the promise of Paradise. The weapons race in all of its horrifying nuclear, chemical, and biological manifestations grows deadlier by the hour. The triggering of war either by plan, accident, or panic, has become the omnipresent nightmare of national leaders both in the West and in the East. We cannot here go into a discussion of that sinister numbers game of guess and calculation about the possible mutual effects of deterrence—balanced, preventive, or other types—with which the military statisticians so coolly amuse themselves. What is clear, however, to sober scientists and observers is that if war breaks out, either by miscalculation or otherwise, universal destruction and possibly the total annihilation of life, are distinct probabilities.

At the same time—and this is the strange contradiction in the present predicament—the amazing advances in the sciences and in the various forms of technology make it distinctly possible, not only in the remote future, but within the next generation, peaceably to provide plenty for all. We may suggest that the essence of this Age of Revolution is that we are in a race between war and social improvement, in either of which alternative the technological advances of our time may be utilized. Today the poor constitute two-thirds of the human species. Their personal income averages less than one hundred dollars a year. Ignorance and illiteracy keep them untrained and unavailable for the skilled types of labor required by a modern automating society. Their nutrition is below the bare minimum. Life expectancy is between twenty-nine and thirty-nine. There have always been the poor and the rich. Today, to use the title of Barbara Ward's recent book, there are also "the poor nations and the rich nations," with the birthrate of the poor nations outrunning their food, goods, and resources. The scandal of this is that it is altogether unnecessary. The social scientists have been telling us that automation and the computer process known as "feedback" can render poverty not only obsolete, but likewise both the Communist and Capitalist ways of coping with it. Gerald Piel writes: "Human want has now become as immoral as slavery, for the reason that want is technologically obsolete . . . there is no technological reason why the capacity of the industrial system should not already be equal to meeting the real needs of all the people." It is significant that the editor of the *Scientific American* made these remarks in connection with his sharp criticism some years ago of the American decision to develop the hydrogen bomb. In the same passage he continues: "If we would comprehend the true source of our security, the productive capacity of the world's most advanced industrial system can be mobilized to secure the abolition of want and the peace of the world before the end of the century." How to resolve the paradox of poverty in the midst of plenty which if unresolved will surely send mankind down the road to nuclear catastrophe; how to set our sights upon the right goals of human salvation—these require the vision, the capacity to plan and to make sacrifices, and perhaps above all the will to justice. This calls for the kind of moral and theological reorientation of our thought patterns which today ought to be the prime concern and consideration of religion.

As in all crisis situations of the past, there is now no lack of variety of religious responses. There is the by now well-advertised religious revival, especially in the United States, with its phenomenal growth in Church and Synagogue affiliation, the investment of huge funds in religious plants, and the intensified interest in popular religious books and films. This is accompanied by a professed concern with the atheism of Communist countries and with their persecution of "true believers." The religious revival, about which some healthy skepticism is developing, offers us a complete catalogue of the familiar ritual, mystic, and apocalyptic responses of the past as well as some modern variations. We can permit ourselves only a brief resumé of them.

There are the popular evangelists, the purveyors of quick salvation for the soul via a return to the literal truth and simple faith of the biblical gospel. These promise us an answer to all questions and a solution, or at least an anodyne, for all problems. Along with them are the salesmen of "positive religion" offering health and well-being, success and wealth to those who get on the right side of God, the direction "right" being not at all fortuitous. Then we have the ritualists, the High Churchmen, the reconstructionists, who contend that religion, being the bridge to the Eternal (sometimes not the Lord of Hosts but the Value of Values), must be built of pageantry, rites, magic, folklore, and myth. There is another very special kind of faith promoter today, the proponents of the counselling and pastoral ministry, the schadchanim of religion and psychiatry, who argue that the major function of religion must be to sooth the ruffled egos of the children of the Age of Anxiety. Finally, on a different and perhaps deeper level, are the philosophers of irony and despair, the Neo-Orthodox theologians of the dogmas of human depravity and inherent sin. There are, too, the varieties of religious Existentialism, all of them having this in common, that they make the individual man who is born, suffers, and dies, the center of concern. Man, they say, cannot be comprehended apart from the condition of sin, guilt, anxiety, despair, and death. Wm. Barrett rightly sees the origin of Existentialism in Greek religion, as symbolized by the tragedies of Aeschylus. The Furies must be placated. This is, of course, a confusion of the darker moods of religion with religion itself. The somber mood is present in the Bible, in Job: "Hast Thou poured me out as milk, and curdled me like cheese." (Job 10.10). And in the Psalms: "For my life is spent in sorrow, and my years in sighing . . ." (Ps. 31.11). It is even found in the Prophets, eloquently in the confessions of Jeremiah. But it is also pertinent to point out that it is the prophets who are the most effective refutation of the present attempts to make of the Bible an existential textbook. The hallmark of the existentialist is that he is hopeless about the solution of human problems. He despairs of the help of God. He argues that man's reason is too weak and his will too confused by mixed motivations of good and evil ever to prevail over his difficulties; and God too remote and inaccessible to help him. Barrett trenchantly describes Existentialism as the counter-Enlightenment. This alone, it may be parenthetically observed, makes it altogether incompatible with liberal Judaism. Although Barrett is personally somewhat sympathetic with the Existentialists, he advertently acknowledges their inadequacy for a time of crisis when he writes: "I for one am personally convinced that man will not take his next great step unless he has drained to the lees the bitter cup of his own powerlessness. The trouble is, however, that the chastening experience may come only with the destruction of his world—a calamity in which the tragic hero also destroys himself." The philosopher and the epic poet may view such a denouement with equanimity and perhaps even with a certain amount of satisfaction. The Jew steeped in the prophetic tradition, never!

None of the responses which we have just described, except when they are exploited by the pitchmen and the fakers, are in any sense illegitimate. They are all worthy, necessary, and legitimate insofar as they satisfy the spiritual and emotional needs of individuals. The trouble is that neither singly nor together do they fill the requirements of this "time of trouble." They are all in one sense or another escapist, some assuming a thicker habiliment of semantic profundity than others. They neither challenge nor compel men to face the real problems of the real world. They may almost be described as the very opposite of prophetic religion.

The one response needed to help us cope with and thrust our way out of the present predicament is the prophetic response. Yet its voice today is singularly weak. It is nevertheless the right response for this Age of Revolution. The very essence of prophecy is that man must confront the social situation, not remain cloaked in his own private unease. The human condition consists not only of sickness, pain, loss, and death, but more widely and oppressively in our time, of injustice, inequality, cruelty, war, and the inhumanity of man to man. Personal anxiety cannot be altogether removed, but it can be measureably diminished when the fear of economic insecurity is relieved, the indignity of inequality removed, the pain of illness, the loneliness of old age, the dread of dying in poverty and solitude alleviated, and perhaps above all the horror of being destroyed in the fiery furnace of atomic war eliminated. The confrontation of God is incomplete without the confrontation of man by his fellowman, and the dialogue with God is a whispered conspiracy unless it concerns itself with the wellbeing of the parties not present, the other members of the human race. The prophetic dialogue with God took place so that the prophets might speak to men in His name and transmit His will to them. The prophets were no philosophers spinning out metaphysical fancies in ivory towers, nor were they mystics counting beads in whitewashed cells. When they complained to God about their anguish, it was not out of an existentialist despair with life, but out of a sense of frustration with their inability to persuade men to live in accordance with God's law.

The prophets were the first to declare their belief in what Robert Heilbroner calls "the legitimacy of the idea of human betterment." Only they were much more emphatic. This

striving after betterment is what God requires of man, they
declared. It is the primary goal of human effort. The
prophets saw the future in terms of a better life if men
would only obey God's laws of justice. They were thinking
of that future not in abstract but in concrete terms of human
welfare—of food, clothing, and shelter—of racial equality—
of equity as between rich and poor—of justice in the law
courts—of protection for the rights and dignity of workers—
of peace between nations. For at least one-third of the population of our own country, and for three-fourths of the population of the globe, the terms have not changed. Poverty,
monopoly, the exploitation of labor, the persecution of mi-
norities, and the deprivation of human rights are as prevalent
today as they were in Israel and Judah and in the empires
of antiquity. "Restore, I pray you, to them, even this day,
their fields, their vineyards, their oliveyards and their houses,
also the hundred pieces of silver, and the corn, and the wine
and the oil, that ye exact of them." (Nehemiah 5.8-11).

Prophetic religion today would be unhesitant in condemning the sins of Communism. Not merely because it closes the
churches, deprives them of their secular power and wealth,
and strips the ecclesiastics of their special privileges (the
prophets might have gotten some melancholy satisfaction
out of that); but because it exalts new forms of idolatry—
of the state, the leader, and the party—in the eyes of the
prophets the cardinal sin. It sets up new high places where
human sacrifices are made. Marxism, certainly in its Len-
inist derivation, attempts to achieve social ends through the
use of naked power and through the manipulation of human
beings and the distortion of their minds, hearts, and wills.
Men are given unlimited power over the destinies of other
men and inevitably end up using them as objects. The image

of man is defaced, and with it God's image, when men are compelled to do cruel and vile deeds to each other. Truth is deformed and made to bend to the necessities of convenience and the whim of rulers. It is no accident that a system such as this refuses to grant the existence of God. It dare not admit the existence of any transcendental authority. Robert Heilbroner says: "Every student of early Capitalism is shocked at the inhumanity of its condition of labor and at the heartlessness of its ruling classes. We see a similar grinding of the human personality in Communism today." The prophets would certainly reject and denounce such a system. They would contend that men will feel responsible for the welfare of other men only in proportion to their sense of responsibility to God. In the words of Eric Kahler,—"for responsibility, if it has any meaning at all, implies a responsibility to a criterion higher than self. Such human responsibility for one's whole being is of course a transcendent responsibility, that is to say, it is beyond any law and any convention." The prophets saw God alone as the pattern for man's emulation.

Prophetic religion would be equally bold, however, in its criticism of the shortcomings of Western Capitalism. It would, first of all, expose the hypocrisy and hollowness of a prosperity which is unshared by two-thirds of the people in the most advanced Capitalist country, the United States, by far more than this proportion in Western Europe, and enjoyed by only a minute privileged minority elsewhere, while the rest of the population lives at subsistence or lower levels. It would point the finger of scorn at the blighting slums of the cities. It would call attention with pity to the plight of the chronically unemployed and the undereducated. It would underline the horrifying statistics on crime and juvenile delinquency, the backwardness of our penal methods, and the shameful neglect of the aged and the mentally ill. It would expose the denial of rights and of opportunity to racial and minority groups. It would employ the word, the burning word of God, to sear the citadels of privilege. It would not hesitate to sound the death knell of a civilization which so perverts justice. Concerned as it must be with the inner life of man as well as with the social framework within which he functions, prophetic religion would focus the spotlight upon the inadequacies of a system which extols the creature comforts which only a few enjoy as the ultimate goal for all, and advocates selfish competitiveness in which the majority are bound to fail, as the sanctified way of life. "Hear this word, ye kine of Bashan, that are in the mountain of Samaria, that oppress the poor, that crush the needy, that say unto their lords: 'Provide the means that we may carouse!'" (Amos 4.1). Amos preached in a time of national prosperity, yet he saw the decay in the midst of the luxury, the spiritual poverty at the heart of wealth, especially in a social situation in which the benefits are limited to the few. Prophecy would demand justice. But it would also go beyond that to urge us not merely to build the economic man seeking plenty and the satisfactions of his material ends, but the moral man who seeks the fulfillment of every aspect of his spirit. Especially is this pertinent in a rapidly automating economy in which work itself may one day be outmoded. The common heresy of both Communism and Capitalism is that they assume that once material needs are satisfied, men will automatically become unselfish, kind, and intelligent; that they will seek the true, the good, and the beautiful. Men will pursue these ends only if they are motivated to believe in them as eternally worth-while, that is, as transcendent values, as purposes beyond the satisfaction of instincts and hungers. But first of all there must be justice! Once again quoting Heilbroner: "The ugly, obvious, and terrible wounds of mankind must be dressed and allowed to heal before we can begin to know the capacities, much less enlarge the vision of the human race as a whole."

It is a major task of prophecy today to rally humanity to oppose those who would lead us down the road to war, a war which can solve nothing. It would lay bare the fallacies and irrationality of "balance of terror" theories, as Eric Fromm and David Riesman among others have done so brilliantly. Refuting these theories and arguing in favor of universal disarmament, Eric Fromm says: "To sum up: it is true that the aim of universal controlled disarmament is exceedingly difficult to reach; maybe it is unrealistic, as its opponents say. But to believe that a strategy of mutual threats with ever more destructive weapons can, in the long run, prevent a nuclear war, and that a society following this road could preserve its democratic character, is a great deal more unrealistic." Rising above national interests, prophetic religion would be critical of bomb making and bomb testing, no matter by whom, the poisoning of the atmosphere and the food supply, the crippling of the genes of unborn children, and the barbaric experimentation with the means of chemical, bacteriological, and space warfare. It would indicate how easily we can be led to succumb to the illusion that preparedness means security, when so often what it really means is the effort to keep the economy on an even keel.

Prophetic religion, however, must do more than denounce. Prophecy believes in the possibility of repentance, therefore of moral reform and of social reconstruction. Jonah was rebuked by God because he was skeptical of the capacity of the Ninevites for repentance and wanted them destroyed. The prophet is often the messenger of doom when he has become convinced of the improbability of change for the better, but he must also hold out hope for the future even in the face of imminent disaster. In the dreadful aftermath of the destruction of Jerusalem, Jeremiah forecast the rebuilding. In the thermonuclear age, that may be unjustified optimism, but that is the prophetic burden.

In the meanwhile, prophetic religion must exhaust every effort and utter every last word to the end that the "day of Yahweh" may be averted. It must constantly urge the leaders of the advanced nations to share their knowledge and to pool their resources, using the means now so wastefully employed in the arms race, in the assistance of undeveloped regions. "There are no fixed and immutable limits to what is historically possible," says Heilbroner. This optimism, based upon the amazing achievements of today's men of science, can be confidently proclaimed. Prophetic religion must ceaselessly urge negotiation and compromise between the world's contending forces. Its voice must constantly be raised against the use of violence, which in our day has become so contagious. It should condemn the employment of terror, torture, and brain-washing. Prophetic religion must appeal to what C. P. Snow has called, "the conscience of the rich," to support the peaceful changes and evolutionary reforms which alone can obviate violent revolution. Moreover, the social conscience and sense of responsibility of scientists need to be prodded. We can no longer afford to have them take the naive, simplistic, objectively technological approach to the monstrous weapons systems which they are creating. In sum, to the extent to which it is possible, modern prophecy must hold itself independent and critical of nation, class, and ideology, constantly demanding that moral means be employed to gain right ends. Only a religion of the prophetic type can exercise the moral power and perspective to challenge men to realize that now there is at last a real prospect, perhaps a final chance, for the genuine betterment of the human condition,—and it must not be missed.

What follows is by way of postcript. Surely it must be apparent from what has preceded that the first impulse to the revival and articulation of prophetic religion must come from Judaism, which has always understood that God's will is fulfilled in man's ascending career on earth. Now if ever we must turn toward the world the image of ourselves as a prophet-people. Certainly we in the liberal wing of our faith should be in the vanguard. Although I am aware that what I am about to suggest would probably arouse intense disagreement among many of my colleagues, I am nevertheless persuaded that our rabbinate must endeavor to recover that prophetic function and zeal which I fear has become nearly atrophied through disuse. We must learn again to speak forthrightly in the name of God, and in a "time of trouble" of what does one speak to men and nations if not of peace and justice? We must recapture the voice of dissent, the eloquent and passionate voice that flames out from the fire that rages within the bosom. Hundreds of rabbis speaking from pulpits throughout this land can make their voices reverberate in the hearts and consciences of men. They may fail for the moment, as the prophets did—they may become lonely men, as the prophets were, but ultimately God will vindicate their words. Mankind will either repent, or perish, must be the burden of their preaching.

We rabbis are guilty of our own forms of escapism. Feeling helpless or afraid in the path of the raging seas of social change, we are induced to accept the roles of pastors, comforters, counsellors, and amateur psychiatrists. Or we try to serve as interns at theological births, functioning in the natal chambers of Empiricism, Positivism, and Existentialism, helping to bring forth the, for Jews, curious offspring of Dewey, Niebuhr, and Tillich. Or we operate as ecclesiastical technicians busily engaged in manufacturing rituals and ceremonies. All of this is interesting, helpful, and it may even be important. But the agonizing query which cannot be repressed—at least I cannot repress it, is—what does all this mystification and speculation, this pomp and pageantry, have to do with the heart of Judaism, prophecy?

One is saddened, too, by another form of escapism in which we are indulging ourselves, the feverish, activity-crazed expansionism which has overtaken not only our local houses of worship, but our national institutions, the Union of American Hebrew Congregations, the Central Conference of American Rabbis, and the Hebrew Union College-Jewish Institute of Religion. If I speak in critical tones, it is out of the deepest love for these historic institutions, and especially for the College. We are all of us strangling in the nets of activities, regions, branches, committees, and mailings. The authority of the Central Conference of American Rabbis, individually and collectively, to speak prophetically, to speak urgently on matters of social moment, has been lost in a jungle of organizations and enmeshed in a machinery of commissions, its voice silenced in masses of wordy and often irrelevant resolutions which are buried in the back pages of newspapers. How to recover voice and authority is today the major and most pressing problem of our rabbinical calling. Pleading that we are neither prophets nor the sons of prophets is begging the question. If we do not make at least an effort to function as the sons of the prophets or members of the "prophetic guild," then we are becoming a snare and a delusion to the people.

Perhaps we should look for at least part of the answer to the fountainhead of our learning and tradition, the College. We are graduating competent and personable young rabbis, but one misses in them the ardor of social idealism, the passion to preach the word of God, and the informed ability to apply the ideas of Judaism to the problems of our day. One senses, too, in both our older and younger men a kind of weary skepticism about the utility of preaching altogether. Dr. Solomon B. Freehof recently wrote: "When in the last generation the stress was on social idealism and social service, this, too, gave new life to the sermon. The doctrine of social betterment and ideals was deemed to be a direct mandate of the Biblical prophets, whose greatest expression was in public eloquence—But when the main task becomes personal relationship and guidance, then public utterance seems like a scattered volley of bird shot aimed in the general direction of the target. Public utterance seems to be an old-fashioned instrument for an outworn purpose."

Where is the passion of the prophet, where are the voices urgently speaking both in the accents of chastisement and of hope? Must we not answer that question, or betray our heritage?

THE PROPHETIC CRITICISM
OF ISRAELITE WORSHIP

Dr. J. Philip Hyatt, *Professor of Old Testament*
The Divinity School, Vanderbilt University
Nashville, Tennessee

THE GOLDENSON LECTURE OF 1963

EVERY READER OF THE BIBLE HAS COME across passages in the prophets, as well as in some other books, that express strong criticism of the prevailing worship, or of specific practices in Israelite worship.[1] Such passages stand out boldly because they appear to contradict the clear teaching of other parts of the Bible regarding the ways in which man should worship God.

One of the best-known and strongest of such criticisms is Amos 5:21-24. Speaking in the name of the Lord, Amos says:

> I hate, I reject your feasts,
>> and I take no delight in your festive assemblies.
> Even if you offer me your burnt offerings and cereal
>> offerings
>> I will not accept them,
> and the "peace offering" of your fatted beasts
>> I will not look upon.
> Take away from me the noise of your songs,
>> and the melody of your harps to which I do not listen,
> in order that justice may roll down like waters,
>> and righteousness like an everflowing stream.[2]

A similar passage is Hosea 6:6. Hosea 5:15—6:6 is a single message of the prophet. At its beginning, Hosea expresses the displeasure of Yahweh with the easy-going

confidence of the people of Israel in the constant presence and aid of their deity, and with their facile repentance from sin. The prophet says their love of God is only
"like a morning cloud, like the dew that goes early away."
The Lord has therefore "hewn them by the prophets . . .
slain them by the words of my mouth," because his real
demand can be expressed in these words:

> I desire steadfast love and not sacrifice,
>> the knowledge of God, rather than (or, without)
>> burnt offerings.

The third passage we quote is perhaps the most famous of
all the passages in the prophets; its climax is one of the most
often quoted verses in the whole Bible. This is Micah 6:1-8;
whether it is actually from the eighth century Micah or not
is of little consequence for our present purpose.

In this oracle the prophet says that Yahweh has a controversy (a law-suit) with his people, one that is to be tried
before the mountains and the enduring foundations of the
earth. What has Yahweh done to Israel? Wherein has he
failed the nation? Did he not bring them up from Egypt
and lead them through the desert? Why then have they
forgotten the "saving acts (ṣidqôth) of the Lord?" Then
the prophet represents an individual Israelite, speaking in
the name of the nation, as inquiring what he should do in
order properly to "come before the Lord"—that is, to worship him:

> With what shall I come before the Lord,
>> and bow myself before God on high?
> Shall I come before him with burnt offerings,
>> with calves a year old?
> Will the Lord be pleased with thousands of rams,
>> with ten thousands of rivers of oil?

Shall I give my first-born for my transgression,
   the fruit of my body for the sin of my soul?

The response of God comes through the prophet:

He has told you, O man, what is good,
   and what the Lord requires of you:
only to practice justice and faithful love,
   and walking wisely with your God.[3]

I.

It is appropriate at this stage of scholarly study of the Bible to consider the meaning and importance of these prophetic criticisms of Israelite worship, because Biblical scholars have for some time been placing great emphasis on the role of the Israelite cult in producing and preserving much of the literature of the Bible. (This is true for both the Old and New Testaments.)

It should be perfectly obvious that the Psalms were created for, and used in, the worship of the Israelites— their corporate worship in the sanctuaries and probably also their private devotions. It is not so obvious that many other parts of the Bible may have originated in the cult, and been preserved by the priesthood in the temples.

As an example of a widely accepted theory, we may cite the view of Gerhard von Rad concerning the origin of the Torah (the Pentateuch).[4] He believes that the original nucleus of the Torah can be found in the short creed or confession of faith now embedded in Deuteronomy 26:5-10, which begins, "A wandering Aramean was my father; and he went down into Egypt and sojourned there," etc. This originated, and was used in worship, in the period of the settlement of Canaan, before the establishment of the monarchy. A longer version of this confessional statement can

be found in Joshua's speech in Joshua 24:2-13, which von
Rad can call a "Hexateuch in smallest form." Thus the
Torah—or, more specifically the Hexateuch—is an expansion
(a very large expansion!) of a short creed used in very early
Israelite worship.

It may be that some scholars have over-emphasized the
dependence of the Biblical literature on the cult, but we
must not forget that the sanctuaries performed a very significant role in pre-exilic Hebrew life, far more than any synagogue or church plays in American life today. The sanctuaries were centers of learning and perhaps of great wealth;
it is most likely that literacy and learning were largely
confined to the personnel of the temples.

We can do justice to ancient Hebrew religion if we substitute the word "worship" for the word "cult," for the
latter has become a somewhat derogatory term. "Cult" often
suggests to us primitive, ancient notions that we believe we
have outgrown, but in general the word means simply what
we now mean by worship in the formal sense.

Modern studies have shown that many of the prophets
were attached to sanctuaries. They were part of the temple
personnel, as priests were. Thus it is proper to speak of "cult
prophets." The evidence for their existence comes in part
from comparison with the religion of other Near Eastern
nations,[5] and from the Bible itself.[6] The function of such
prophets was to consult oracles and thus to secure the "will
of God" for the people on various matters, and also to represent the people before God in intercessory prayer. The function of the priests was to offer sacrifice, superintend the
sanctuaries, and teach and preserve *tôrāh* (or *tôrôth*). The
prophet's primary concern was with the "word of the Lord,"
but he also taught *tôrāh*. The *tôrôth* (instructions) of the
priests related to ceremonial matters, such as the making

of proper distinctions between the clean and the unclean or the holy and the common, and the regulation of specific cult practices. The *tôrôth* of the prophets were directed primarily, if not exclusively, to moral problems and the enunciation of God's will on matters of individual and national conduct. Between most of the prophets and most of the priests there was no antagonism, since they worked together in the sanctuaries of the nation.

We can properly call some of the canonical prophets cult prophets. Haggai, Zechariah, and Malachi were so much concerned in their messages with the rebuilding of the temple and the proper cult observances within it that we can see no reason for denying them the title. Among the prophets who lived before or during the exile, there is hardly a one who has not been called by some modern scholar a cult prophet. Some have even maintained that Amos was such a prophet![7] The evidence for this is very slender. Among the pre-exilic prophets the one most likely to have been a cult prophet is Nahum. However, in ancient Israel, there was a very large number of prophets, and the simple word *nāvî'* encompasses a disconcertingly large variety of types of persons. Some were ecstatics, and hardly more than dervishes or shamans; others were men of great stature, probably not subject to ecstatic possession. Some were members of organized societies or attached to sanctuaries, while others were solitary individuals. Some were closely associated with the royal court, while others engaged in revolutionary activities that led to the change of dynasties. The very small group of men whose books have been preserved as the Prophets in the Bible represent only a tiny minority. They were free, independent-minded, charismatic individuals. It really matters little whether we think of them as "cult prophets" or not. Perhaps some of them were, and their strong polemic against the worship of their day arose from their intimate knowledge of it from the inside.

II.

As a problem in the historical interpretation of the prophets, these strong criticisms of Israelite worship have puzzled interpreters, and there is no general agreement among scholars as to what precisely was the attitude of the prophets toward the cult. We do not have in mind, of course, all of the prophets, but only those who criticized the worship of their day. Did they think that the cult as such was wrong, an offense to Yahweh, and thus should be abolished? Or, did they intend only to criticize the abuses of the cult, and so want it purified or simplified or in some manner made acceptable to God?

The majority opinion of scholars today probably is the latter. They have been influenced by studies of the Israelite cult, and believe that the prophets did not wish to see it abolished. The principal arguments advanced in favor of this opinion are as follows: (1) The prophets surely *could not* have envisioned a religion without cultic practices. That is *a priori* impossible, for no ancient religion existed without some kind of cult. The prophets were not interested in making of religion simply an ethical culture society. (2) If one groups together all of the strong criticisms of the cult, then he must conclude that the prophets did not even approve of prayer. They directed their polemic not only against elaborate sacrifices, noisy festivals, and the like, but even against praying to the Lord. Isaiah says in 1:15:

When you spread forth your hands,
   I will hide my eyes from you;
even though you make many prayers,

> I will not listen;
> your hands are full of blood.

(3) It is characteristic of Hebrew idiom to say "not this, but that," when in reality the meaning is, "that is more important than this." Thus we are to interpret Hosea's words, "I desire steadfast love and not sacrifice," as really meaning "I desire steadfast love more than sacrifice," but sacrifice itself is not excluded. This idiom, a form of hyperbole, has been called "relative negation."[8]

On the other hand, some scholars have said that the prophets' attitude toward the cult was one of radical and complete rejection. T. H. Robinson has said in interpreting their attitude: "The God of Israel, alone among the deities worshipped by men, made no ritual demands; to Him sacrifice was always a weariness, and, when substituted for morality, an abomination."[9] Those who hold to this view urge arguments such as these: (1) The words of the prophets are really very strong, and must be taken at face value. One could hardly imagine a polemic against worship stronger than that of Amos. (2) The arguments of those who take the view just discussed are mostly *a priori* arguments, and overlook the seriousness of the prophets' words. Such scholars seem to be more concerned with what they think a prophet should or could have said, rather than what he actually did say. (3) The prophets should be considered as "radicals" in the sense that they wished to get at the root *(radix)* of the evils they saw. For them the worship as it was practiced was a root evil, a barrier between men and God, and so they wished to see it eradicated. They were not theologians or philosophers; nor were they pastors. Since most of them expected the imminent coming of doom upon the nation, they did not think in terms of purifying the cult, but only of proclaiming God's word of judgment and summoning men to repentance.

The most recent full-scale treatment of the prophets' attitude is that of Richard Hentschke, *Die Stellung der vorexilischen Schriftpropheten zum Kultus*.[10] He examines in detail the words of Amos, Hosea, Isaiah, Micah, Zephaniah and Jeremiah, and concludes that their polemic went far beyond the criticism of individual cultic abuses. Those prophets opposed the cultus as a means by which men sought for themselves salvation and security. They taught that Yahweh demands the unconditional surrender of men to his sovereignty. The cult stood in the way of such surrender, for it was understood as a quasi-magical, automatic means by which men could secure divine blessing. Thus the prophets did not advocate cultic reform, but called upon the Israelites to repent, to remember the wonderful acts of Yahweh on their behalf, and to give him their obedience. Thus their opposition to the cult meant radical rejection.[11]

I find myself in agreement with the latter point of view, but we must remember that the message of each prophet was conditioned in part by the historical situation of his age. Each prophet spoke to the concrete problems faced by the people to whom he prophesied. In the post-exilic age the problems were different, and thus the message of the prophets was different. It is important for our present purposes to try to determine the grounds on which the prophets objected to the worship of their age, and to ask why they criticized it. This may lead us to see what the prophetic criticism of ancient Israelite worship can mean to us in our own worship. The ultimate Biblical and prophetic view is not that cultic worship can be completely dispensed with. So, we may end by asking, what kind of worship benefits from the ancient prophets' criticism?

III.

There were five factors in the popular worship of their time against which the pre-exilic prophets protested in the name of their God. In their denunciation they made no distinction between the "official" and the "popular" interpretation of worship, but denounced what they saw taking place before their eyes.

1. The prophets protested against the worship because it often placed the activity of God exclusively or mainly in the past. The people of Israel believed that Yahweh had performed mighty deeds on their behalf: he had brought them out of slavery in the land of Egypt, made a covenant with them at Sinai, led them wondrously through the desert, and fought on their behalf in the conquest and settlement of Canaan. They celebrated those deeds in their cult. But there was often a tendency to think of Yahweh as a God of the past, and thus to forget that he is also active in the present and the future. The prophets wished to assert that he is active in the present and to emphasize the belief that he is sovereign Lord of the present and future as well as of the past.

In his presidential address before the Society of Biblical Literature in 1960, R.B.Y. Scott said: "Whereas to the priests Israel's tradition meant that Yahweh had chosen her to be a priestly kingdom and a continuing religious community and that he was ever-present at her shrines, to the prophets Israel was Yahweh's people primarily in the context of his historic purpose, past and present. To them he was not so much a holy Presence dwelling in Israel's midst, as an active, righteous Being ever demanding that his word be heard afresh. The priests spoke of what Yahweh is, because of what he had done. The prophets spoke of what Yahweh will do, because of what he is. They confronted men in the present with the God of Israel's past."[12]

2. The prophets protested against the cult because many elements in it, as it was actually carried out, made it appear to be magical or quasi-magical,—that is, it was believed to work mechanically or automatically to benefit the worshipper.

The essential difference between magic and religion is that magic is believed to work automatically, and it seeks to coerce the deity into doing something for man. Religion, on the other hand, requires a free relationship between a human person and a divine Person; there can be no coercion on either side. Magic denies the sovereignty of God, and seeks to place sovereignty and control within man himself. Magic wishes to manipulate the divine; religion demands man's surrender to the divine.

The official interpretation of the cult, especially of the sacrificial acts which were central to the cult, did not see it as magic or quasi-magical in its operation. At its best the Israelite cult was conceived as a sacramental system by which the grace of God was mediated to men. The Priestly code demanded that, where sacrifice was offered for sin, there should be confession of sin; and where there was offense against another person and restitution could be made, the law demanded restitution (Leviticus 5:5f; Numbers 5:6f).

But the cultic system was always subject to two dangers, which can be expressed in two Latin phrases: *opus operatum* and *do ut des*. The meaning of the first is well-known, and it expresses the notion that the mere carrying out of certain actions can influence God and benefit man, whether or not man is penitent and acknowledges God's sovereignty. *Do ut des* means "I give in order that you may give"; it suggests that man makes a gift to God simply in order to receive a gift from him. Religion can in this manner be reduced to a virtually commercial transaction, in which God is placed under obligation to man. This leads to the externalizing and depersonalizing of man's relationship to God.

H. H. Rowley is correct when he says that "no sacrifice is represented in the teaching of the Bible as effecting salvation by the mere performance of an outer rite." But he goes on to say: "That many people thought of them [the sacrifices] in such terms is unquestionable, and that they were so thought of outside Israel is not to be denied. But the prophets continually challenged the idea that by the offering of abundant sacrifices the well-being of individual or community was assured, and the Law no more than the prophets was content with a merely formal act."[13]

Repentance was for the prophets of paramount importance; it meant a national and individual turning to God in penitence and in obedience. They must have seen in the elaborate rites around them little or no evidence of repentance, and of the bringing forth of fruits appropriate to repentance. They set themselves against those things which resulted in the externalizing and depersonalizing of man's relationship to God.

3. The prophets protested against worship which was too much centered around man and his wishes and needs, rather than around the demands of God. Many of the forms of worship appeared to them to be man-centered rather than God-centered, the substitution of man-made devices for the ordinances of God.

It is possible to translate Micah 6:8 as follows:

Man has showed thee what is good,
    but what does Yahweh require of thee
but to practice justice etc.

This is linguistically possible, but is not accepted by many scholars. If correct, however, it makes crystal clear that the author of this passage looked upon the usual manner of approaching God with sacrifices—burnt offerings, rams, oxen, oil, and even one's own most precious possession, his first-born son—as a man-made approach; the true requirement of the Lord is something different—justice, mercy, and proper living in God's presence.

Ludwig Köhler, in his *Old Testament Theology,* heads the section dealing with the cult with the title: "Man's Expedient for His Own Redemption: the Cult." He begins the discussion by saying: "There is no suggestion anywhere in the Old Testament that sacrifice or any other part of the cult was instituted by God. It knows only the regulation of already existing sacrifice by divine instruction. . . . (The cult) is begun and continued and accomplished by man; it is works, not grace; an act of self-help, not a piece of God's salvation."[14] This is an extreme point of view, and I think the opening sentence is mistaken, for the Bible does in fact look upon the cult as a divine institution. Yet this exaggerated point of view shows how the Israelite cult strikes one modern interpreter.

Amos and Jeremiah spoke words which imply very clearly that they thought the worship of Israel in the ideal period of Moses did not contain sacrifices and offerings; or at least that they were not commanded by Yahweh (Amos 5:25; Jeremiah 7:22). This view is contrary to statements in early narratives of the Pentateuch (e.g. Exodus 18:12; 24:5-6), and is not historically accurate. But these prophets were correct if they meant that there was nothing unique about the offering of sacrifices, for they were found in all the religions of the ancient Near East. They were in no sense uniquely Yahwistic. Modern research has shown that many of the cultic practices were borrowed from the Canaanites, and it was probably in the area of such practices that the Hebrews were most indebted to Canaan.

The prophets saw the cult as man-made or man-centered in that it was the source of self-satisfaction and pleasure to those who participated in it. In a passage filled with irony, Amos says (4:4-5):

Come to Bethel—and transgress;
   to Gilgal—and multiply transgression;
bring your sacrifices every morning,
   your tithes every three days;
offer a sacrifice of thanksgiving of that which is leav-
   ened,
   and proclaim freewill offerings, publish them:
   for so you love to do, O people of Israel!

A passage in what is sometimes called "Third Isaiah" is difficult to interpret, but it is rendered in the Revised Standard Version as follows (Isaiah 66:3):

He who slaughters an ox is like him who kills a man;
   he who sacrifices a lamb, like him who breaks a
     dog's neck;
he who presents a cereal offering, like him who offers
     swine's blood;
   he who makes a memorial offering of frankincense,
     like him who blesses an idol.
These have chosen their own ways,
   and their soul delights in their abominations. . . .

The contrast to this is expressed in the preceding verse: "This is the man to whom I will look, he that is humble and contrite in spirit, and trembles at my word" (Isaiah 66:2).

4. The prophets protested against elements in the cult

which implied too great familiarity with Yahweh, an exaggerated anthropomorphizing of his nature. This meant
too great a stress upon the immanence of God, too little
upon his transcendence and sovereign majesty.

The Canaanite Baal was a nature deity, a god of fertility
and vegetation who was very popular in Canaanite religion.
Baal was the immanent deity, whereas El was the transcendent and remote god. When the Israelites came under the
influence of Canaanite religion, Yahweh came to be considered as a deity like Baal. Some scholars speak of a baali-
zation of Yahweh. In this process Yahweh came to be a more
immanent deity, dwelling among the people, his presence
being symbolized by the sanctuaries which were numerous
in the land before Josiah's reformation.

One of the original motives in the offering of sacrifices
probably was to give sustenance or food to the deity. In the
religions of Egypt and Mesopotamia, the idols of the gods
were often treated as if they were human. The temple was
the house in which the god dwelled. The priests fed him
his meals, put him to bed at night, wakened him in the
morning, took him on procession through the streets, and
so on. Thus the deity was crudely thought of as if he were
human in his needs.

The most vigorous protest against this kind of anthropomorphizing of Yahweh is found in one of the Psalms, which
must have been influenced by the prophets. In Psalm 50:
12-13, the Lord is represented as saying:

If I were hungry, I would not tell you;
   for the world and all that is in it is mine.
Do I eat the flesh of bulls,
   or drink the blood of goats?

This Psalm protests that the God who is creator and

sustainer of man's world has no need of this kind of attention from man. On the contrary, man should call upon God for help and deliverance, and give him the offering of thanksgiving and of right living before God.

Jeremiah says, in a long passage directed against the false prophets: "Am I a God at hand, says the Lord, and not a God afar off?" (23:23). The context stresses the presence of God in all the heaven and earth, so that no man can hide from him anywhere. Man should not be too familiar with such a God, but he cannot hide from him.

In a passage in Job which describes the activity of God in creation, words are uttered (26:14) with which many of the prophets would have agreed:

Lo, these are but the outskirts of his ways;
  and how small a whisper do we hear of him!
  But the thunder of his power who can understand?

5. Much of the prophetic criticism of the worship of their time can be summed up in the statement that they objected to its failure to proclaim the moral demands of a sovereign God who wished to be worshipped by the whole of Israel's life, and not simply by that which took place within the formal cult.

This is a point on which all scholars agree, whether they think the prophets sought the abolition of the cult or only its modification and purification. The great weakness of the worship, according to the prophets, was that it did not stress Yahweh's moral demands and issue in righteous and obedient conduct. Again and again the prophets placed over against the prevailing worship Yahweh's demand for justice, righteousness, steadfast love, moral purity, humility, contriteness of heart, and the like.

Martin Noth has said, in writing of the early worship of

Israel in the period of the settlement of Canaan: "From the very beginning . . . Israel's speciality did not consist in a particular and unique form of worship at the central shrine but in the fact that it was subject to a divine law which was recited at the tribal gatherings at regular intervals and to which Israel committed itself in constantly renewed acts of affirmation."[15] From the reading of the eighth and seventh-century prophets we must conclude that this unique feature or speciality of Israelite religion was too often ignored by the people in favor of those elements in the cult which were more congenial to their tastes. The role of the prophets was to recall this earlier emphasis, and to challenge Israel to live up to the unique features of its religion.

The prophetic emphasis on this point can be seen in other books of the Bible. For example, in Proverbs 15:8 we read:

The sacrifice of the wicked is an abomination to the Lord,
    but the prayer of the upright is his delight.

Similar words can be found in the apocryphal books (e.g. Sirach 34:18f.) and in rabbinic literature. Long before the time of Moses, an Egyptian sage wrote: "More acceptable is the character of one upright of heart than the ox of the evildoer" (about 2100 B.C.).[16]

Before closing this part of our discussion, we should emphasize that the prophetic criticism of Israelite worship does not imply a neat and simple cleavage between priests and prophets. The truth is more likely that there was antagonism between some prophets and some priests. A few priests may have agreed with some of the prophetic denunciation of the prevailing worship; many prophets probably did not agree with that denunciation at all. Priests as well as prophets were interested in morality and in proclaiming the moral demands of Yahweh. They helped to preserve the

words of the prophets we have been quoting as criticisms of
the worship. The issue was not a simple antithesis between
a "prophetic" and a "priestly" conception of the ancient
Israelite faith.

IV.

Can we learn anything for our own worship from the prophets' criticism of ancient Israelite worship? In order to answer
this question, we must first inquire whether the human
condition of our time is similar to that of ancient times. In
many respects it most certainly is. Modern man is very much
like the man of Israel to whom the prophets addressed their
message.

Modern man prefers magic and mechanically working
methods that seem to be swift and sure, rather than the slow
and difficult procedures that lead to establishing a relationship with a divine Person. We live in an age of pushbuttons
and innumerable automatic gadgets; one of the most-often
heard words today is automation. Pushbuttons and the devices of automation do not nurture the spirit of worship.

Modern man finds it more comfortable to celebrate the
past—the mighty deeds of God in the past—than to submit
himself to the will of God in the present and recognize his
sovereignty over the future. Our life is very largely anthro-
pocentric, man-centered, rather than theocentric, centered
around God.

Modern man wants his God to be a familiar deity, with
whom he can chat in his prayers and whom, on occasion,
he can use to do his bidding. In the current popular revival
of religiosity, we can glibly speak or sing of God as "the
Man upstairs." We find it difficult to accept the mystery of
God's being, because there are so many mysteries we have

been able to penetrate by our scientific methods. We find it congenial to try to manipulate the divine, rather than surrender ourselves to a transcendent Deity.

Modern man likes to compartmentalize his worship, as he does his religion as a whole. For him worship is what he does in special places and at special times. He is inclined to make a sharp distinction between the sacred and the secular, with his worship confined to a small corner of the sacred.

The prophets would say to us that authentic worship means the acknowledgment of the sovereignty of God over the whole of life. It calls on us to recognize that there is a Being and a Mystery that transcends our own little life, upon whom we depend and to whom we owe our ultimate loyalties. At the same time, in authentic worship man affirms himself as a person who is responsible to God as a supreme Person, and likewise responsible to his fellowmen.

It is significant that several of the words in both Hebrew and Greek that are translated "worship," originally had a much wider significance, and continued to have a broad significance even when they were used specifically to designate worship. You are well aware of the fact that one of the words in Hebrew is 'avôdāh. It originally meant labor or service of various kinds, and in later books of the Bible was applied to the service of God in the cult. In post-Biblical usage it had this meaning, and prayer was designated as "service [of God] with the heart" ('avôdāh shebballēv).[17]

In the Greek New Testament, one of the common words for worship is leitourgía, from which we derived the English "liturgy." This word began in classical Greek by meaning service performed by an individual for the state, often free of charge. It came to mean public service of the gods. In the Greek New Testament, it always has a religious connotation, but it applies to various forms of service which one can perform for God, not simply that which he does in what we call "liturgy." The Greek *latreía* had a somewhat similar history.

If we look at it from the Biblical point of view, then, worship can be divided into two parts: cultic worship, that service which we perform in our public and private ceremonies and rites, in our liturgy; and non-cultic worship, our service to God in ethical obedience. It is to cultic worship that we usually give the name, but that is really too narrow a definition.

Authentic worship can be rendered only in part by words and by repeated actions that we call religious rites. These can indeed have an important part in our religious life. We can worship God in synagogue or temple or church; yet we can worship also as we study, as we engage in commerce, as we live in our homes, and in all the activities of life, if we seek in all of them to serve God and his purposes.

Prophetic criticism of cultic worship should lead us to see that its primary motive should be gratitude—gratitude to God for what he has done and is doing, and for what he is. It should lead us to see that the primary ingredient of all true worship is integrity. Where there is integrity in worship, there is unity between what we profess and what we do; between our daily activities and our Sabbath observance; between what we do in public and what we are in private. Authentic cultic worship strengthens and invigorates our moral endeavor, and does not become a substitute for it; at the same time, prophetic criticism saves our religion from being simple moralism or only ethical culture. Authentic worship in the full sense is responsible existence under a sovereign God. It is love of God, and acceptance of his will and his love, both for ourselves and for our neighbors.

Much of the prophetic view of worship can be summed

up in two quotations. One of them is from the Old Testament, and one from the New Testament.

The first is Psalm 51:15-17. This is a Psalm attributed to David on the occasion of his rebuke by the prophet Nathan after his notorious sin with Bathsheba:

> O Lord, open thou my lips,
>> and my mouth shall show forth thy praise.
> For thou hast no delight in sacrifice;
>> were I to give a burnt offering,
>>> thou wouldst not be pleased.
> The sacrifice acceptable to God is a broken spirit;
>> a broken and contrite heart, O God, thou wilt not despise.

I hope that you will allow me to end with a quotation from the apostle Paul, who before his conversion to the Christian faith was a Hellenistic Jew. He described himself once as "a Hebrew of the Hebrews" and had received a Pharisaic education. He expressed a prophetic viewpoint when he said in Romans 12:1: "I appeal to you therefore, brethren, by the mercies of God, to present your bodies as a living sacrifice, holy and acceptable to God, which is your spiritual worship." The words here rendered "spiritual worship" in the Revised Standard Version are *tēn logikēn latreían*. The King James Version translated the phrase "reasonable service." The New English Bible, in its margin, renders the whole verse as follows:

> "Therefore, my brothers, I implore you by God's mercy to offer your very selves to him: a living sacrifice, dedicated and fit for his acceptance, for such is the worship which you, as rational creatures, should offer."

NOTES

[1]The more important passages are Amos 3:14; 4:4-5; 5:21-27; Hosea 4:4-14; 5:6; 6:6; 8:11-13; Isaiah 1:10-17; 66:2-4; Micah 1:7; 3:11-12; 6:1-8; Psalms 40:6-8; 50:7-15; 51:16-17; Proverbs 15:8; 21:27; Ecclesiastes 5:1; I Samuel 15:22-23.

[2]For defense of this translation, see my article, "The Translation and Meaning of Amos 5: 23-24," *Zeitschrift für die alttestamentliche Wissenschaft,* 68 (1956), 17-24. The verb at the beginning of vs. 24, *weyiggal,* is an imperfect with simple *waw* used to express purpose.

[3]For this translation see my article, "On the Meaning and Origin of Micah 6:8," *Anglican Theological Review,* 34 (1952), 232-39. The phrase *haṣnēa' léketh* apparently does not mean "walk humbly" as usually rendered, but "walk wisely, circumspectly, properly" or the like. Cf. Gerhard von Rad, *Theologie des alten Testaments,* Vol. II (Munich, 1960), p. 197, n. 17; D. Winton Thomas, in *Peake's Commentary on the Bible,* rev. by Matthew Black and H. H. Rowley (Nelson, 1962), p. 633.

[4]See especially his "Das formgeschichtliche Problem des Hexateuch," in *Gesammelte Studien zum Alten Testament* (Munich, 1958), pp. 9-86.

[5]Cf. A. Haldar, *Associations of Cult Prophets among the Ancient Semites* (Uppsala, 1945).

[6]The best recent treatment in English is Aubrey R. Johnson, *The Cultic Prophet in Ancient Israel,* second edition (Cardiff, 1962); cf. H. H. Rowley, "Ritual and the Hebrew Prophets," in *Myth, Ritual, and Kingship,* ed. by S. H. Hooke (Oxford, 1958), pp. 237-60.

[7]John D. W. Watts, *Vision and Prophecy in Amos* (Grand Rapids, 1958); A. S. Kapelrud, *Central Ideas in Amos* (Oslo, 1956).

[8]C. Lattey, "The Prophets and Sacrifice: a Study in Biblical Relativity," *Journal of Theological Studies,* XLII (1941), 155-165. See, for an example of this point of view in general, H. H. Rowley, *The Unity of the Bible* (New York, 1957), pp. 38-48.

[9]W. O. E. Oesterley and T. H. Robinson, *Hebrew Religion: its Origin and Development* (New York, 1930), p. 202.

[10]*Beiheft zur Zeitschrift für die alttestamentliche Wissenschaft* 75 (Berlin, 1957).

[11]In a recently published book J. Lindblom expresses general agreement with the position of Hentschke, though not in all details; *Prophecy in Ancient Israel* (Oxford, 1962), pp. 351-60. It is worthwhile to note the warning of W. Eichrodt, that we must not be too free in pronouncing all the prophets to have been cult prophets, and dismiss their criticism of the cult as "an unimportant trifle"; *Theology of the Old Testament,* Vol. I (Philadelphia, 1961), p. 367, n. 1.

[12]"Priesthood, Prophecy, Wisdom, and the Knowledge of God," *Journal of Biblical Literature,* 70 (1961), 1-15; see pp. 8-9.

[13]*The Faith of Israel* (London, 1956), p. 95.

[14]*Old Testament Theology* (Philadelphia, 1957), p. 181.

[15]*The History of Israel* (New York, 1958), p. 101.

[16]In the Instruction for King Meri-ka-re; see J. B. Pritchard, ed., *Ancient Near Eastern Texts Relating to the Old Testament* (Princeton, 1950), p. 417.

[17]Ismar Elbogen, *Der jüdische Gottesdienst in seiner geschichtlichen Entwicklung,* third ed. (Frankfurt, 1931), pp. 1, 4.

THE SO-CALLED
"SUFFERING SERVANT"
IN ISAIAH 53

Dr. Harry M. Orlinsky, *Professor of Bible*
Hebrew Union College –Jewish Institute of Religion
New York, New York

THE GOLDENSON LECTURE OF 1964

T HERE ARE A NUMBER OF BIBLICAL CONCEPTS
that are of prime importance to the modern student of the
Bible but which, it would seem, were actually non-existent,
or were only of the slightest significance, in biblical times,
when the inhabitants of the land of Israel were in the process of creating what ultimately became Sacred Scripture.
Among these, apparently only allegedly, biblical concepts
are the existence of a "soul" (the traditional, but incorrect
translation of Hebrew *nefesh*), the "virginal" character of
the *'almah* in Isaiah 7:14, the prophets' hostile attitude toward sacrifice in the worship of the Lord, the international
outlook of the biblical writers (including the prophets)—
and the *'ebed* in Isaiah (52-53) as the Suffering Servant par
excellence, who, innocent of sin, suffered vicariously in
order that others, guilty of sin and hence deserving of punishment, might thereby be atoned for and spared the punishment.

For history is full of the supercommentary of eisegesis
grafted upon the original exegesis which differed from it
altogether; yet it is the primary task of the historian to re-
move the layers and crust of subsequent explanation and
distortion and reveal the authentic kernel of truth created
by the original author. The present essay is part of a larger
work that will attempt to deal with a number of biblical
concepts in their historical development.[1]

227

In chapter 8 of the Book of Acts in the New Testament, we are told of an Ethiopian eunuch who was reading the Book of Isaiah when Philip the evangelist asked him whether he understood what he was reading. The specific passage in question was Isaiah 53:7-8:

> As a sheep led to the slaughter
> Or a lamb before its shearer is dumb,
> So he opens not his mouth.
> In his humiliation justice was denied him;
> Who can describe his generation?
> For his life is taken up from the earth.

The eunuch asked Philip, "'About whom, pray, does the prophet say this, about himself or about someone else?' Then Philip opened his mouth, and beginning with this scripture he told him the good news of Jesus."[2]

There are a number of important aspects to the problem of the "servant" in Isaiah 52-53, and they have been the subject of theological and scholarly discussion and argument for two millennia. We shall deal here with five of these aspects: Do the last three verses of chapter 52 (vv. 13-15) really belong with chapter 53, to constitute a single unit with but one servant involved? Is the servant of Isaiah 53 the people Israel, either actual or idealized, or an individual person? Is the servant in Isaiah 53 really a *vicarius,* a substitute for someone else, and is he really the "Suffering Servant" par excellence, one who deserves the use of capital "S" in both "Suffering" and "Servant"? Are there really pertinent Near Eastern parallels for the servant in 53? And finally, though but briefly, who is the servant in chapter 53?

Scholarship has been virtually unanimous in the belief— more correctly, in taking it for granted—that the last three verses in chapter 52 and all of 53 constitute a single composition.[3] There are several cogent reasons for questioning this, quite gratuitous assumption.

(1) The very first phrase in 52:13, הִנֵּה יַשְׂכִּיל עַבְדִּי, "Behold My servant will prosper," indicates through the pun–יִשְׂרָאֵל יַשְׂכִּיל that it is the people Israel that is the servant here. Like his follow prophets, and the biblical writers generally, our prophet was given to punning. As for the pun on "Israel" here, compare 44:2 where *Yeshurun* represents Israel ("Fear not, My servant Jacob, // Jeshurun whom I have chosen") and 42:19 where *Meshullam* is so intended ("Who is blind like Meshullam, // Blind like the servant of the Lord?").[4] And one is reminded of the same use of the term *Yeshurun* three times in Pentateuch (Deuteronomy 32:15; 33:5, 26) and of the term *Yesharim* once, in Numbers 23-10.[5]

(2) Independently, and at the same time bearing out the equation *"yaskil*=Israel," the expressions "(powerful) nations" (גּוֹיִם רַבִּים) and "kings" (מְלָכִים) in v. 15, as also the description of the woebegone servant in v. 14, point to the people "Israel" rather than to an individual person as the servant: Israel will be exceedingly exalted and honored,[6] after shocking the mighty with its wretched condition,[7] by the same powerful nations and kings who would never have believed possible what they will themselves see and hear.[8] (Parenthetically it may be noted that Second Isaiah employs such terms as "nations" [גּוֹיִם] and "kings" [מְלָכִים] in contrast not to the prophet himself but to the people Israel, or to Cyrus, God's conquering hero in behalf of Israel; see further below, nn. 18, 19.)

Second Isaiah[9] has much to say about the degraded condition of Israel in exile; indeed, the raison d'être of his career revolved precisely about Israel's inferior standing and God's decision and ability to restore Israel to her original home and status. Compare, e.g., the prophet's opening words in chapter 40, where Israel's very presence in Babylonia is described as "her term of service, of penal servitude" (צְבָאָהּ) and her punishment as far more severe than her sin warranted, so that the entire situation justified fully the exulting clarion cry of consolation and liberation:

> Comfort, oh comfort My people,
> Says your God . . .
> Ascend a lofty mountain,
> O Zion, herald of joy;
> Raise your voice with power,
> O Jerusalem, herald of joy—
> Raise it and have no fear,
> Announce to the cities of Judah:
> Behold your God!

In 41:10-12 Israel is told:

> Fear not, for I am with you,
> Be not frightened, for I am your God;
> I strengthen you and I help you,
> I uphold you with My victorious right hand.
> Shamed and chagrined shall be
> All who contend with you;
> They who strive with you
> Shall become as nought and shall perish . . .
> Less than nothing shall be
> The men who battle against you.

In 42:22 God's servant Israel is described as

> A people robbed and plundered,
> All of them trapped in holes
> And hidden in prisons;
> They have become a prey with none to rescue,
> A spoil with none to say, "Restore!"

And so on.

(3) The situation is quite different in chapter 53. Nothing is said there of nations and kings. The treatment is entirely

individualistic. Unlike the people Israel, which did not keep
silent in the face of destruction, which was not cut off from
the land of the living, and which deserved the divine punishment of destruction and exile because of transgression of the
covenant, the servant in 53 is one who did not complain,
who apparently did not survive, and who experienced suffering through no guilt of his own.[10]

(4) As a matter of fact, a closer examination of the last
three verses of 52 in relation to what precedes will reveal
that they constitute a suitable ending for all of chapter 52.
The entire chapter — actually the theme begins already in
chapter 51 preceding—is a proclamation and exhortation to
Zion-Jerusalem to prepare for the triumphant return of the
exiles, a triumph even greater than the Exodus from Egypt.
Thus v. 12 asserts, with obvious reference to the Exodus:

> But you shall not depart in haste,
> You shall not leave in flight;
> For the Lord is marching before you,
> The God of Israel is your rear guard.

It is with this dramatic proclamation that our section is to be
associated: God's degraded servant, His people Israel, will
astonish everyone by the great restoration he will achieve.

(5) As for the very few verbal similarities between 52:13-15
and 53:1-12 (even allowing for the relatively few verses involved), e.g., תֹּאַר and מַרְאֶה (each in vv. 14 and 2), and רַבִּים
(in vv. 14:15 and 11-12), and the use of "the root שמע as the
link-word"[11] (viz., the verb שָׁמְעוּ in 15 and the noun שְׁמֻעָתֵנוּ
in 1)—they help to indicate why 53:1 ff. was placed after
52:13, and may even help to prove that the author of the one
section was responsible also for the second; they do not,
however, prove that the two sections constitute a single unit.[12]

(6) It has been noted that—as against the (rather late)
chapter division—Jewish tradition begins a section with 52-13

(to the end of 53).[13] However, neither the one division nor the other—when the two traditions fail to agree—is automatically to be followed; each instance has to be decided on its own merits. Interestingly, the complete Isaiah Scroll treats both 52:13 and 53:1 as the beginning of sections.[14] Isaiah Scroll II, however, which coincides far more frequently than Scroll I with the masoretic division (as with the preserved Hebrew text[15]), has a space-division at 52:13 only (none at 53:1).

In fine, be that as it may so far as 52:13-15 and 53:1-12 are concerned, our own analysis of the so-called Suffering Servant will be based on chapter 53 alone.

A fundamental, and moot, problem in Isaiah 53 that requires solution is whether the subject of the chapter is an individual person or the people Israel. Let it be stated here, at the outset, that it cannot possibly be the people Israel that is involved.

It is a fact that the central figure in this chapter experienced suffering and punishment for no transgression or guilt of his own;

> Although he had done nothing lawless
> And there was no deceit in his mouth

is how the latter half of v. 9 put it. This alone at once excludes the people Israel from further consideration.

The devastation of Judah, the destruction of the Temple, and the exile of so many of her finest citizens to Babylonia was the greatest national tragedy yet experienced by Israel. To account for this unprecedented catastrophe to God's chosen, covenanted people, Second Isaiah asserted—and this is the very core of his message—that God was the only Deity in the universe, omnipotent and just. As a just God, He punished Israel for transgressing the covenant, and in His omnipotence He used the army of Babylonia as the means of bringing this justified punishment upon His people. Now, however, the penalty having been paid by Israel in the fullest measure, God will restore His people to their homeland, to "Jerusalem, holy city" (52:1).[16]

Those who hold—and they constitute a vast, perhaps the majority of biblical scholars — that Israel is the subject of Isaiah 53 and that innocently and meekly it went into exile to make, or rather to constitute expiation for the gentile nations, must explain away or pass over the numerous passages in Second Isaiah that assert clearly, or assume, that it is Israel's own sins that led to her captivity. I have in mind such passages as 40:2, where Jerusalem is told

> That she has completed her term,
> That her iniquity is expiated,
> For she has received at the hand of the Lord
> Double for all her sins.[17]

Or 42:24-25:

> Who gave up Jacob to the spoiler,
> Israel to plunderers?
> Was it not the Lord, against whom we sinned,
> In whose ways they would not walk
> And whose instruction they would not obey?
> So He poured upon him His hot anger
> And the fierceness of battle . . .

Or 43:24-25:

> You did not buy Me fragrant reed with money
> Nor sate Me with the fat of your sacrifices.
> Nay, you burdened Me with your sins,
> Wearied Me with your iniquities.
> It is I, I, who—for My sake—
> Wipe your transgressions away,
> And remember your sins no more.

Or 44:21-22:

> Remember these things, O Jacob,
> O Israel, for you are My servant . . .
> I wipe away your sins like a cloud,
> And your transgressions like mist;
> Come back to Me, for I redeem you.

Or 48:1-8:

> Hear this, O house of Jacob,
> You who are called by Israel's name . . .
> Who swear by the name of the Lord
> And invoke the God of Israel—
> But not in truth or justice . . .
> I know that you are stubborn:
> Your neck is an iron sinew
> And your forehead copper . . .
> I knew that you would deal treacherously,
> "A rebel from birth" you were called.

In 48:18 God tells Israel:

> If only you had obeyed My commandments,
> Your welfare would have been like a stream
> And your triumph like the waves of the sea . . .

Or, finally, 50:1, where the Lord says:

> It is for your sins that you were sold,
> For your crimes that your mother was dismissed.

It is unheard of in the Bible that Israel, God's "treasured people" (עַם סְגֻלָּה), His partner in the covenant, should suffer innocently for the sins and in behalf of any non-Israelite people.[17a] But leaving aside for the moment the problem of Israel as a *vicarius,* a substitute for gentile nations, let us deal with the matter of alleged sin on the part of these nations: precisely what sins are the gentile nations supposed to have committed to warrant punishment from God, punishment that Israel will allegedly suffer in their stead?

Biblically, gentile nations committed two kinds of crimes which justified God's intervention: (a) transgression against the so-called Noahide Laws, what might be called crimes against natural law or humanity; (b) crimes against God Himself or against Israel, God's covenanted partner whom He promised to protect and prosper. Thus Amos (1:3-2:3) arraigned Israel's neighboring nations, the inhabitants of Damascus, Gaza, Tyre, Edom, Ammon, and Moab for crimes against humanity; Judah and Israel, however, alone in the world, are arraigned for transgression of the covenant (2:4 עַל־מָאֳסָם אֶת־תּוֹרַת יְהוָה) "because they rejected the instruction of the Lord"). Isaiah—First Isaiah, in 37:23 ff.—condemned Sennacherib king of Assyria for having blasphemed the Lord by proclaiming his own power, rather than God's, the source and cause of his victories; and cf. 10:6 ff. Jeremiah (chap. 27) promises destruction for those nations who, contrary to God's decision, will not submit to "Nebuchadnezzar king of Babylonia, My servant." Or cf., e.g., Isa. 14:12-16; Jer. 50-51 *passim.*

In Second Isaiah, however, the situation is quite different. If the nations will be smitten by God, if the gentile peoples are repeatedly denounced by the prophet, if Babylonia herself will be utterly destroyed—and all this is exactly what the prophet asserts—that was not because they had sinned but simply because they were the means by which God would show Israel and the whole world His uniqueness and omnipotence, and His abiding love for His people Israel. Passage after passage makes it crystal clear that the gentile nations were to be subjected to ignominy and defeat not because of any sins charged to them but only because God was to show His might in behalf of Israel. One recalls at once the identical fate of Egypt and its Pharaoh in the days of Moses and the Exodus, when God hardened and stiffened Pharaoh's

heart so that He could perform His miracles in the land and
"so that the Egyptians may know that I am the Lord"
(Exodus 7:3-5).

Thus, in chapter 40:9-11 our prophet proclaims joyfully
that God will raise His mighty arm against the gentiles—
hardly to spread His covenant and commandments among
them—in order to gather in His lambs, exiled Israel:

> . . . Behold the Lord God comes in might,
> His arm winning triumph for Him . . .
> Like a shepherd He pastures His flock:
> He gathers the lambs in His arms
> And carries them in His bosom;
> Gently He drives the mother sheep.

In verses 15-31 the nations are belittled and mocked, their
idols ridiculed, and the leaders threatened with extinction,
simply because they are not covenanted partners of God,
whereas the Judean exiles who have faith in the Lord will
be restored:

> The nations—they are a drop in a bucket,
> Reckoned as dust on a balance;
> The countries—He lifts them like motes . . .
> All nations are as nought before Him,
> Accounted by Him as less than nothing . . .
> He brings potentates to nought,
> Makes rulers of the earth as nothing . . .
> Why do you say, O Jacob,
> Why declare, O Israel:
> "My way is hid from the Lord,
> My cause is ignored by my God"? . . .
> They who trust in the Lord shall renew their strength
> As eagles grow new plumes:
> They shall run and never weary,
> They shall march and not grow faint.

Everyone knows that the traditional Hebrew text of
chapter 41 is not altogether clear and that several individual

words are hardly original; yet the context as a whole is clear: the gentile "nations" and "kings" will be subdued (vv. 2-3), the "coastlands" and "the ends of the earth" will tremble in fear (v. 5), and all of Israel's enemies will be destroyed.[18] Here is how the prophet himself has put it (vv. 8-16):

> But you, O Israel, My servant,
> Jacob, whom I have chosen,
> Seed of Abraham My friend—
> You whom I led from the ends of the earth
> And called from its far corners,
> To whom I said: You are My servant;
> I chose you, I have not rejected you—
> Fear not, for I am with you,
> Be not frightened, for I am your God;
> I strengthen you and I help you,
> I uphold you with My victorious hand.
> Shamed and chagrined shall be
> All who contend with you;
> They who strive with you
> Shall become as nought and shall perish.
> You may seek, but shall not find
> Those in conflict with you;
> Less than nothing shall be
> The men who battle against you.
> For I the Lord am your God,
> I hold you by the hand,
> I say to you: Have no fear;
> I will be your help.
>
> Fear not, O worm Jacob,
> O men of Israel:
> I will help you—declares the Lord—
> I your Redeemer, the Holy One of Israel.
> I will make of you a threshing-sledge,
> Sharp, new, with many spikes.
> You shall thresh the mountains to dust,
> And make the hills like chaff.
> You shall winnow them

> And the wind shall carry them off,
> The whirlwind shall scatter them.
> But you shall rejoice in the Lord.
> And glory in the Holy One of Israel.

Yet throughout this inspired statement—not a word about the nature of the sin committed by the gentile nations whom God will cause to perish and become as nought. And the same is true, e.g., in 42:23-24, where God Himself is stated to have handed over "Jacob to the spoiler, Israel to plunderers"; clearly all that the gentile nations did was to serve as tools of God's punishment of sinful Israel.

Even nations not involved in Israel's exile, Egypt, Cush, and the Sabeans, our prophet asserts, will come under Israel's authority, for it is only Israel who has God on her side (43:4-6 and 45:14-17):

> For I, the Lord, am your God,
> The Holy One of Israel delivers you:
> I give Egypt as your ransom,
> Cush and Seba in return for you.
> Because you are precious in My sight
> You are honored, and I love you;
> I will give mankind in your stead
> And peoples in exchange for your life.
> Fear not, for I am with you:
> I will bring your seed from the east
> And I will gather you from the west;
> I will say to the north, "Give up!"
> And to the south, "Hold not back!"
> Bring My sons from afar,
> And my daughters from the ends of the earth.[19]

and

> Thus said the Lord:
> The wealth of Egypt and the substance of Cush and
>   the Sabeans . . .

Shall pass over to you and be yours;
They shall follow you,
They shall come over in chains;
They shall bow low to you
And make supplication to you:
God is with you alone,
There is no other, no god besides Him . . .
All of them are shamed and chagrined . . .
But Israel is rescued by the Lord
In everlasting triumph . . .

In chapter 47, for the first and only time in all of Second Isaiah, a reason is given for the downfall of a gentile nation, Babylonia; it is the same as that given in chapter 37 (and the parallel section in II Kings 19) for the downfall of Sennacherib and Assyria, namely that Babylonia ignored the central role of God in making her merely the rod of His punishment of Israel, and, instead, regarded herself as the all-powerful one; in addition, she maltreated Israel ruthlessly, and unnecessarily; for that she will be punished (verses 5-15):

. . . Sit in silence, and go into darkness,
O daughter of the Chaldeans;
For you shall no more be called
The mistress of kingdoms.
I was angry with My people,
So I profaned My heritage;
I gave them into your hand,
But you showed them no mercy;
On the aged you laid heavy yoke.
You said, "I shall be mistress for ever . . .
I shall not sit as a widow
Or know the loss of children . . .
You said in your heart: I am,
And there is no one besides me."
But calamity shall come upon you . . .
Disaster shall fall upon you . . .

> And ruin shall come upon you suddenly,
> Of which you know nothing . . .

Without citing here any additional passages in the same vein, there is ample justification for the assertion that, on Second Isaiah's view, Israel suffered destruction at home and captivity in Babylonia abroad only because she had transgressed her covenant with God; Babylonia, on the other hand, having no covenant with God and being under no legal obligation to Him, committed no such transgression. It was but the rod of God's anger and punishment against sinful Israel, and the helpless witness and victim of God's might and of God's restoration of His beloved and chosen Israel to her homeland.

There is, of course, so much more to be said about Second Isaiah's attitude toward Babylonia and whatever other nations he may have had in mind. But one additional aspect must be brought out clearly, namely, that nothing could have been farther from the prophet's mind than that Israel was in existence for the welfare of the nations, or that other nations would achieve equality with Israel in God's scheme of things. This may be a very noble and worthy concept, one that would do credit even to the nations of our own twentieth century; but it is unfair and historically unjustifiable to read this concept back into Israelite thinking two and a half millennia ago.[20]

The Israelite composers of the Bible recognized God as the only God in the universe. He was the Creator, the sole Creator, of the whole world; He and He alone, brought all peoples into being and determined their careers; everyone and everything—even though they were not cognizant of it—were beholden to Him. At the same time, however, not one of all these peoples, apart from Israel, was God's covenanted people. So that while God was—to the biblical writers

—a universal God, He was not an international God, but a national God, the God of no nation in the universe but Israel.[21] Let us see how this concept manifested itself in Second Isaiah.

You will recollect how Babylonia is referred to as "spoiler" and "plunderers" (42:24). God, we are told in chapter 40, verse 10,

> Like a shepherd He pastures His flock:
> He gathers the lambs in His arms . . .

whereas (v. 17)

> All nations are as nought before Him,
> Accounted by Him as less than nothing.

Throughout, Second Isaiah uses terms of endearment in reference to Israel.

> Comfort, oh comfort My people,
> Says your God.
> Speak tenderly to Jerusalem

is how he begins his message. In Chapter 41 he will talk of

> Jacob whom I have chosen,
> Seed of Abraham My beloved . . .
> Less than nothing shall be
> The men who battle against you.
> For I the Lord am your God,
> I hold you by the hand,
> I say to you: Have no fear;
> I will be your help.
> Fear not, O worm Jacob . . .
> I will help you—declares the Lord—
> I your Redeemer, the Holy One of Israel.

This hardly sounds like an appeal to Babylonia or any other gentile nation to recognize God and become part of His covenanted people. Or as the prophet put it in the verses (14-15) immediately following:

> I will make of you a threshing-sledge,
> Sharp, new, with many spikes.
> You shall thresh the mountains to dust,
> And make the hills like chaff.
> You shall winnow them
> And the wind shall carry them off,
> The whirlwind shall scatter them.[22]
> But you[23] shall rejoice in the Lord,
> And glory in the Holy One of Israel.

Whether or not the reference to "Cyrus" in 44.28 and 45.1 is original, the fact is that the gentile "nations" and "kings" will be—not saved or converted—but mercilessly overcome, all for the sake of God's name and Israel's welfare; as put in the first part of the Chapter:

> ... For the sake of My servant Jacob,
> Israel My chosen ...
> That it may be known,
> From the rising of the sun and from the west,
> That there is none besides Me,
> I am the Lord, there is none other ...

When we read in Chapter 43:

> For I the Lord am your God,
> The Holy One of Israel who brings you triumph ...
> Do not fear, for I am with you:
> I will bring your offspring from the east,
> And from the west I will gather you;
> I will say to the north, Give up,
> And to the south, Do not withhold ...

it is hardly "good tidings" that the prophet was announcing to the gentile peoples of the earth. And the same is true, e.g., in chapter 48, where God calls out:

> Hearken to Me, O Jacob,
> Israel whom I called ...
> The Lord loves him.

whereas, so far as Babylonia is concerned,

He shall perform His will on Babylon
And His arm on the Chaldeans.

Or take chapter 49. Verse 7 asserts clearly:

Thus says the Lord,
The Redeemer of Israel and his Holy One,
To one deeply despised, abhorred by the nations,
The servant of rulers:
"Kings shall see and stand up;
Princes, and they shall prostrate themselves,
Because of the Lord, who is faithful,
The Holy One of Israel, who has chosen you."

Lest, however, the reader jump to the conclusion that the expression "they shall prostrate themselves" (וְיִשְׁתַּחֲוּוּ) points to conversion, to acceptance of Israel's God and His teachings, let him but continue to read on, to the end of the chapter (verses 8-26). He will read, e.g., in v. 13,

Sing for joy, O heavens, and exult, O earth!
Break forth, O mountains, into song!
For the Lord comfort His people,
Will show compassion to His afflicted ones,

whereas, the Lord assures His people (v. 22),

I will lift up My hand against the nations
And raise My standard against the peoples.

Indeed, it is in this very context that the most vigorously nationalistic statements of the prophet are expressed:

And they[24] shall bring your sons in their bosom,
And your daughters shall be carried on their shoulders.
Kings shall be your foster fathers,
And their queens your nursing mothers.
With their faces to the ground they shall bow down to you
And lick the dust of your feet[25]. . .
I will make your oppressors eat their own flesh,
And they shall be drunk with their own blood as with wine.

> Then all flesh shall know
> That I the Lord am your Savior,
> And your Redeemer, the Champion of Jacob!

And something of a climax is reached in chapter 52, which begins with the exhortation:

> Awake, awake,
> Put on your garb of might, O Zion,
> Put on your robes of splendor, O Jerusalem, holy city,
> For no one uncircumcised or unclean
> Shall enter you any more.

because (vv. 10-11):

> The Lord will bare His holy arm
> In the sight of all the nations,
> And the very ends of the earth shall see
> The victory of our God.
> Away, away,
> Depart from there!
> Unclean! Touch it not!
> Depart from her midst,
> Cleanse yourselves,
> You who bear the vessels of the Lord![26]

If there is any purpose in Israel's presence in Babylonia, other than Israel's punishment for her sins, it is that the gentile nations (i.e., Babylonia and the world in general) may witness and experience, to their great chargrin and discomfiture, God's might in behalf of Israel, His boundless and exclusive love for His people Israel, exclusive because the gentile nations were never associated with God's love.[27] We are now ready to turn to chapter 53.

All scholars agree that the original Hebrew text of our brief chapter of 12 verses is not altogether intact; there are several verses that cannot be translated, that make no sense, as they stand; and other verses hardly belong there in the first place. However, we shall propose no emendations, and we shall deal with the passages that concern us in their preserved, traditional form.

The crucial passages in our chapter are certainly verses 4-6 and 7-9. The former reads:

> Surely he has borne our sickness,
> And carried our pains;
> Yet we thought him stricken,
> Smitten, and afflicted by God.
> But he was wounded because of our transgressions,
> Crushed because of our iniquities;
> The chastisement of our welfare (or, that made us whole)
>   was upon him,
> And through his stripes we were healed.
> All we like sheep had gone astray,
> We had turned each to his own way;
> And the Lord caused to fall upon him
> The guilt of us all.

It is evident at once that neither Babylonia nor any other gentile nation can be involved here: they had experienced no sickness and no pain, they were guilty of no transgression or iniquity, and they were not going to be healed. Quite the contrary: the prophet held out for them nothing but shame and ignoble defeat. There is only one party who had experienced sickness and pain, who had transgressed and sinned, and who would be healed of its wounds, and that was the people Israel, now in exile. They were like sheep who had gone astray, who had turned away from God each his own way. And if Israel is the party of the first part, then it is only an individual person, be it the prophet himself or someone else, who can be the party of the second part.

There is, in addition, a second aspect to this section of three verses that must be determined, namely, the aspect of vicariousness. It is true that this aspect has been associated

with our chapter by theologian and scholar alike for nigh
on two millennia. But does this association have any basis
in our text? Is the person in 53 a *vicarius*? Did he really act
as a substitute for the guilty who deserved punishment because of their iniquity, but who escaped it because this
servant, while himself innocent of sin, bore their punishment
for them?

It is our contention that there is not to be found either
here or elsewhere in the Bible any justification for the concept of vicarious suffering and atonement, a concept that
arose in Jewish and especially Christian circles of postbiblical
times.[28] I know of no person in the Bible, nor has any scholar
pointed to any such, who took it upon himself or who considered himself or who was appointed or considered by
others to be a *vicarius* for wicked people deserving of punishment. This should hardly be surprising in the light of the
covenant.

All scholars agree, and rightly so, that the covenant lay at
the heart of biblical thought. God and Israel voluntarily
entered into a pact according to which God promised on
oath to prosper Israel if she remained faithful to Him, and
Israel undertook to worship Him alone in return for His
exclusive protection. This altogether legal contract, then, assured both the obedient and the rebellious, both the guiltless
and the wicked, their proper due. Nothing could be farther
from this basic concept of *quid pro quo,* or from the spirit
of biblical law, or from the teachings of the prophets, than
that the just and faithful should suffer vicariously for the
unjust and faithless—that would have been the greatest injustice of all, nothing short of blasphemy, that the lawless
be spared their punishment at the expense of the law-abiding. Nowhere in the Hebrew Bible did anyone preach a
doctrine—which would have superseded the covenant!—

which allowed the sacrifice of the innocent in place of and as an acceptable substitution for the guilty.

Thus, the prophet Ezekiel, immediately before Second Isaiah, observed (chapter 14) that if the three models of righteousness, Noah, Daniel, and Job, were dwelling in wicked Jerusalem, they themselves would escape harm in the catastrophic destruction of the city, but the inhabitants of the city, transgressors of the Lord's commandments, would suffer the punishment due them. It would have occurred to no one in the Bible that such blameless persons as Noah, Daniel, and Job bear vicariously the suffering and punishment coming to the wicked populace of Jerusalem.

Even in the well-known story in Genesis 18, where Abraham bargains with God in the matter of the impending destruction of Sodom and Gomorrah, there is not to be found the slightest hint of vicariousness. Abraham asks God whether He would insist on destroying these wicked cities if some innocent men (*tsaddiqim*) were found dwelling in their midst, be they 50, 40, 30, 20, or even 10 in number. God replies that He would spare the guilty for the sake of (*ba'abur*) the innocent; but in no case is there any question of a *tsaddiq* being a *vicarius* for the wicked (*rasha'*).

Or, finally, in Exodus 32, when Moses came down from Mount Sinai to behold Israel rejoicing in the golden calf. For this idolatrous act, God wanted to destroy His people Israel. According to verses 9-10 God said to Moses, "I see that this is a stiffnecked people. Now let Me be, that My anger may blaze forth against them and that I may destroy them, and make of you a great nation." But Moses dissuades God from such drastic action (verses 11-14), reminding Him of what the Egyptians would say and of the oath that He swore to the patriarchs. In another version of this same event, verses 30 ff., Moses said to God, "Alas, this people is guilty

of a great sin . . . And yet, if you would only forgive their
sin! If not, erase me from the record which You have written!" But the Lord said to Moses, "He who has sinned
against Me, him only will I erase from My record . . ." Here,
too, then, there is no hint of anything vicarious being sought
or offered by either party.

Turning back, now, to our passage in Isaiah 53, it will probably come as an anticlimax to learn that in point of fact the
text has nothing to say in the first place about vicariousness;
this was only read back into the text many centuries after
Second Isaiah's time. All that our text says is that the individual, whoever he was, suffered on account of Israel's
transgressions. Let us try to comprehend this statement in
proper historical perspective.

　　Throughout the Hebrew Bible, whoever came in the name
of God to the representatives of the people to rebuke them
for breaking faith with God—and for what other reason did
a spokesman for God make public appearance?—automatically suffered because of the nature of his mission. No
prophet ever appeared in order to tell Israel's leaders that
they were just and upright in the eyes of God. On the contrary: it was when they had to be rebuked and condemned,
and be made to repent and return to God, that a prophet
appeared on the public scene. And because of their "uncompromising vehemence, the prophets continually risked and
suffered abuse and even death at the hands of those they attacked . . . Elijah had to flee for his life because of his
vehement denunciations of Ahab and Jezebel. Micaiah was
hit on the jaw and thrown into prison . . . Amos the Judean
risked life and limb . . . at Bethel, and he minced no words
in telling the royal house and its supporters what lay in store
for them as retribution for their rebellion against the Lord.

Because he bitterly denounced the domestic and foreign policy of his government, Jeremiah's life was threatened, he was beaten, he was put in stocks, and he was thrown into a dungeon, so that he was constrained to cry out, 'and I was like a docile lamb that is led to the slaughter' (11:19, וַאֲנִי כְּכֶבֶשׂ אַלּוּף יוּבַל לִטְבּוֹחַ) . . . Ezekiel was told by God, 'And you, son of man, be not afraid of them [namely, your fellow Judean exiles in Babylonia], neither be afraid of their words, though briers and thorns be with you and you dwell among scorpions' . . . Uriah the prophet was killed by King Jehoiakim . . . and . . . Zechariah was stoned to death (II Chron. 24:20-21)."[29]

Every one of these spokesmen of God suffered because of the nature of their calling; it was their occupational hazard. None of them had committed any sin for which they were suffering, for which they were experiencing punishment. It was simply that, innocent as they themselves were of any transgression against the Lord, their extremely unpopular occupation and mission as God's spokesmen necessarily brought into their wake suffering, and abuse, and jail, and even death. In this respect, the servant of Isaiah 53 was no more a sufferer than so many of those who preceded or followed him as a spokesman of God.

Read straightforwardly, then, all that the pertinent verses in our chapter actually assert is that the servant in question bore the griefs and carried the sorrows of the people, having been wounded for their transgressions and bruised for their iniquities. Like all spokesman and prophets of God, from first to last, this person too suffered on account of and along with the people at large, the latter directly because of their trangressions and the former, though not guilty of transgression, because that was, unfortunately, his lot, the consequence of his calling, of his unpopular mission.[30] And when the people were made whole again, when their wounds were healed, it was only because the prophet had come and suffered to bring them God's message of rebuke and repentance. That, and that alone, is the meaning of such a verse as "The chastisement of our welfare (or, that made us whole) was upon him, and through his stripes we were healed . . . And the Lord caused to fall upon him The guilt of us all."

And this fundamental fact, too, should not be lost sight of, that neither elsewhere in the Bible nor in this chapter do the sinful people get off scot free, at the expense, as it were, of the prophet. Quite the contrary; the people whom the prophet was addressing had experienced the greatest catastrophe in their history: devastation of Judah and Zion, massacre of the populace, captivity in exile. So that the central element in the phenomenon of vicariousness, that the wicked go unpunished, is lacking altogether here.

Not only that. We are now able to see clearly that the prophet in Isaiah 53 does not deserve the title "Suffering Servant" with capital "S". This is an utterly gratuitous appelation bestowed upon him only after, and because vicariousness had, no less gratuitously, been associated with him.[31] His biblical career was essentially no different from that of Elijah, or of Jeremiah, or of Uriah, or of Zechariah.

The attempts to discover elsewhere in the ancient Near East pertinent parallels to our problem in Isaiah 53 have been less than successful, partly because there are none and partly because our own biblical problem was not comprehended correctly in the first place: for having assumed that a suffering servant and vicarious suffering and atonement were involved in our chapter, and that the servant accepted the suffering in meekness, humility, and uncomplaining silence (see on this below), scholarly procedure dictated a search in comparative materials for parallels.

Unfortunately, the parallels that have been discovered scarcely stand up as such even under casual scrutiny. Thus the generalizing statement has been made, lacking all pertinence to the problem at hand, "Humility, silence, and meekness became increasingly characteristic of ancient oriental piety after the late second millennium B.C."[32] But how this sweeping statement bears upon our specific problem is not made clear; for what does this prove, even if only chronologically, for the period of Second Isaiah over half millennium later? Or when the same scholar follows immediately with the statement, "The inscriptions of the Neo-Babylonian kings (sixth century B.C.) often begin with the words (following the titulary), 'the meek and humble one,'" the sceptical question leaps at once to mind, "So what? What does this prove?" Everyone knows that such inscriptions are generally characterized from the very beginning by formulaic humility, conventional meekness and politeness. These are but official formulas, and have no pertinence for Isaiah 53 which has no association with royal historical inscriptions; or is one to assume that the—likewise only alleged—meekness and humility of Jeremiah ("But I was like a gentle lamb led to the slaughter . . .," followed in the very next verse by, "But, O Lord of Hosts . . . let me see Your vengeance upon them . . . !") derived likewise from Neo-Babylonian royal inscriptions?

Again, attention is drawn to the fact that "The words 'I am a humble man' appear at the commencement of an inscription of a king of Hamath about 800 B.C." But apart from the fact that the reading and meaning of the original are not beyond dispute,[33] how can the alleged concept in

Isaiah 53 be proved by finding the word for "humble" in the dialect of another culture, region, and period?

And, finally, the statement is made, "Humility is also a characteristic of the worshipper in late Egyptian and Assyrian prayers to the gods"—as though this were not the case in all prayers among all peoples in all times, including the prayers in the Bible itself. (And since when is Isaiah 53 a prayer, and where is the worshipper?)[34]

In fine, there are no Near Eastern parallels to our problem.[35]

In 1892 B. Duhm unwittingly performed a great disservice to the correct understanding of Second Isaiah when he pulled out of their context four "Servant" sections and treated them as something of a homogeneous group which was composed not by Second Isaiah but by an unknown writer[36]; nothing could be farther from the truth.[37] But this problem, outside the scope of this essay, will be treated in some detail elsewhere (see n. 31).

Suffice it to state here that each of the four so-called "Servant Songs" must be treated *per se* within its own context; there is no more reason to associate any one *'ebed* passage, outside its specific context, with any other in Second Isaiah, than there is to group together, regardless of their place in the text, the *'ebed* passages, say, in the book of Kings: for just as God's *'ebed* in the latter Book may be Moses, or David, or Ahijah, or Elijah, or Jonah, or prophets in general, so may God's *'ebed* in Second Isaiah be Jacob (= the people Israel) or the prophet himself, with Cyrus of Persia (described as God's "shepherd" and "anointed") playing the same role for Israel's God in Second Isaiah (44:28; 45:1) as "Nebuchadnezzar, king of Babylon My servant" does in Jeremiah (25:9; 27:6; 43:10).

In dealing with the identity of the person in Isaiah 53, several facts must be kept in mind. Firstly, the meaning of several of the passages is uncertain—and this on any theory—because the preserved text is corrupt. Secondly, several passages, especially verses 11-12, suffer from misplaced or editorially inserted clauses. Thirdly, regardless of how this person is identified, the problem of identification is of no crucial importance for the overall understanding of Second Isaiah's message to his fellow Judeans in exile, any more than it is in the other three so-called servant sections. And fourthly, some of the expressions are to be taken as poetic exaggeration rather than as literal fact, so that, e.g. (cf. n. 35 above), the language of the suffering, and even of the death, of the person involved is but hyperbole. Thus we know that Jeremiah, who was taken down to Egypt against his will and of whose life and death there we know nothing, tells of himself, while yet in Judah, "I was like a docile lamb led to the slaughter, I did not know it was against me they devised schemes, saying, 'Let us destroy the tree with its fruit, let us cut him off from the land of the living, that his name be remembered no more' " (11:18-20). But everyone knows Jeremiah was neither docile as a lamb nor was he slaughtered in Judah and cut off from the land of the living. Yet precisely this is the language employed in vv. 7-8 of Isaiah 53: ". . . and like a sheep that before its shearers is dumb, so he opened not his mouth...he was cut off from the land of the living..."[38]

When it is realized (1) that the person in Isaiah 53 did not die but would live long enough to see children and grandchildren and enjoy triumph over his adversaries, (2) that his career as spokesman of God was essentially the same as that of so many prophets in the Bible, and (3) that he suffered—in nowise vicariously—at the hands of the very Israelites to whom he was sent by God to admonish and persuade, then it can be none other than our prophet himself, Second Isaiah, who is that person. The career of no other such spokesman of God, say Jeremiah or Moses, fits the picture[39]; in contrast to them, our prophet, while likewise facing insult and probably even some physical violence, would himself witness the fulfillment of what he came to announce: a restored exile and homeland; and he himself—unlike Jeremiah or Moses—would enjoy something of that restoration.[40] By the same token, there is no reason for regarding the person in Isaiah 53 as one utterly unknown to us, the "Great Unknown" as it were: why should this person be different from all other "servant" persons in Second Isaiah?[41] To put it differently; would any scholar have thought of treating chapter 53 differently from any other chapter in our Book had it not been for the theological aura created for it in early Christianity?

CONCLUSIONS

In summary, then, it is our thesis that:

(1) The personage in Isaiah 53 is not Israel (personified or ideal or otherwise) but an individual person, a spokesman of God, and that person is Second Isaiah himself.

(2) The element of vicariousness was completely unknown in connection with this individual person's career, in life and, in the fulness of time, in death, until long after his career had come to an end, indeed, until after the death of Jesus and in consequence of it.

(3) It was, again, long after Isaiah 53 was composed, and only in consequence of the vicariousness that came to be read into Isaiah 53 in conjunction with the death of Jesus, that the servant came to be associated with such extreme and unique suffering as to be dubbed the Suffering Servant *par excellence,* an appelation unknown to the Hebrew Bible and unsupported by it. It was then that our prophet came to be pushed out of the picture as that person, in favor of Jesus, or Israel, or the Messiah; in short, eisegesis has pushed out exegesis.

NOTES

[1] I have dealt with several of these concepts in my *Ancient Israel* (Cornell University Press, 1954; frequently reprinted)—where, however, detailed argumentation and documentation could not be presented. Thus my discussion of "The Tribal System of Israel and Related Groups in the Period of the Judges" (in *Studies and Essays in Honor of Abraham A. Neuman*, ed. M. Ben-Horin, B. D. Weinryb, and S. Zeitlin [Phila.-Leiden, 1962], pp. 375-387; reprinted in *Oriens Antiquus*, 1 [1962], 11-20) is an elaboration of the brief "anti-amphictyonic" treatment of the subject on pp. 58-60 of *Ancient Israel;* and my detailed analysis of "The Seer in Ancient Israel" (to appear shortly in *Oriens Antiquus*) is what really lay behind the popular presentation on pp. 143-148 of *Ancient Israel.* And see now my essay on "Who is the Ideal Jew: the Biblical View," *Judaism*, 13 (Winter Issue, 1964), 19-28.

[2] The English translations used in this essay are either my own or are based upon the Revised Standard Version. In no case have I departed significantly from the traditional rendering of the Hebrew text where my own analysis was involved.

[3] M. Schian, *Die Ebed-Jahwe-Lieder in Jesaias 40-66,* etc. (Halle, 1895), pp. 34 f., 47, 59 f., isolated the two verses 52:13 and 53:1 as a later addition to 53:2-12, in his opinion the original song. In the twentieth century, H. Jahnow (*Das hebräische Leichenlied im Rahmen der Völkerdichtung* [*Beiheft zur Zeitschrift für die alttestamentliche Wissenschaft,* vol. 36, 1923], p. 256), J. Monteith ("A New View of Isaiah liii," *Expository Times,* 36 [1924-25], 498-502), J. D. Smart ("A New Approach to the 'Ebed-Yahweh Problem," *Expository Times,* 45 [1933-34], 168-172), and N. H. Snaith ("The Servant of the Lord in Deutero-Isaiah" [in *Studies in Old Testament Prophecy*—the T. H. Robinson *Festschrift*—ed. H. H. Rowley (Edingurgh, 1950)], p. 199), stand almost alone in questioning this tacitly accepted view.

[4] C. C. Torrey, *The Second Isaiah* (New York, 1928), p. 331, has some pertinent remarks on *meshullam,* as on *yeshurun* (p. 344) and *yaskil* (p. 415), and on the prophet's "constant use of paronomasia" (pp. 193 f.); or cf., e.g., S. H. Blank, *Prophetic Faith in Isaiah* (New York, 1958), p. 79 and nn. 7 and 9 (on p. 216).

K. Budde ("The So-called 'Ebed-Jahweh Songs' and the Meaning of the Term 'Servant of the Yahweh' in Isaiah Chaps. 40-55," *American Journal of Theology*, 3 [1899], 533 f. [=34 f. in *Die sogenannten Ebed-Jahwe-Lieder*, etc. (Giessen, 1900)], followed, e.g., by K. Marti (*Das Buch Jesaja erklärt* [*Tübingen*, 1900], ad loc.) and J. Monteith (*op. cit.*, 499 f.), missed the point completely in emending יַשְׂכִּיל to יִשְׂרָאֵל.

[5]Where (singular!) כָּמֹהוּ correctly refers back to the Israel in *yesharim*, which is parallel to Jacob and Israel. On the rendering "the upright" for *yesharim* in the new Jewish Publication Society version of the *Torah* (Philadelphia, 1962), the explanatory footnote reads: "*Heb* Yesharim, *a play on* Yeshurun (*Jeshurun; Deut. 32.15*), *a name for Israel*."

[6] הִנֵּה יַשְׂכִּיל עַבְדִּי יָרוּם וְנִשָּׂא וְגָבַהּ מְאֹד:

[7] כַּאֲשֶׁר שָׁמְמוּ עָלֶיךָ רַבִּים כֵּן מִשְׁחַת מֵאִישׁ מַרְאֵהוּ וְתֹאֲרוֹ מִבְּנֵי אָדָם:

Scholars agree that parts of this verse, as of v. 15 following, are of uncertain meaning; nor is the text altogether certain. Our own interpretation is based upon the generally accepted understanding of the traditional Hebrew text.

[8] כֵּן יַזֶּה גּוֹיִם רַבִּים עָלָיו יִקְפְּצוּ מְלָכִים פִּיהֶם כִּי אֲשֶׁר לֹא־סֻפַּר לָהֶם רָאוּ וַאֲשֶׁר לֹא־שָׁמְעוּ הִתְבּוֹנָנוּ.

[9]I have never been convinced that there was a Third Isaiah (regarded by many, if not the majority of scholars as the author of chapters 56-66) readily distinguishable from Second Isaiah as the latter is from First Isaiah, allowing, of course, that "The *literary* unity of Is. 40-66 is undoubtedly imperfect, especially in later chapters: naturally the whole will not have been delivered by the prophet continuously, but some alteration, and advance, in the historical situation may be presupposed for its later parts. Thus . . ." (S. R. Driver, *An Introduction to the Literature of the Old Testament*, rev. ed. [New York, 1913], pp. 244 ff.; see in general, pp. 211 f. [on Isaiah 13:1-14:23], 225 f. [on chapters 34-35], and 230 ff. [on chapters 40-66]). I regard the bulk of chapters 40-66 as the product of a single writer. However, so as not to prejudice the argument presented here, I shall limit myself to chapters 40-55 when referring to Second Isaiah.

[10]There is much to be said for the opinion that the author of chapter 53 was resorting to hyperbolic rather than to factual description (cf., e.g., pp. 148 ff. in C. R. North, *The Suffering Servant in Deutero-Isaiah* [Oxford University Press, 1948; revised ed., 1956];

and see further below); so that, in effect, the servant did not really keep silent nor did he die. But there is no way of getting around the straightforward statement (v. 9), עַל לֹא־חָמָס עָשָׂה וְלֹא מִרְמָה בְּפִיו: "Although he had done nothing lawless // And there was no deceit in his mouth," in contrast to which the servant had previously been considered punished for his own sins rather than in consequence of those of others (vv. 4-6; see beginning of next section). Smart (p. 169, § 3) put it bluntly, "Would any prophet of Israel worthy of the name make the statement that Israel 'had done no violence, nor was any deceit in his mouth'? Torrey (p. 421) tries to water this down to mean only that Israel 'was far better than those for whom he suffered,' but the plain meaning remains. The writer of Is. 40-66 was under no such delusions about his people. He reminds them of sins of the past, and assails them for sins of the present . . . " And cf. H. H. Rowley, *The Servant of the Lord and other Essays on the Old Testament* (London, 1952), p. 51.

It is worth noting that even Torrey, who regards 52:13-53:12 as a single major unit—with Israel being the servant throughout, vicariously atoning for the Gentiles (409 f.)—has to distinguish 52:13-15 ("the formal statement," with God as the speaker) from 53:1-9 ("the main body . . . conceived in somewhat dramatic form," with the Gentiles as the speaker) and 10-12 (God again as the speaker).

[11]Snaith, p. 199 bottom. It may be noted that the form שְׁמוּעָה is found only here in all of chapters 40-66 of Isaiah.

[12]This is one of the main aspects of L. J. Liebreich's detailed study of "The Compilation of the Book of Isaiah," *Jewish Quarterly Review*, 46 (1955-56), 259-277; 47 (1956-57), 114-138 (especially 135 f., where נִשָּׂא "be elevated" in 52:13, but נָשָׂא "bore" in 53:4, 12 are cited). And cf. the detailed analysis of the "Language of the Songs" by North, pp. 161-177, 189-191.

[13]Cf., e.g., C. D. Ginsburg, *Introduction to the Massoretico-Critical Edition of the Hebrew Bible* (London, 1897), Part I, Chap. II, "The Sectional Divisions of the Text (the Open and Closed Sections)," pp. 9-24. Thus O. Eissfeldt, *Einleitung in das alte Testament*, 2nd ed. (Tübingen, 1956), 150 f. (3rd ed., 1964, 171 f.), e.g., after discussing some instances in which "Hier ist also die Kapitelteilung besser," continues with "Umgekehrt verdient die Paraschenteilung Gefolgschaft, die Kapitelteilung dagegen nicht, etwas bei dem letzten der 'Ebed-Jahwelieder Jes 52 13-53 12 und bei dem von uns schon als eine Einheit, nämlich also Volksklaglied erkannten Stück Jes 63 7-64 11 . . . "

¹⁴H. Bardtke has discussed "Die Parascheneinteilung des Jasajarolle
I von Qumrān in *Festschrift Franz Dornseiff*, ed. H. Kusch (Leipzig, 1953), pp. 33-75. He has noted (pp. 67 f.) that "Fünf offene
Paraschen lassen sich von 52,7 bis 53,12 feststellen. Diese sind:
52,7-12, 52,13-15, 53,1-8, 9-10a, 10b-12; die erste Parasche wird
im MT nur durch BHK (²) bestätigt und Pesch, die zweite ist
worhanden in Petrop., S, B, A. Von 53,1 an hat MT keine Unter-
gliederung mehr, auch nicht Pesch und B . . . "

¹⁵*The Dead Sea Scrolls of the Hebrew University*, ed. E. L. Sukenik
(-N. Avigad) (Jerusalem, 1955), Plate X; cf. S. Loewinger, "The
Variants of DSI II," *Vetus Testamentum*, 4 (1954), 155-163.

¹⁶On the concept יְרוּשָׁלַיִם עִיר הַקֹּדֶשׁ, see now M. Haran, *Between
Ri'shonot (Former Prophecies) and Hadashot (New Prophecies):
A Literary-Historical Study in the Group of Prophecies Isaiah XL-
XLVIII* ([in Hebrew, בֵּין רָאשׁוֹנוֹת לַחֲדָשׁוֹת, etc.] Jerusalem, 1963),
§30, pp. 96-101.

¹⁷It is curious that the expression "double; twofold" (כִּפְלַיִם) has
sometimes been understood literally. Thus O. Eissfeldt, "The Ebed-
Jahwe in Isaiah xl.-lv. in the Light of the Israelite Conceptions of
the Community and the Individual, the Ideal and the Real" (*Expository Times*, 44 [1932-1933] 261-268), pp. 265 f., would have it
that Jerusalem having "received from the hand of Jahwe double
punishment for all her sins . . . the possibility is at least suggested
that surplus punishment may be credited to others . . . " In immediate reply, Smart has put it this way (p. 168), "Eissfeldt uses
the old explanation that the double punishment mentioned in 40²
was half for the sins of the world. But surely the evident meaning
of 40² is that since the nation has been punished twice over for all
her sins the new day of forgiveness and blessing must be at hand.
The purpose is to emphasize that the time of punishment has been
completely fulfilled." S. Sandmel, *The Hebrew Scriptures: An Introduction to their Literature and Religious Ideas* (New York,
1963), p. 184, n. 7 (on "His compensation" / שְׂכָרוֹ), believes
that "The meaning here is that Jerusalem, having paid double for
its sins, will now receive compensation for its sinfulness which
has been eradicated." P. A. H. de Boer, *Second-Isaiah's Message*
(=*Oudtestamentische Studiën*, vol. XI, Leiden, 1956), p. 115,
would have it that ". . . Second-Isaiah's message is that their (viz.,
Israel's) suffering, beyond their deserved punishment, was accepted
by Yhwh as an atonement for those who remained without punishment . . . " We shall see below that the non-Israelite nations did

not "sin"—they had no covenant with God to transgress!—nor were they atoned for. Our term "double" is employed rhetorically, not mathematically; cf., e.g., Torrey, p. 305.

[17a]Smart (pp. 168 f.), while seeing with everyone else vicariousness in chapter 53, nevertheless recognizes the fact that "The idea of Israēl as a suffering Servant, meekly redeeming the nations, is quite foreign to the thought of the prophet, and has been largely instrumental in obscuring his real thought . . ."

[18]It should be observed here that the expressions "nations," "peoples," "ends of the earth," "seacoasts" (or "isles"), "far corners" (respectively אֲצִילִים; אִיִּים; קְצוֹת הָאָרֶץ; לְאֻמִּים, גּוֹיִם), and the like, do not, as a matter of fact, refer to any nations at all. Our prophet has but one specific nation in mind as Israel's foe, and that is Babylonia. Whom else would he have in mind at this point in history: Egypt? Phoenicia? Edom? Philistia? Assyria? When he used the terms "nations; peoples; ends of the earth," etc., his audience recognized in them at once poetic language for "the whole world; everyone," exactly as First Isaiah, among others, meant to be understood when he began with

> Hear, O heavens,
> Give ear, O earth.

By the same token, when the prophet refers to "kings," "rulers," "chieftains," "potentates," "rulers of the earth" (respectively מְלָכִים; שֹׁפְטֵי אֶרֶץ, רוֹזְנִים; שָׂרִים; מֹשְׁלִים), and the like, or, e.g. (41:11-12), to

> All who contend with you,
> They who strive with you,
> Those in conflict with you,
> The men who battle against you

he has no one (except the Babylonian leaders) specifically in mind.
Again, when the prophet proclaims (42:10-11):

> Sing to the Lord a new song,
> His praise from the ends of the earth—
> You sailors of the sea and its creatures,
> Your coastlands and their inhabitants!
> Let the desert and its towns cry aloud,
> The villages where Kedar dwells;
> Let Sela's inhabitants shout,
> Call out from the peaks of the mountains.
> Let them do honor to the Lord,
> And tell His glory throughout the lands.

he is not referring to the denizens of the sea, or to the inhabitants of Kedar, or of Selạ, or of the desert, and the like; he is resorting to rhetoric pure and simple.

[19]Here too (cf. n. 18 preceding), we probably have rhetoric rather than—as many scholars (cf., e.g., M. Haran, p. 59, ad loc.)— specific geopolitics. Thus Torrey has noted at 43:3 (p. 334), " 'I give Egypt as thy ransom . . . nations in thy stead.' The well-known figure of speech, meaning simply, 'Ye are dearer to me than the other peoples . . .' " And de Boer, e.g., has noted (p. 42, at 40:28 and 41:1, cf. pp. 89 f.), "*coastlands*. This expression possesses the same meaning as the ends of the earth, i.e. the whole earth . . ."; or cf. Sandmel, p. 179, n. 9. This is, clearly, in keeping with the expressions "east . . . west . . . north . . . south . . . from afar . . . ends of the earth."

Although my own interpretation of the problem at large would not suffer, I cannot agree with E. J. Hamlin, who would limit "The Meaning of 'Mountains and Hills' in Isa. 41:14-16" (*Journal of Near Eastern Studies*, 13 [1954], 185-190) specifically to Babylonia and her heathenism; the use of הָרִים and גְּבָעוֹת in both Isaiahs and elsewhere in the Bible, as well as our own immediate context, scarcely justifies this kind of specific restriction.

[20]An excellent case in point is provided by Isa. 56:7, where scholars generally have found the last clause to be the very essence of inter-nationalism: "for My House shall be called a House of Prayer for all peoples" (כִּי בֵיתִי בֵּית־תְּפִלָּה יִקָּרֵא לְכָל־הָעַמִּים). But this inter-pretation can be read into the text only by ignoring and perverting the context, i.e., by eisegesis. For the context (vv. 2-7) asserts un-equivocally that it is only the alien (בֶּן הַנֵּכָר) and the eunuch (הַסָּרִיס) "who join themselves to the Lord, to minister to Him . . . to be His servants . . . and who hold fast to My covenant" whom "I will bring . . . to My sacred mount and let rejoice in My House of prayer . . . for My House shall be called a House of Prayer for all peoples"; in other words, only foreigners who have converted to God's Torah are welcome in His House! As to whether this section of six verses (2-7) is original or the product of a later hand—that is a separate problem and does not concern us here.

Or cf., e.g., Isaiah 14:1-2, where the resident alien in the midst of restored Israel may become attached to the Israelites, whereas, on the other hand, the gentile peoples who had oppressed them will become their slaves

(כִּי יְרַחֵם יְהוָה אֶת־יַעֲקֹב וּבָחַר עוֹד בְּיִשְׂרָאֵל וְהִנִּיחָם עַל־אַדְמָתָם וְנִלְוָה

הַגֵּר עֲלֵיהֶם וְנִסְפְּחוּ עַל־בֵּית יַעֲקֹב: וּלְקָחוּם עַמִּים וֶהֱבִיאוּם אֶל־מְקוֹמָם
וְהִתְנַחֲלוּם בֵּית־יִשְׂרָאֵל עַל אַדְמַת יְהוָה לַעֲבָדִים וְלִשְׁפָחוֹת וְהָיוּ שֹׁבִים
לְשֹׁבֵיהֶם וְרָדוּ בְּנֹגְשֵׂיהֶם:) This, of course, is not universalism at all,
except that it is arbitrarily made universalistic by ignoring the true
force of v. 1 and by suppressing altogether v. 2! — as was done
recently, e.g., by M. Weinfeld, in "Universalism and Particularism
in the Period of Exile and Restoration" (in Hebrew; *Tarbiz,* 33
[1964/5724], 228-242, especially 231 ff.). He likewise misses the
point completely, e.g., when he fails to note in Zechariah 2:15
(and ignores v. 14 altogether) that only the heathens who join
Israel in her homeland can become part of God's people and that
it is only in Zion that God will dwell:

רָנִּי וְשִׂמְחִי בַּת־צִיּוֹן כִּי הִנְנִי־בָא וְשָׁכַנְתִּי בְתוֹכֵךְ נְאֻם־יְהוָה: וְנִלְווּ גוֹיִם
רַבִּים אֶל־יְהוָה בַּיּוֹם הַהוּא וְהָיוּ לִי לְעָם וְשָׁכַנְתִּי בְתוֹכֵךְ וְיָדַעַתְּ כִּי־יְהוָה
צְבָאוֹת שְׁלָחַנִי אֵלָיִךְ: In this he was following uncritically his mentor
Y. Kaufmann; see the several references to the latter's תּוֹלְדוֹת
הָאֱמוּנָה הַיִּשְׂרְאֵלִית, especially (in notes 38, 59, and 60) to vol. 8
(Tel-Aviv, 5716-1956). Even in the extremely difficult latter part of
chapter 19 in Isaiah (vv. 18-25), which is doubtlessly eclectic and
derives from more than one historical background (cf., e.g., G. B.
Gray, *ICC on Isaiah,* 1912, pp. 332 ff.), it tends to be overlooked that
Egypt will first be crushed (vv. 1-17, 22, 23) before it recognizes
Israel's God, and that in forming a triumvirate with Egypt and
Assyria, Israel will constitute a blessing in the world, i.e., through
Israel they will be blessed. But this composite section cannot, as it
stands, serve as the basis for any theory—except for those who would
resort to the principle of *obscurus per obscurius.*

[21]An excellent case in point is provided by Amos 9:7, where the
prophet clearly asserts: "You are like the Cushites to Me, O
Israelites, declares the Lord: I brought up Israel from the land of
Egypt, and the Philistines from Caphtor, and the Arameans from
Kir." Since Israel's God is the only deity in the world, who else but
He is responsible for all events involving nature and man? Ethiopia,
Philistia, Aram—all lands and peoples everywhere are His to act
upon as He sees fit. (Note how Amos expresses the identical con-
cept in 1:3-2:3, discussed briefly above.) But this does not make
God the God of the Ethiopians, Philistines, or Arameans! He is
the God of Israel exclusively, by legal and binding contract, by the
covenant.

For a different approach to the problem, *in re* Second Isaiah, see
S. H. Blank, "Studies in Deutero-Isaiah" (*Hebrew Union College*

Annual. 15 [1940], 1 ff.) and "Israel's God is God" and "And Israel is his Prophet" (respectively chapters IV and V in *Prophetic Faith in Isaiah* [New York, 1958], pp. 49-73 and 74-116); cf. also J. Morgenstern, "Deutero-Isaiah's Terminology for 'Universal God' " (*Journal of Biblical Literature,* 62 [1943], 269-280), and now "The Suffering Servant—a New Solution" (*Vetus Testamentum,* 11 [1961], 292-320, 406-431; 13 [1963], 321-332). S. Sandmel, pp. 189 f., has put it this way," . . . Second Isaiah excels all other prophets in his universalism, while at the same time particularism is not only present but central to his thinking, he is interested in all lands, but he must have Israel restored to Palestine." See in general the section on "Particularism and Universality of the Prophets" in my *Ancient Israel* (Cornell University Press, 1954), pp. 163 ff. (with the references in n. 14 to F. James and N. H. Snaith.)

[22]Of course, as in similar passages (cf. nn. 18 and 19 above), Second Isaiah is not promising here his colleagues in exile military conquest of Babylonia or of any other nation; the exiles, in the midst of their mighty masters, would, with justification, regard him as mad. In good rhetorical manner he is simply assuring them that God and His covenant would prevail over all else. Torrey, his theory of Israel's mission to the gentile nations rather embarrassed by the blunt statement of our passage, resorts to this kind of exposition (p. 317), "Those whom Israel is to 'thresh' and 'shatter' are not the heathen nations in general nor any of the surrounding nations in particular, but *the wicked* [italics in original], of all races and lands; the incorrigible enemies of Yahwè and the religion of righteousness . . . " It is interesting how the utterly nationalistic statements of our prophet are diluted and "extended" in order to make them express internationalism and to support Israel's alleged mission to the world. Thus de Boer (p. 90) recognizes well that "No other conclusion can be drawn from our texts than the statement: Second-Isaiah's only purpose is to proclaim deliverance for the Judean people. 'Yhwh bares his holy arm before the eyes of all the nations, and all the ends of the earth see the salvation of our God, ['] lii 10. Foreign nations are but mentioned as peoples to be conquered, in whose hands the cup of wrath will be put, li 23; or as the instrument of Yhwh to deliver his people; or, in rhetorical manner of speaking, to be witness of Yhwh's glory. Yhwh's glory will be shown only in his elected people, raised up from their humiliation. If the interpretation which reads a world-wide missionary task of the servant in the so-called first and second song of Yhwh's

servant and in chapters li and lv is right, we must state that the expressions where upon this interpretation is based are a *corpus alienum* in the book of Second-Isaiah. Are they an alien element indeed? . . . " One may well ask: Would anyone, prior to the rise of post-biblical Judaism and Christianity, have thought of creating such a *corpus alienum* and then introducing it into the text and context of Second Isaiah as the basic, original element?!

[23]Note the pronoun וְאַתָּה and its emphatic position.

[24]Viz., the gentile nations, i.e., the whole world.

[25]It is almost beyond comprehension how the plain meaning of this chapter is sometimes subverted by the "universalists" in order to attribute to the prophet the idea of " . . . the 'restoration,' the conversion of the heathen nations, and the final status of Jews and Gentiles in God's kingdom . . . " (Torrey, pp. 380 f.). Far from thinking of the alleged "conversion of the heathen nations," Second Isaiah expresses but contempt for them; cf., e.g., the scorn manifested for them precisely in passages where Israel is exhorted to prepare for liberation (52:1 and 10):

עוּרִי עוּרִי לִבְשִׁי עֻזֵּךְ צִיּוֹן לִבְשִׁי בִּגְדֵי תִפְאַרְתֵּךְ יְרוּשָׁלַיִם עִיר הַקֹּדֶשׁ כִּי
לֹא יוֹסִיף יָבֹא־בָךְ עוֹד עָרֵל וְטָמֵא: סוּרוּ סוּרוּ צְאוּ מִשָּׁם טָמֵא אַל־תִּגָּעוּ
צְאוּ מִתּוֹכָהּ and :הִבָּרוּ נֹשְׂאֵי כְּלֵי יְהוָה . Again, Torrey asserts (p. 387), "The phrase עֲפַר רַגְלַיִךְ יְלַחֵכוּ [49:23, "They shall lick the dust of your feet"] means no more (and no less) that the omnipresent 'he kissed the ground before him,' in the stories of the *Thousand and One Nights,* wherever king or caliph is approached by one of his subjects"; of course not only is this "explanation" less than convincing in context, but the statement three verses farther on ("I will make your oppressors eat their own flesh, And they shall be drunk with their own blood as with wine") is similarly dismissed with the statement (p. 388), "But the poet would have been horrified by the thought that any one would take his words here as a literal prediction or wish"! It is clear that this is hardly a *literal* prediction or wish; but then neither is it exactly an expression of affection on the part a conquered and humiliated people for her mighty and insolent conqueror! One may rightly wonder by which statement the poet would be horrified, by his own or by Torrey's.

[26]Torrey (p. 406) asserts that " 'There shall no longer enter thee the uncircumcised and the unclean' . . . means simply: Jerusalem will be pure and holy, the abode of upright and God-fearing men; not foul and wicked, as it is at present . . . The sentence has in it

no hatred of Gentiles, nor does it express a wish that Jerusalem may be reserved for Jews only; see on the contrary 60:11 and the many similar passages . . . " One may well ask what עָרֵל וְטָמֵא in v. 1 and טָמֵא אַל־תִּגָּעוּ in v. 11 signify, if not the alien and heathen peoples, which is likewise the only—and natural—frame of reference in which the term עָרֵל, fits. As to 60:11 ("Your gates shall always stay open, Day and night they shall not be shut, To let in the wealth of nations, With their kings conveying it [or, led in procession]"), not only is v. 10 immediately preceding ignored in context (" Aliens shall rebuild your walls, Their kings shall wait upon you, [For in anger I struck you down, But in favor I take you back]"), and not only is v. 12 immediately following ("For the nation or the kingdom That does not serve you shall perish; Such nations shall be laid waste") obliterated as "an addition by a later hand, an exegetical appendage to נְהוּגִים (misunderstood)" (p. 451), but the clear force of hiph'il ("to bring in; be brought in, let in"; as against qal "to come in") is suppressed, חַיִל is rendered "throng" (as against "wealth"), and נְהוּגִים arbitrarily interpreted as "conducted in state; personally conducted"!

As a matter of fact, not only will the uncircumcised and unclean never again enter Israel's Holy City, but even those heathens who had previously conquered and occupied the territory of Israel will now be forced to quit her land. This is how our prophet put it (54:3-4; the historical background is II Kings 17:24 ff.):

> Enlarge the site of your dwelling,
> Let the cloths of your tent be extended;
> Do not stint!
> Lengthen the ropes, and drive the pegs firm.
> For you shall spread out to right and left,
> As your offspring shall dispossess nations
> And settle the desolate towns.

[27]In contrast to his attitude toward the non-Israelite world, our prophet constantly uses terms of endearment, compassion, and consolation for his fellow Israelites and for the devastated homeland. Without attempting here the compilation of a complete list of these terms, attention may be drawn, e.g., to such expressions as "Comfort, oh comfort My people . . . Speak tenderly to Jerusalem" (40:1-2; there is never any comfort or tenderness for non-Israelites); Israel alone as God's flock and lambs whom He will gather (v. 11); the Israelite exiles—never the gentile peoples—as weary and spent, but whose trust in God will bring them renewal of strength (v. 31); Israel—never any gentile nation—as "My servant," "Jacob, you

whom I have chosen," and Abraham as "My friend" (אֹהֲבִי; 41:8); Jacob as God's "worm" and God as Israel's—never anyone else's— "Redeemer" and "Holy One" (v. 14); the Israelites as "the poor and the needy, seeking water . . ." (v. 17); the exiles as blind and imprisoned (42:17); Israel—never the other peoples—frequently exhorted not to fear; God as Israel's "maker," "Creator," and "Fashioner" (43:1; 44:21, 24); and so on.

[28]It is remarkable how virtually every scholar dealing with the subject has merely taken it for granted that the principle of vicariousness is present in Isa. 53; thus, e.g., North has no discussion of it at all, nor Torrey, et al. No one proves it, everyone assumes it. So that when Eissfeldt, e.g., asserts ("The Ebed-Jahwe," etc., p. 265), "Finally, the last Servant Song, which by its unique content (the discovery of the significance of vicarious death) stands on a pinnacle by itself . . . ," it is actually he himself, in common with the other members of the theological and scholarly guilds in postbiblical times, who has made the discovery, not the author of Isa. 53. Not only that, the gratuitous assumption of vicariousness in this chapter has led directly and uncritically to the widespread opinion that this is "the most wonderful bit of religious poetry in all literature" (Torrey, p. 409); or cf. North's approval (p. 176) of L. Köhler's statement that " 'he opened not his mouth' (ver. 7) . . . is 'the most beautiful and expressive *Nachklang* in the whole writing . . . ' " What would the scholars have said of Jer. 11.19, and many other passages had vicariousness been discovered there?

E. J. Kissane (*The Book of Isaiah*, 2 vols. [Dublin, 1941-1943]) is typical of scholarship in assuming vicariousness in Isa. 53. Thus he writes (vol. II, p. 178), and correctly so, "There is still less reason for identifying the suffering servant with the prophets or the teachers. Individual prophets were innocent and suffered (e.g. Jeremiah), but their suffering was not the expiation of the sins of men . . . " Yet he assumes "vicarious suffering of the servant" in verses 3d-5 (p. 186), and asserts sweepingly (p. 177), in verse 10b-d, "Here the servant is a sacrificial victim chosen by God to make expiation for the sins of men by his suffering and death . . . Jahweh's purpose . . . is fulfilled by the servant's vicarious suffering and death." In point of fact, however, these verses have nothing at all to say about either vicariousness or death (cf. n. 34a below).

To realize the absence of vicariousness in Second Isaiah, one need but read carefully C. Lattey, "Vicarious Solidarity in the Old Testament" (*Vetus Testamentum*, 1 [1951], 266-274), where the statement is made (p. 272), "From the scapegoat I turn naturally to Isa. liii, which hardly calls for much exposition, being such a clear case of vicarious solidarity . . . "; or S. H. Hooke on "The Theory and Practice of Substitution (*Vetus Testamentum,* 2 [1952], 2-17). There is, actually, nothing there to connect the Mesopotamian data adduced, or the biblical scapegoat (Azazel), with our chapter 53. On the scapegoat, note T. H. Gaster's statement (s. "Azazel," *Interpreter's Dictionary of the Bible,* vol. I, p. 26), ". . . in view of the very fact that sin and impurity are unloaded upon them [viz. the scapegoats], they can be (and are) used only as vehicles of elimination, but not of propitiation."

[29]This quotation derives from the section "The Fate of the Prophets and Their Teachings" (in chapter VII: "The Hebraic Spirit: The Prophetic Movement and Social Justice") in my *Ancient Israel,* pp. 156-7. As to Zechariah, see S. H. Blank, "The Death of Zechariah in Rabbinic Literature" (*Hebrew Union College Annual,* 12-13 [1937-38], 327-346), where three different Zechariahs, including the prophet, are involved.

It should be noted here that insufficient attention has been paid to the clear distinction between vicariousness and atonement, or even martyrdom. Thus "vicariousness" is treated together with and subsumed under "Atonement" in *Jewish Encyclopedia* (vol. II, pp. 275-284; article by Kaufmann Kohler) and in *Interpreter's Dictionary of the Bible* (vol. I, pp. 309-313; article by C. L. Mitton — most inadequate for the Old Testament) — and quite confused with it. Or cf. "Suffering and Evil" (pp. 450-453; article by O. A. Piper), where, again, it is simply assumed (§ 2a) that "the Servant of God has taken vicariously upon himself the punishment of his nation (Isa. 53:2-12)." In general, it is most unfortunate that so many of the "theological" articles in the *Interpreter's Dictionary of the Bible* involving the Old Testament were written by scholars who are specialists only in the New Testament.

[30]Cf. A. Guillaume, "The Servant Poems in the Deutero-Isaiah" (*Theology,* 12 [1926], 5), "The difference between the sufferings of the nation and the sufferings of the Servant is fundamental. The nation suffered because of its disobedience to Jehovah: the Servant because of his obedience. All his countrymen had wandered from the path of obedience like silly sheep, and Jehovah brought down upon the Servant the guilt of them all. Through these verses the emphasis and antithesis of the *we* and the *he* are everywhere marked, so that the sense is '*we,* not *he,* wandered from the right way, and *he,* not *we,* bore the guilt.' No explanation of this vicar-

ious atonement is offered by the writer except that it was the pleasure or will of God to save Israel and the world in this way . . . The Servant's suffering was voluntary: he could have escaped it by disobedience to God and refusal to deliver his message. But he chose to suffer without protesting. Like a lamb borne to the slaughter: and like a sheep before her shearers." As to the correct understanding of the expression "bore the guilt"—according to which there is no vicarious atonement in the first place and consequently no explanation necessary, nor was the saving of the world involved—see immediately below. Rowley (p. 51, n. 4) refers approvingly to the first part of Guillaume's statement.

L. Waterman, "The Martyred Servant Motif of Is. 53" (*Journal of Biblical Literature,* 56 [1937], 27-34) — this article has been utterly ignored, even when bibliographically listed (as, e.g., by North)—has put it very bluntly (p. 28), "The Christian tradition seized upon the factor of vicariousness and seeing only Christ in the servant figure lifted it bodily out of its context and gave to the language unwarranted implications that cling to it to this day"; and after discussing vv. 4-5 he concludes that "the element of actual vicariousness thus disappears from the verse and the context" (p. 29)—this despite the fact that Waterman himself argues in favor of an "ideal servant" and "a world service that transcends nationalism . . ." (p. 32).

[31]It is outside the scope of this essay to determine when and under what circumstances Jesus came to be associated with the sufferer of Isa. 53. There are scholars who hold "that the ascription to Jesus of an interpretation of His mission in terms of the Servant is an unhistorical creation of the post-resurrection church" (Rowley, p. 55, n. 1, with references to B. W. Bacon, C. T. Craig, and F. J. Foakes Jackson-K. Lake; to which may be added, e.g., Craig's discussion of "The Problem of the Messiahship of Jesus," in *New Testament Studies,* ed. E. P. Booth [New York-Nashville, 1942], pp. 95-114). Thus Foakes Jackson-Lake, in their chapter (IV) on "Christology" (§ III *Primitive Christianity*) in *The Beginnings of Christianity, Part I: The Acts of the Apostles,* vol. I (1920), pp. 345-418, have asserted (p. 385), ". . . in none of these, however, do the writers appear to have had in mind any prophetic description of a great Sufferer and certainly had no idea of relating their descriptions of suffering to the Davidic Messiah or to the Son of man in the Apocalypses"; or (p. 386), "In Mark and in Q there are no clear signs of any identification of Jesus with the sufferer of Isaiah, liii . . ."

B. W. Bacon, "New and Old in Jesus' Relation to John" (*Journal of Biblical Literature*, 48 [1929], 40-81; part of a symposium on *Primitive Christianity and Judaism*), p. 61, put it this way, " . . . Nevertheless the earliest intimations are all opposed to Jesus' application of the figure to himself. Not the 'Servant' but 'the Son of Man' is Jesus' self-designation . . . uniformly the identification of him with the Isaian suffering Servant is represented as a post-resurrection discovery . . ." And C. T. Craig begins his survey discussion of "The Identification of Jesus with the Suffering Servant" (*Journal of Religion*, 24 [1944], 240-245), as follows: "From countless pupits, congregations are told that Jesus found the clew to his ministry in the fulfilment of the Suffering Servant prophecies of the Book of Isaiah. Indeed, many modern scholars have affirmed the same belief . . . On the other hand, it seems to me that at few points has wishful thinking dominated the judgment of scholars more than in the consideration of this issue . . ."

The concept "Servant of the Lord," no more than any of the so-called "Ebed-Yahweh" sections (or "Servant Songs") of Second Isaiah, had no special significance for anyone until after the career of Jesus had come to an end; the attempts to find this significance in an earlier period flounder on the simple fact that mere reference to passages in Second Isaiah, even to chapters 52-53, do not yet demonstrate technical terms and significant concepts such as "Servant of the Lord" and "Suffering Servant." This fact may be determined from a careful analysis of the references compiled, e.g., in C. R. North, Part I., chaps. II-III (pp. 6-27); Rowley, chap. I (pp. 3 ff.); W. Zimmerli — J. Jeremias, *The Servant of the Lord* (=*Studies in Biblical Theology*, No. 20, 1957; this is the English version of their article "παῖς θεοῦ" in *Theologisches Wörterbuch zum Neuen Testament*, ed. G. Kittel-G. Friedrich, 1954, 633-713), chaps. III and IV. In the last named, it is interesting to note how the absence of either all reference or any specific reference to Isa. 53 is frequently turned into proof that it is precisely Isa. 53 that was uppermost in the mind of those who failed to cite from it or gave it no special prominence. Thus, it is conceded that "In the N. T. Jesus receives the title παῖς θεοῦ strikingly seldom . . . " (p. 80) and that "There are strikingly few N. T. passages where in specific quotation a word relating to the servant of Deut. Isa. is applied to Jesus . . . " (p. 88); to the question: "Can Jesus have known himself to be the servant of God?" Jeremias gives immediate reply: "The gospels say so . . . " (p. 98); " . . . the silence of Jesus before his judges (Sanhedrin, Pilate, Herod) . . . " (p. 99) in reference to his role as Deutero-Isaiah's "Servant of the Lord"—all these serious problems are solved with one stroke by the gratuitous assumption, and in the face of reasonable analysis of the data available (or altogether absent), that " . . . Jesus only allowed himself to be known as the servant in his esoteric and not in his public preaching. Only to his disciples did he unveil the mystery that he viewed the fulfillment of Isa. 53 as his God-appointed task . . . " (p. 104). There is far more of eisegesis than exegesis to be found here; thus when Jermiahs asserts, "The gospels say so," one has but to examine carefully each passage quoted from the gospels along with each alleged source in Isa. 53, and it will be seen at once that Jeremias has simply pulled out individual and isolated words or common expressions— virtually never, incidentally, from the Septuagint text of Isaiah 53!— and made these justify his dogmatic assertion, "The gospels say so." Indeed, the gospels do *not* say so; it is only Jeremias who says that they say so. Jeremias' treatment of this all-important subject is an unjustifiable retrogression from the scholarly treatment given it, e.g., by Foakes Jackson-Lake three and a half decades earlier. (I plan to deal elsewhere, in the article "Servant of the Lord" [*'Ebed YHWH*] for Israel's *Encyclopaedia Miqra'it*, with the wholly unjustified and detrimental vogue of dealing with Second Isaiah from the point of view of the so-called "Ebed-Yahweh" sections; they are but a modern scholarly fiction.

Interestingly, in pre-New Testament times it is *yaskil* (52:13), not *'ebed*, that is seized upon for purpose of identification and interpretation. Thus it has long been recognized that the *maskilim* in Daniel (11:33,35; 12:3, 10) derive from our own *yaskil;* but nothing vicarious is involved here, nor any such concept as a Suffering Servant of the Lord. And this is true also of the Dead Sea Scroll material, into which some scholars have tried, beyond the call of scientific duty, to read their own notions of Isaiah 52-53 and Jesus as the fulfillment of them (cf., e.g., A. Dupont-Sommer, *The Essene Writings from Qumran* [Meridian Books, 1962], chap. VIII, §2 "The Man of Sorrows," pp. 364-366; this whole section is a homiletical disservice to the Scroll material, with n. 1 on p. 366 being particularly revealing); nothing vicarious is involved there. Indeed, it is, again, only by wishful thinking (viz., eisegesis) that Qumran's "Righteous Teacher" is identified with Second Isaiah's "Servant"; cf., e.g., M. Burrows, *More Light on the Dead Sea Scrolls* (New York, 1958), pp. 66, 316 f., 328, 335 f.—reiterating with greater emphasis the brief statements in his earlier volume, *The Dead Sea Scrolls* (New York, 1955); F. M. Cross, Jr., *The Ancient Library of Qumran and*

Modern Biblical Studies (Anchor Books, rev. ed., 1961), p. 222, n. 52. I suppose that it would not be easy to associate the concept of vicariousness with a group that could produce a treatise dealing with the ruthless and total war of the righteous (children of light) against the wicked (children of darkness).

[32]W. F. Albright, *From the Stone Age to Christianity: Monotheism and the Historical Process* (Baltimore, 1940), p. 254. This quotation follows immediately upon, ". . . The combination of these two concepts, vicarious suffering and purification through suffering, lies behind Deutero-Isaiah's doctrine of salvation. The most obvious characteristic of the Servant of Yahweh is his humility and meekness in the presence of his tormentors"—differently, one might well ask, from Jeremiah and so many other prophets? Indeed, this is the least obvious characteristic of Second Isaiah's *'ebed,* unless one insists on disregarding altogether the characteristic and vigorous nationalism of our prophet, in relation to both his own people and to the non-Israelites.

[33]Line 2 of the Zakir inscription is generally read (*'ish*) *'aneh* (*'anah*) and translated "(A) humble (man am I)." M. Black, on the other hand (*Documents from Old Testament Times*) *ed.* D. Winton Thomas [1958; now a Harper Torchbook]), pp. 242 ff. (following M. Lidzbarski, *Ephemeris für semitische Epigraphik* [Giessen, 1909-1915], vol. III, p. 6), renders "I am a man of 'Anah" (p. 248, "'*Anah* seems more likely to have been a place name than an adjective"), and observes that "The name could also, however, be read as *'akko* (the middle letter is uncertain) and identified with a place of this name in Phoenicia." Reproductions of the Zakir inscription are given, e.g., in H. Pognon, *Inscriptions sémitiques de la Syrie,* etc. (Paris, 1907), plates IX and XXXV (with the discussion of our word on p. 159); col. 198 of Albright's article on "Hamath" in *Encyclopaedia Miqra'it,* vol. III (1958), cols. 193-200 (with recent bibliography).

[34]One may safely treat with the same reserve the concluding statement by Albright (p. 255), ". . . When not only the leaders themselves, but also every pious Israelite is ready to give himself as a vicarious victim for his people, then God will restore Israel and will give it a glorious future. In this interpretation the different aspects of the Servant of Yahweh receive due consideration. The Servant is the people of Israel, which suffers poignantly in exile and affliction; he is also the pious individual who atones for the sins of the many by his uncomplaining agony; he is finally the coming Savior of Israel . . ."

[35]Whatever Second Isaiah's style and thought may owe to the specifically Babylonian part of his environment, I cannot take seriously the attempts to associate chap. 53, say, with the mythology and cult of Tammuz (see the survey in Rowley, pp. 42 ff.; the unevenness in C. Lindhagen's volume on *The Servant Motif in the Old Testament: A Preliminary Study to the 'ebed Yahweh Problem' in Deutero-Isaiah* [Uppsala, 1950] is due in part to the influence of the Scandinavian school; contrast the sober study of *The Servant Songs in Deutero-Isaiah* [Lund, 1951] by J. Lindblom). As a matter of fact, Tammuz (or the Ugaritic material) would never have suggested itself in this connection to anyone had it not been for the "dying-and-rising" element. Yet verse 10 flatly precludes any resurrection in chap. 53: what else can the expression "he shall see offspring, he shall prolong his days" (יִרְאֶה זֶרַע יַאֲרִיךְ יָמִים) mean, except that the person in question did not actually die but, instead, would live long on earth? (Would he, after dying and rising, die again, and remain dead forever?!) Cf., e.g., Job 42:16-17, "After this, Job lived a hundred and forty years, and he saw (וַיַּרְא) his children and their progeny, four generations. And Job died in ripe old age"; and the expression "to prolong days" (הַאֲרִיךְ יָמִים) is characteristic of Deuteronomy (cf. Driver, *Introduction*, p. 99), where afterlife and resurrection are unknown. Accordingly, the expressions (vv. 7-12) "like a lamb that is led to the slaughter (note the "non-fatal" expression immediately following, "and like a sheep that before its shearers is dumb") . . . for he was cut off from the land of the living . . . and he made his grave with the wicked, and his tomb (on which see now S. Iwri, *Journal of Biblical Literature,* 76 [1957], 232) with the rich . . . and bared (meaning of הֶעֱרָה quite uncertain) his life to death . . ." indicate, rhetorically, nothing more than that the person in question suffered much in the cause of his mission from God to Israel, but did not die in consequence of it; instead, he would live long after that chore, long enough to enjoy several generations of progeny and victory over his opponents. And they may be right who believe that the career of ancient Job—not in the (later) dialogue but in the very much earlier background of the prologue-epilogue (cf. N. Sarna, "Epic Substratum in the Prose of Job," *Journal of Biblical Literature,* 76 [1957], 13-25)—could have suggested this to Second Isaiah.

The universal tendency to see resurrection in vv. 10-12a following death (vv. 8-9, 12aβ), reminds one at once of Job 25:27-29, where the irrevocably corrupt text is made by some scholars to yield resurrection, in spite of all the other perfectly clear data to the contrary; cf. Chap. III, §C, "Alleged Concept of Afterlife," in my "Studies in the Septuagint of the Book of Job" (*Hebrew Union College Annual*, 32 [1961], 241-249; 19:25-27 is treated on pp. 248 f.).

[36]While he had presented this view already in 1875 (in *Die Theologie der Propheten als Grundlage für die innere Entwicklungsgeschichte der israelitischen Religion*, §38, "Jahves Knecht," pp. 287 ff.)—with the four sections designated as 42:1-7; 49:1-6; 50:4-9; 52:13-53:12— it was really his commentary in 1892, *Das Buch Jesaia* (in W. Nowack's series, *Handkommentar zum alten Testament*, pp. xviii, 284 ff., 365 ff., that made such great impact upon biblical scholarship. Scholars (including Duhm himself, in subsequent editions of his commentary) differ on the precise verses to be included in each of the four sections; as put, e.g., by J. Muilenburg, commentary on Second Isaiah in *The Interpreter's Bible*, vol. V (1956), 406, "Precisely at this point a problem is raised that has exercised the minds of scholars perhaps more than any other single Old Testament question . . . One of the first things to strike the reader of this literature is the want of unanimity as to the number and scope of the servant passages . . ." Or cf., e.g., A. Bentzen, *Introduction to the Old Testament*, 2 vols. (Copenhagen, 1958), vol. II, p. 110.

[37]Cf. Snaith (p. 187), "Some few scholars have argued against their (viz., the Servant Songs') segregation from the main body of the prophecy . . . The great majority, however, have followed Duhm, to such an extent that the existence of the four Servant Songs has come to be regarded as one of the firm results of modern O. T. study . . ." Although Snaith's article appeared only fifteen years ago (1950), several of the points that he has made there should have received already more attention than they have; Muilenburg (pp. 406b-408a) has argued vigorously against dealing with the Servant sections outside their context and in favor of regarding them as original with Second Isaiah.

[38]It is hardly necessary to seek further, and outside the Bible, additional parallels. One calls readily to mind, e.g., the well known Mesopotamian composition, *Ludlul bel nemeqi* ("I will praise the lord of wisdom"), where the "righteous sufferer" lives to lament:
The grave was open still when they rifled my treasures,
    While I was not yet dead, already they stopped mourning
(pp. 212-216 in T. Jacobsen's chapter in *The Intellectual Adventure of Ancient Man*, ed. H. and H. A. Frankfort [1946; appeared in 1949 as a Pelican Book, without the chapters on the Hebrews,

under the title, *Before Philosophy*]; or cf. R. H. Pfeiffer's translation on pp. 434-437 in *Ancient Near Eastern Texts relating to the
O. T.,* ed. J. B. Pritchard [1950]).

[39]It has long been noted what extensive use Second Isaiah made of
Jeremiah; cf. recently Blank, *Prophetic Faith in Isaiah,* chap. V, §5,
"After the Manner of Jeremiah," pp. 100-104 and the notes on pp.
218-220; O. Eissfeldt, *Der Gottesknecht bei Deuterojesaja (Jes.
40-55) im Lichte der israelitischen Anschauung von Gemeinschaft
und Individuum* (=*Beitrage zur Religionsgeschichte des Altertums,*
Heft 2 [Halle/Saale, 1933], 27 pp.)—on which see Blank, *Hebrew
Union College Annual,* 15 (1940), 21 and n. 35.

[40]As noted by R. H. Pfeiffer, *Introduction to the Old Testament*
(New York, 1941), p. 461, §3, "The autobiographical interpretation of the Servant poems was considered possible by the Ethiopian
eunuch of Acts 8:34"; but of course this was possible only in the
belief that the prophet could experience resurrection, a belief unknown to Biblical Judaism. Cf., e.g., A. A. Neuman, *The Immortality of Man: A Jewish Viewpoint* (Lancaster, Pa., 1949), 26 pp.
On "Die Deuterojesajanischen Gottesknechtlieder in der juedischen
Auslegung," see H. A. Fishel, *Hebrew Union College Annual,* 18
(1944), 53-73 (with a useful chart on pp. 74-76).

[41]Cf. recently Sandmel, p. 190, "The Suffering Servant poems (50:4-11
and 52:13-53:12) are two rather brief fragments preserved from a
lost larger work. They are discussed here only because they are
found in Second Isaiah and not because they bear any relationship
to it in either time or content. We do not know where or when
they were written . . . " For some recent literature along these lines,
see O. Eissfeldt, *Einleitung in das Alte Testament,* 2nd ed. (Tübingen, 1956), pp. 402 ff.; (3rd. ed., 448 ff.).

JERUSALEM AND THE PROPHETS

Reverend Roland De Vaux, O.P.
Visiting Professor at Harvard Divinity School
Head of Ecole Biblique at Jersulem
Pioneer in Discovery and Study of Dead Sea Scrolls

THE GOLDENSON LECTURE OF 1965

THE DOUBLE GLORY OF JERUSALEM IN THE
Old Testament is that of being the political capital of the
kingdom, the seat of the dynasty of David, and the religious
capital where the people come to worship their God who
inhabits the Temple. Jerusalem is the City of David and
the City of Yahweh. These two aspects are bound together
historically and the second seems subordinated to the first,
for it is David who introduced Yahweh to Jerusalem. However, the religious importance of Jerusalem very soon out-
weighed its political importance which was diminishing.
After the glorious but short period of the empires of David
and of Solomon, Jerusalem was only the capital of the
little kingdom of Judah, then a vassal city of Assyria and
Babylonia, finally a provincial city of the Persian, Greek
and Roman empires. In reverse, the religious importance
of Jerusalem continued to increase. In spite of the separation of the two kingdoms and the attempt of Jeroboam
to establish a concurrent sanctuary in Bethel, Jerusalem
remained the religious center of Yahwism. After the destruction of the temple, the exiles of Babylon wept when
they thought of Jerusalem (Ps. 137); they returned to
Jerusalem not to re-establish a kingdom but to rebuild the
temple. It was facing in the direction of this temple that
all the Jews of the Diaspora prayed. Long after the fall of
the dynasty of David and until the end of Jewish history,

Jerusalem remained the sanctuary of the memories and of the spiritual hopes of the people. Repository of the traditions of the past, she was the new Sinai; repository of the promises of the future, she was the image of the heavenly Jerusalem. The prophets are the privileged witnesses of this greatness of Jerusalem and in a certain way the artisans thereof. We are going to try to follow their development of this theology of Jerusalem.

* * * *

A prophet intervenes at the very beginning of the history of Jerusalem as an Israelite city; it is Nathan. It is not possible or necessary to discuss all the interpretations which have been given concerning the "Prophecy of Nathan" (II Sam. 7). It is sufficient for me to say that I refuse to single out several sources in this chapter.[1] The account may have been subjected to editorial changes and have received minor additions — the most notable being v. 13a which announces the building of the temple by Solomon.[2] But this account goes back to a unique and homogeneous source[3] which comprised not only the prophecy with its two elements, the refusal of a temple and the promise of a dynasty (v. 5-16), but the introduction which gives the circumstances of the oracle (v. 1-4), and the prayer of David which is his answer to the oracle (v. 18-29). The whole chapter is linked to what precedes: the project of building a temple is a natural result of the transfer of the ark to Jerusalem (I Sam. 6:1-19), and the promise of a dynasty is an answer to the question raised by the sterility of Michal (II Sam. 6:20-23). The chapter is equally articulate with what follows. The dynastic promise is like a preface to the great history of the succession to the throne which fills II Samuel 9-20; I Kgs. 1-2.

In II Sam. 7 the name of Jerusalem is never mentioned, but the thought of the city is present everywhere with the concern of its double destiny. The promise made to David of a house and of a royalty which will continue forever, of a throne which shall be established forever (v. 16; cf. 11b-12) consecrates Jerusalem as the capital of a kingdom. But more important is what concerns its character as a religious center. David has brought back to Jerusalem the Ark of the Covenant which is the symbol of the presence of Yahweh in the midst of his people, and he has deposited it under a tent (II Sam. 6:17). He wishes now to make a more stable habitation for it and to build a temple to Yahweh (II Sam. 7:1-2). In the Ancient Orient the building of a temple is a royal task, but it can only be accomplished by the order or the consent of the gods.[4] Now Yahweh, by the intermediary of his prophet Nathan, rejects this human initiative. "Who are you, you a man,[5] to build for me a house where I shall live, I, your God." Yahweh wishes to continue to live under a tent as He has done heretofore (v. 5-8). The refusal is categorical and lasting: Yahweh does not wish a temple. For this refusal many explanations have been proposed.[6] The most recent and the most contestable is that Nathan represents the Jebusite party who did not wish a sanctuary concurrent to that of the Canaanite god of Jerusalem whose worship would have survived the conquest.[7] But it is in the Israelite tradition itself that one must seek the reason for this refusal. It has been proposed to recognize in it the first expression of a trend of hostile opinion to the temple of Solomon.[8] Such a trend actually existed. It was translated concretely in the manner of life of the Rekabites who lived in tents, did not build houses for themselves, and did not want any for their God, and whom Jeremiah had to talk with before persuading them to accompany him to the temple (Jer. 35:2). This trend is shown later and in another way by the building on Mt. Garizim of a Samaritan sanctuary rival to that of Jerusalem. This same trend is expressed explicitly by a prophet after the Exile at the time of the rebuilding of the temple: "What is the house which you would build for me?" (Is. 66:1), and later in the speech of St. Stephen who quotes explicitly this last text. But the case of Nathan is different. If verse 13a is set aside as an addition — and that has seemed necessary to us—, if one accepts as historical the circumstances in which the oracle was pronounced — and this historicity is not contradicted by any valid argument—, there can be no question of hostility to the temple of Solomon, which did not yet exist. Nathan does not represent a reactionary trend; he represents a conservative trend, which wishes the preservation of the religious traditions of the League of the Tribes.

The "Sitz im Leben" of the account is the sanctuary of the ark in Jerusalem. It is there, before Yahweh, that David says his prayer of thanksgiving (II Sam. 7:18). The ark had been the pedestal on which Yahweh, invisible, became present in the midst of his people; the ark was also the receptacle which contained the tablets of the Law, the documents of the covenant Yahweh had concluded with his people. The ark had been, during all the period of the Judges, the center of the common worship which was the only effective bond between the tribes. Now the political conditions have changed, the Federation of the Tribes has become the Kingdom of David; but the religious conditions — the relation between the people and their God — remain the same. Although the word *berit* is not mentioned, the prophecy of Nathan is the equivalent of a treaty; it establishes the covenant between Yahweh and the House of

David[9], and this covenant is only the adaptation of the covenant of Sinai to the new circumstances.[10] The first covenant had made of Israel the vassal people of Yahweh. Now the king who is the *nâgîd* (II Sam. 7:8), the "vicegerent" of Yahweh over his people, becomes the vassal of Yahweh.

In fact, the references to this sacred past abound in the chapter. The religious and historical traditions which were bound to the ark, those of the period of the desert as those of the period of the Conquest and the Judges, are recalled in verses 6-7 and 23-24. Nathan speaks in the name of Yahweh Sabaoth (v. 8) and David, in his prayer, twice uses (v. 26-27) this same name which was especially attached to the ark.[11] He praises the name of "Yahweh Sabaoth, God in Israel" (v. 26). This Israel which comes back in v. 7, 8, 10, 11, 23, 24 is not the tribes of the North which constitute one of the elements of the kingdom of David; he is king of Israel *and* of Judah (II Sam. 5:5 cf. I Kgs. 1:35). This people of Israel is the "people of God," that of Sinai and of the Federation of the Tribes.[12]

In receiving the ark Jerusalem had become the heir of all this past, and she must preserve it intact. The building of a temple in a manner of a royal sanctuary of the Canaanites could appear as a rupture of tradition which would put this heritage in danger. The sanctuary of the ark must remain what it had been for the Federation of the Tribes — the spiritual center of "all Israel." Paradoxically, the refusal of the temple signified, and meant to preserve, the religious importance of Jerusalem.

Contrary to this expectation, it is the building of the temple by Solomon which definitely established the character of Jerusalem as a holy city. This construction is presented in I Kgs. 5:17f. as an initiative of Solomon fulfilling the

vow of his father; more clearly in I Chr. 28: 10-19 as the
execution of a plan carefully prepared by David. One
would expect a divine intervention conforming with the
rules of establishment of the sanctuaries of the Ancient
Orient — (the best known example is the building of the
temple of Ningirsu by Gudea) — and in the Bible itself
Moses received from Yahweh the order to build the
tabernacle according to the model which He gave him
(Ex. 25-27). It is possible[18] that in the primitive tradition
such an intervention from God was related to the dream
of Solomon at Gibeon (I Kgs. 3:4-15). In any case Yahweh
accepts the new sanctuary. When the ark is introduced
in the Debir, the glory of Yahweh who manifests himself
in the cloud fills the sanctuary (I Kgs. 8:10-11), as it had
filled the tabernacle of the desert where the ark was deposited (Ex. 40:34-35). The God of Sinai took possession
of the temple of Solomon and the continuity of the tradition
was assured. No prophetic opposition had this time hindered
the building, not even on the part of Nathan who disappears
from the history after having procured the accession of
Solomon to the throne (I Kgs. 1).

Another prophet was soon to bear witness to the value
of the temple for the religious significance of Jerusalem.
Already before the death of Solomon, a prophet of Shiloh,
i.e. Ahijah, predicted to Jeroboam that Yahweh was to
detach ten tribes from the kingdom of Solomon and give
them to him. The lineage of David will be humiliated
and will preserve only one tribe, Benjamin, outside the
paternal tribe of Judah (I Kgs. 11:29-39). The political
schism, which was accomplished just after the death of
Solomon (I Kgs. 12:1-20) has thus its justification (cf. v. 15).
But Jeroboam builds afterwards a sanctuary at Bethel and
installs there a "golden calf" to prevent his subjects from

continuing to frequent the temple of Jerusalem (I Kgs. 12:26-33). It is not a change of religion; the God whom Jeroboam asks his subjects to adore is the one who made Israel come up out of Egypt (I Kgs. 12:28). The "golden calf," or rather the young bull, is not an idol in the mind of Jeroboam. It is, according to the most probable interpretation, a symbol and the pedestal of the invisible divinity — in other words, an equivalent of the ark. In adopting this image Jeroboam perhaps revived an old tradition of some Yahwish groups of the North who claimed Aaron as leader. In the setting of the same religion Jeroboam opposed only one temple to another temple — that of Jerusalem — and one symbol to another symbol — the ark of the covenant. But the same Ahijah who had offered the kingdom of Jerusalem to Jeroboam from Yahweh now turns against him. To the wife of Jeroboam who comes to consult him at Shiloh, he announces that Jeroboam and all his house are condemned for this religious reform (I Kgs. 14:1-18). These accounts have been rewritten by a Deuteronomic editor whose hand is easily recognized and especially when they speak of Jerusalem as the city which Yahweh has chosen among all the other tribes of Israel (I Kgs. 11:32), the city where Yahweh has chosen to put his name (I Kgs. 11:36). These passages would be of immediate interest for our purpose, but we cannot use them because they reproduce textually the formulas of Deuteronomy (Deut. 12:5, 11, 14, etc.). However, these accounts are certainly ancient in the main and they come from a prophetic history. One can easily understand that a prophet who lives in the kingdom of the North should approve the movement of independence of the Ten Tribes and the political separation, but why did he not approve the religious reform? An ingenious explanation has recently

been proposed.[14] Ahijah of Shiloh would be this same
Ahijah, son of Ahitub, a descendant of Eli who carried
the *ephod* in the time of Saul (I Sam. 14:3). He had applauded the political separation; he might have applauded
the rupture with the temple of Jerusalem from which the
family of Eli had been excluded to the advantage of the Sad-
ducees since the banishment of Abiathar by Solomon. (I Kgs.
2:26-27). He would have applauded if Jeroboam had revived the sanctuary of Shiloh which had been served by
his family. But the choice of Bethel disappointed his hopes
and he turned against the king. This hypothesis is contradicted by the fact that Ahijah, the son of Ahitub, is called
"priest" while our Ahijah is "prophet" and that, according
to I Sam. 22:20, all the descendants of Eli had been mas-
sacred by Saul's order except Abiathar who will become
the priest of David. The opposition of the prophet of Shiloh
must be explained in another way;[15] there was in the kingdom of the North a trend which distinguished between
the political significance of Jerusalem and its religious
significance. This trend had no interest in the destiny of
the Davidic dynasty and in Jerusalem as seat of this dynasty,
but remained attached to the temple which sheltered the
ark of the covenant, and to Jerusalem as the religious
center of all Israel. We cannot measure the extent of
this trend, but it persisted and it reappears occasionally.
It is not doubtful that the faithful of the kingdom of the
North have always continued to frequent the temple of
Jerusalem; one could not otherwise explain that after
the destruction of Jerusalem by Nebuchadnezzar, men of
Schechem, of Shiloh, and of Samaria had come to bring
their offerings on the ruins of the temple (Jer. 41:5).

So much for the kingdom of the North, but it is to be
noted that this pre-eminence of the religious role of Jerus-

alem over its political role had also been recognized in
the kingdom of Judah. In fact, it is a consequence of the
theocratic conception of the State. Yahweh is the real king,
the only king of Jerusalem. The Psalms which celebrate
his royalty are decidedly earlier than the Exile and the
doctrine is very old, anterior even to the institution of the
monarchy (cf. Ex. 15:18; Jg. 8:23; I Sam. 8:7; 12:12).
The earthly king, the descendant of David, is a beneficiary
of the promises made to his ancestor, but like him he is
only the vassal of Yahweh.

On the other hand, it was the same Yahweh who had
chosen Jerusalem for his dwelling and who had chosen
David to reign there and these two choices were related
in the thought of Israel (cf. Ps. 78:68-70; 132:11 and 13;
I Kgs. 11:32). One could conclude from this that the
political and religious fates of Jerusalem were indissolubly
united, and the conclusion was drawn that Jerusalem,
political city, was inviolable because it was the city where
Yahweh lived. The astonishing fact is that they had also
distinguished between the fate of the dynasty of David and
that of Jerusalem, the city of Yahweh. This distinction
made already by the prophet of Shiloh is found in the
great prophets of Judah.

A first point is to be noted.[16] According to Am. 9:11f.
the tottering house of David will be raised up; according
to Is. 9:6 the tribe of David and his royalty are assured;
according to Is. 11:1 a shoot will come forth from the
stump of Jesse; according to Mi. 5:1, the future king is to
be born from Ephrata; according to Jer. 23:5, a legitimate
branch will be born to David; finally Ezekiel announces
the new David, shepherd of the people of God (Ez. 34:23;
37:24). None of these prophecies which announce a Messiah
of the race of David mentions Jerusalem; only the later

text of Zech. 9:9 predicts the entry of the Messiah into Jerusalem. It is very likely that these prophets pictured the future king as reigning in Jerusalem, but it did not seem to them necessary to mention the role of Jerusalem as a royal city in the messianic context. It is an indication that they did not consider as essential the bonds which united the dynasty of David to Jerusalem.

In the eyes of the prophets the permanent glory of Jerusalem is that it is the City of Yahweh, and under this religious aspect it is given preferably the name of Zion. Such had been the name of the Jebusite acropolis of the city conquered by David, and Zion had become the City of David (II Sam. 5:7). The prophets, like the Psalms, have resumed this archaic name to designate the City of Yahweh. It is found 29 times in the first part of Isaiah; 17 times in the second part; 15 times in Jeremiah; 15 times in Lamentations; 9 times in Micah; 8 times in Zechariah; 7 times in Joel, twice in Amos and Zephaniah and once in Obadiah.

Jerusalem-Zion is the city of Yahweh. No pre-exilic prophet states explicitly that Yahweh has chosen Jerusalem and this term will appear only in Zechariah: Yahweh has formerly chosen Jerusalem (Zech. 3:2) and he will renew this choice (Zech. 1:17; 2:16). This doctrine is that of the Deuteronomic school. In Deuteronomy itself the city remains anonymous but is mentioned by its name in the Deuteronomic edition of the Books of the Kings and in certain Psalms which made the choice of Jerusalem parallel and related to the election of David (Ps. 78:68-70; 132:11-13). But the prophets have the equivalent and even better. According to Is. 14:32 Yahweh "founded'" Zion as one says that He founded the earth or the universe:[17] Zion is the creation of Yahweh.

Yahweh lives in Jerusalem. Amos says that "Yahweh roars from Zion and utters his voice from Jerusalem." (Am. 1:2). According to Isaiah "Yahweh Sabaoth dwells on Mt. Zion" (Is. 8:18); He is "Yahweh whose fire is in Zion and whose furnace is in Jerusalem." (Is. 31:9). It is in the temple that Yahweh lives. The mountain of Zion is "the mountain of the house of Yahweh" (Is. 2:2; Mi. 4:1). It is on the "mountain of Yahweh" that "the house of the God of Jacob" stands (Is. 2:3; Mi. 4:2). It is in the setting, real or imaginary, of the temple that Isaiah has his inaugural vision. He sees Yahweh sitting upon a throne, high and lifted up, and his train fills the temple (Is. 6:1). This throne is the ark which the tradition of Shiloh, adopted by Jerusalem, calls "the ark of Yahweh-Sabaoth who is enthroned on the cherubim" (I Sam. 4:4 and II Sam. 6:2), and it is to the presence of the ark that the temple and Jerusalem owe, above all, their holiness.

But this holiness survived the ark which disappeared at the latest in the destruction of the temple in 587, and perhaps before that.[18] The Book of Lamentations does not mention it. Ezekiel does not foresee the ark in the future temple and there was none in the post-exilic temple. Jeremiah 3:16-17 says that another ark will not be built and that it will not even be regretted, for the whole of Jerusalem shall be called "Throne-of-Yahweh." This recalls immediately the name which Ezekiel gives to the future Jerusalem: "Yahweh-is-there" (Ez. 48:35). There is, however, one difference. In Ezekiel the reconstructed temple shall be the center of the future Jerusalem and it is in the temple that he sees the return of the glory of Yahweh (Ez. 43:1-5). Besides, it is during the reconstruction of the temple that the prophet Zechariah announces that Yahweh is returning to live in the midst of His people (Zech. 2:14), that He is returning to Zion and wishes to live in the midst of Jerusalem (Zech. 8:3). But Jeremiah in calling the whole of Jerusalem the "Throne of Yahweh" makes no allusion to the temple. Besides, the "mountain of the temple" (Is. 2:2 and Mi. 3:12; 4:1) will become in later prophecies simply the "holy mountain" of Yahweh. (Is. 27:13; 66:20). This last text is significant; from all the nations the survivors of Israel shall be brought as an offering to Yahweh, to the holy mountain Jerusalem — just as the Israelites bring their cereal offerings to the temple of Yahweh. Just as the presence of Yahweh and the holiness of Jerusalem had become independent of the ark, so they are no longer connected with the buildings of the temple.

Nevertheless, they continued to be joined in the eyes of many of the faithful until the Exile, and they might have seemed joined forever. If Yahweh who resides in Jerusalem is "the King of glory, Yahweh, strong and mighty, Yahweh, mighty in battle" (Ps. 24:8), are not the city and the temple in which he lives inviolable? It has been said by some scholars that the idea of the inviolability of Jerusalem was a conclusion drawn from the miraculous deliverance of the city at the time of the attack of Sennacherib in 701.[19] It has also been said on the contrary that it was already a pre-Israelite belief attached to the temple of El-Elyon, "El the Most High" who was worshipped in Canaanite Jerusalem.[20] The truth is probably between these two extreme solutions. In the Canticles of Zion (Ps. 46, 48, 76) the peoples assaulting Jerusalem are stopped by Yahweh who breaks the bow, the lance and the shield. The same schema is found in Isaiah, especially Is. 17:12-14: "The nations roar like the roaring of many waters, but Yahweh will rebuke them and they will flee far away chased . . . like whirling dust before the storm." But also in Is. 29:1-8: the multitude of the foes of Ariel (symbolic name for Jerusalem) in an instant suddenly shall be visited by Yahweh Sabaoth and shall be like small dust, like passing chaff. It is possible indeed that these Psalms use material originating from Jerusalem and predating David,[21] but this use of Canaanite themes does not suffice to prove that they are very ancient. However, it is likely that these three Psalms are pre-exilic (the most doubtful is Psalm 48), and in this case they could have influenced Isaiah. In any case, Isaiah and the Psalms represent a tradition which pre-dates the prophet and which consequently pre-dates the attack of Sennacherib.

In several circumstances Isaiah had to confront this tradition with the events of history, and his position is then much more qualified. In 734, Rezin of Damascus and Pekah of Israel marched against Jerusalem. Their intention was to dethrone Ahaz and carry Judah along into a coalition against the Assyrians. The king and the people are desperate. Isaiah announces to the king that Yahweh will destroy his enemies but he makes one condition for the saving of Jerusalem: "If you will not believe, surely you shall not stand." (Is. 7:9). Ahaz lacks faith; he refuses the sign which the prophet offers him on the pretext of not tempting God. Then the holy ire of Isaiah explodes: Yahweh himself will give you a sign . . . A son will be born, his name will be Emmanuel. Before the child knows how to refuse the evil and choose the good the land of the two kings will be deserted. But Yahweh will call the king of Assyria against Judah; all the land will be briars and thorns (Is. 7:10-24). Ahaz chose the ways of human politics: Tiglat Pileser of Assyria was already marching against Damascus and Israel. Ahaz sent him all he could collect in the treasure of the temple and the palace and he declared himself his vassal. He had avoided war; he had perhaps saved Jerusalem; but the Assyrian threat henceforth hung over Judah. To this occasion Isaiah did not invoke the doctrine of the inviolability of Jerusalem; he demanded faith, and in the absence of it, he foresaw ruin. But beyond ruin he sees the light of hope: "Everyone that is left in the land will eat curds and honey" (Is. 7:22). The name of the child announced will be Emmanuel, "God is with us." The son of Isaiah who accompanies him on his mission to Ahaz also bears a symbolic name: Shear Yashub, "A remnant shall return" (to Yahweh) (Is. 7:3).

Another circumstance was the attack of Sennacherib in 701 under Hezekiah. The account of the events, the intervention of Isaiah and the oracles which he pronounces are found in Isaiah 36-37. These chapters come from the book of Kings (II Kgs. 18:13 to 19:37) from where they have been added to the book of Isaiah (likewise the chapters 38-39). But is is very evident that in the book of Kings itself these chapters come from a tradition which was derived from Isaiah. Their interpretation is very debated — first the sequence of events and the historicity of the deliverance of Jerusalem; then the authenticity of the oracles attributed to Isaiah. I cannot enter here into this discussion and I must content myself by giving the solution which seems to be the most probable. It is historically certain that Sennacherib made a campaign in Palestine in 701, that he conquered the fortified cities of Judah and that Jerusalem was spared because Hezekiah paid a heavy tribute. The account of II Kgs. 18:13-16 (Isaiah 36:1) is fully confirmed by the Assyrian annals, but the book of Kings and Isaiah give later two parallel accounts (II Kgs. 18:17-19:9a and II Kgs. 19:9b-36); 19:37-38 is a common conclusion to the two accounts. They tell of an embassy which Sennacherib sends from Lakish to exact the surrender of Jerusalem. The

city is saved because Sennacherib receives news which forces
him to go back to Nineveh, according to one of the accounts, or because the Angel of Yahweh destroys the
Assyrian army, according to the other account. It is not
likely that this double tradition of an unexpected deliverance — and considered as miraculous — should have come
only from the fact that Hezekiah had saved Jerusalem
from destruction by paying tribute to Sennacherib.[22] The
account of Kings contains too many details which have
not been invented and which correspond, at least partially,
to the indications of extra-biblical sources. It is possible that
this deliverance of Jerusalem could have taken place during
a second campaign of Sennacherib toward 688 B.C.[23] The
intervention of Isaiah in such a circumstance is very likely;
it agrees with what we know already of the career of the
prophet. The oracles which are attributed to him have a
style which is distinctly Isaiah's and they express ideas
which are found in the prophecies — surely authentic —
especially those which are directed against Assur. In the
account in prose itself, the faith of Hezekiah (Is. 37:3-4,
15-20) is that faith which Isaiah had asked in vain of Ahaz
as a condition of salvation (Is. 7:9b), but it is equally clear
that these oracles have been altered and that these accounts
have a theological intention precisely on the point which
interests us. One of the accounts makes the messenger of
Sennacherib say that the inhabitants of Jerusalem are mistaken in putting their confidence in Yahweh and in listening to Hezekiah who said to them "Yahweh will surely
deliver us; this city will not be given into the hands of
the king of Assyria" (Is. 36:7-15). In the parallel account
Sennacherib writes to Hezekiah, "Do not let your God on
whom you rely deceive you by promising that Jerusalem
will not be given into the hands of the king of Assyria"

(Is. 37:10). The belief in the inviolability is clearly expressed. It is turned to derision by the Assyrians but it is affirmed by Yahweh in the words attributed to Isaiah (37:6-7 and 29), and especially 37:34b-35: "He shall not come into this city," says Yahweh, "for I will defend this city to save it for my own sake and for the sake of my servant David."

In no other place has Isaiah expressed himself so firmly. It does not seem that he had ever excluded the possibility of the ruin of Jerusalem.[24] Sometimes he seems even to have foreseen it (Is. 6:9-13) and it is the general message with which he is charged (3:8-9, 16-26). Indeed, he is divided between fear and hope but the realization of this hope seems to be reserved for the messianic times: in Is. 14:32 (with the mention of the "poor of Yahweh"), in 16:5 (clearly messianic), in 28:16 (the angular stone which is laid at Zion is that of the religious community of the future.) Another indication that this passage is not from Isaiah is the mention of David as the motive of divine protection assured to Jerusalem, which is an idea foreign to this prophet. We can thus recognize in this affirmation that Jerusalem is inviolable, the hand of the disciples of Isaiah.

When Isaiah himself refers to the ancient and vague tradition of the inviolability of Jerusalem, which we have pointed out in his prophecies and in certain Psalms, he modifies it on two important points.[25] First, as we have already said, he puts faith in Yahweh as the condition of the protection and the salvation (Is. 7:9b). He condemns those who go down to Egypt for help but who do not look to the Holy One of Israel (31:1). "In returning and rest you shall be saved; in quietness and in trust shall be your strength" (30:15). He asks trust in the works and the acts of Yahweh who alone can save the city, but the inhabitants do not recognize the action of Yahweh; "they do not regard the deeds of Yahweh or see the work of his hand" (Is. 5:12, cf. 19).[26] This work of God may seem strange and foreign (Is. 28:21) for — and this is the second point where he changes the tradition — Isaiah puts the assault of the enemies against Jerusalem in the very field of the action of God. Asshur is the rod of God's anger against his people (Is. 10:5) but when Yahweh has finished all His work on Mt. Zion and on Jerusalem he will punish the king of Assyria (10:12). In the prophecy against Ariel it is Yahweh himself who attacks Jerusalem: "I will encamp against you . . . and will besiege . . . and will raise siegework against you." (29:3). But suddenly Yahweh turns against the enemies which were fighting Mount Zion (29:5-8).

Isaiah, citizen of Jerusalem and devoted to his native city, saw with astonishment how the double plan of punishment and salvation of God concerning the city was developing. His contemporary, Micah, native of Hebron, was much more radical in his judgment. The princes, the priests, the prophets "built Zion with blood and Jerusalem with wrong" and they say, "Is not Yahweh in the midst of us? No evil shall come upon us." But Micah makes this announcement: "Because of you, Zion shall be plowed as the field, Jerusalem shall become a heap of stones and the Mountain of the Temple a wooded height." (Mi. 3:9-12). This oracle was certainly given before the deliverance of Jerusalem at the time of the attack of Sennacherib.

This deliverance must have appeared as a denial of the words of the prophet and it reinforced the belief in the inviolability of Jerusalem. We have pointed out the expression of this belief in Isaiah 37:35 where the hand of disciples of Isaiah is recognized. A century after Isaiah, Jeremiah attests that this belief was firmly established in Jerusalem. The inhabitants repeated, "The temple of Yahweh, the

temple of Yahweh, the temple of Yahweh" (Jer. 7:4).
But the prophet reminds them that they cannot steal,
commit murder and adultery, burn incense for Baal, follow
other gods and then present themselves at the temple before
Yahweh and say: "We are delivered," (Jer. 7:9-10). He
gives them this message from Yahweh: "If you will not
listen to me . . . I will make this temple like Shiloh, and
I will make this city a curse for all the nations of the earth,"
(Jer. 26:5-6; cf. 7:12-14). For these words the priests and
the prophets call for the death of Jeremiah, but he is saved
by the intervention of the elders who recalled the oracle
of Micah whom we have cited (Jer. 26:11, 16-19).

The ruin of Jerusalem and the destruction of the temple
in 587 were a terrible ordeal for the faith of Israel. We
have the echo of it in the book of Lamentations. They put
down as an intolerable contrast the glorious figure of Jerusalem which the Psalms presented, "the perfection of beauty,
the joy of all the earth" (Lam. 2:15, cf. Ps. 48:3; 50:2) and
the image of the ruined city. The whole world is stupefied.

> The kings of the earth did not believe,
>   or any of the inhabitants of the world,
> That foe or enemy could enter
>   the gate of Jerusalem.—LAM. 4:12.

The key to the theology of Lamentations is in fact found
in the tension between specific religious conceptions and
historical realities, between the confident belief of the Zion
traditions in the inviolability of the temple and city, and
the actual brute facts.[27] For faith recognizes that this ruin
is not due to the lack of power in Yahweh; it is the work
of Yahweh, a judgment of God who punishes the infidel-
ities of the daughter of Zion (Lam. 1:18-20).[28] If she con-
fesses her fault, the hand who struck her can raise her up:

> For Yahweh will not cast off for ever,
> > but, though he causes grief, he will have compassion
> According to the abundance of his steadfast love.
> > > > > —Lam. 3:31-32.

> Restore us to thyself, O Yahweh, that we may be
> > restored!
> Renew our days as of old!—Lam. 5:21.

It is a prayer, but it already expresses hope. This hope expresses itself more clearly with the prophets of the Exile. Ezekiel sees the glory of Yahweh return in the renovated temple (Ez. 43:1-5). Especially Deutero-Isaiah, forseeing the approaching restoration, strikes up a hymn of jubilation: the ordeal of Jerusalem is over, her iniquity is forgiven (Is. 40:1-2) and this joy resounds in the whole of the "Book of Consolation."

> Behold, I have engraved you on the palms of my hands;
> > your walls are continually before me.—Is. 49:16.

> Awake, awake,
> > put on your strength, O Zion;
> Put on your beautiful garments,
> > O Jerusalem, the Holy City.—Is. 52:1.

> Hark, your watchmen lift up their voice,
> > together they sing for joy;
> For eye to eye they see
> > The return of Yahweh to Zion.—Is. 52:8.

On the return from Exile, the reconstruction of the temple, accomplished in a modest manner and through many difficulties, was only an imperfect realization of this hope, but it continues to express itself with the two contemporary prophets of the reconstruction. Haggai announces that "the latter splendor of this house shall be greater than the former" (Hag. 2:9). Zechariah says: "Sing and rejoice,

O daughter of Zion; for lo, I come and I will dwell in
the midst of you . . . Yahweh will again choose Jerusalem"
(Zech. 2:10, 12).

Finally a disciple of Deutero-Isaiah displays all the splen-
dors of the future Jerusalem in Is. 60-62. All the peoples
of the earth bring their presents. There is no longer need
of the sun nor of the moon, for God will be her light. This
dazzling description has no longer any connection with
earthly realities:[29] Jerusalem transcends history; in her is
summed up the whole history of salvation.

A closer connection is forced upon us with a text of
the first part of Isaiah:

It shall come to pass in the latter days
    that the mountain of the house of the Lord
Shall be established as the highest of the mountains,
    and shall be raised above the hills;
And all the nations shall flow to it,
    and many peoples shall come, and say:
"Come, let us go up to the mountain of the Lord,
    to the house of the God of Jacob;
That he may teach us his ways
    and that we may walk in his paths."
For out of Zion shall go forth the law,
    and the word of the Lord from Jerusalem.

One knows that this text of Isaiah (2:2-4) is found almost
identically in Micah 4:1-3. On account of its universal and
eschatological doctrine, it is sometimes attributed to an
anonymous prophet, in Exile or after the Exile, depending
on Deutero-Isaiah.[30] However, good reasons have been proposed in favor of the Isaiah authenticity of this passage
which is inspired as other texts of Isaiah from the tradition
of the Canticles of Zion.[31] This oracle expresses two ideas
which are important for our object and which are ancient

in Israel. Jerusalem is the new Sinai and she is the mountain
of God.

Because Yahweh resides in Jerusalem and because the
temple shelters the ark of the covenant which contains the
Ten Commandments, Jerusalem is the new Sinai: "For out
of Zion shall go forth the Law." Already Amos had said,
"Yahweh roars from Zion and utters his voice from Jerusalem." The connection is explicitly expressed in a Psalm:

> O divine mountain, mountain of Bashan,
> O many-peaked mountain, mountain of Bashan!
> Why look you with envy, O many-peaked mountain,
> at the mount which God desired for his abode,
> yea, where Yahweh will dwell forever?
> . . .
> Yaheh came from Sinai into the holy place.
> Ps. 68:15-17.

But here as in Isaiah 2:2-4 the memory of Sinai is joined
to another tradition, that of the mountain of God.[32] In the
Canaanite mythology there were mountains of the gods —
Bashan (perhaps Mt. Hermon, which overlooks the country
of Bashan) was one; Zaphon, the "North", was another
(cf. Is. 14:12-13.). The ugaritic texts mention Zaphon, which
was the abode of Baal and the place of assembly of the
gods and which was identified with Mount Casios to the
north of Ras-Shamra. But the real Zaphon is the Mount
Zion:

> His holy mountain, beautiful in elevation
>   is the joy of all the earth,
> Mount Zion, the remotest part of Zaphon,
>   the city of the great King.—Ps. 48:2-3.

Jerusalem is transfigured. The modest hill of Zion which
is overshadowed by the surrounding heights becomes the
highest of the mountains. Ezekiel says that Yahweh will

plant the new branch of Israel "upon a high and lofty mountain; on the mountain height of Israel." (Ez. 17:22-23). God says that it is "my high mountain, the mountain height of Israel." (Ez. 20:40). He sees the new Jerusalem "upon a very high mountain" (Ez. 40:2).

The last step was to make Jerusalem the center of the earth. It is already prepared by Ezekiel: "Thus says Yahweh God: This is Jerusalem; I have set her in the center of the nations, with countries around about her." (Ez. 5:5). The idea is developed in the apocryptal books of the Old Testament in late Judaism and with the Fathers of the Church.[33] It is expressed visually in certain maps of the Middle Ages, which place Jerusalem in the center of the inhabited world.

* * * *

The prophesies are accomplished. Three thousand years after the entry of the ark of God into Jerusalem, Jerusalem remains the Holy City, a spiritual center for the three monotheistic religions of the earth.

Living in Jerusalem for thirty years and considering it my second home, I love Jerusalem for the reasons given by the Prophets. I may be allowed to say here that, being a Christian, I have another reason: Jerusalem, city of David and city of the Prophets, is also the city where my Lord Jesus Christ offered himself for the redeeming of all mankind, Jews and Christians alike. Being presently far away from Jerusalem, I say what the Israelites in Exile said by the waters of Babylon:

> If I forget you, O Jerusalem let my right hand wither
> Let my tongue cleave to the roof of my mouth
> If I do not remember you
> If I do not set Jerusalem above my highest joy.
> — Ps. 137:5-6.

NOTES

[1] Especially L. Rost, *Die Ueberlieferung von der Thronnachfolge Davids (BWANT III 6)*, 1926, 47-75 = *Das Kleine Credo und andere Studien zum Alten Testament*, 1965, 159-183.

[2] This is the common opinion. However the verse is hold as genuine by S. Mowinckel, 'Natanforjettelsen, II Sam. 7', in *Sv. Ex. Arsb.*, 12 1947, 220-229, and A. Caquot, 'La prophétie de Nathan et ses échos lyriques', in *Congress Volume Bonn 1962 (Suppl. to VT, IX)*, 1963, 213-224.

[3] See M. Noth, *Ueberlieferungsgeschichtliche Studien²*, 1957, 64 ff., and 'David und Israel in II Samuel 7', in *Mélanges Bibliques rédigés en l'honneur de André Robert*, s.d. (1957), 122-130 = *Gesammelte Studien zum Alten Testament²*, 1960, 334-345.

[4] A.S. Kapelrud, 'Temple Building, a Task for God and Kings', in *Orientalia*, 32 1963, 56-62.

[5] And not: "You, David" as opposed to Solomon who will build the Temple (add. of v. 13a).

[6] The main opinions concerning the rejection of the Temple are listed and discussed by J. Schreiner, *Sion - Jerusalem Jahves Königssitz. Theologie der Heiligen Stadt im Alten Testament*, 1963, 80-88.

[7] G. W. Ahlström, 'Der Prophet Nathan und der Tempelbau', in *VT*, 11 1961, 113-127.

[8] See mainly M. Simon, 'La prophétie de Nathan et le Temple', in *RHPR*, 32 1952, 41-58, and 'Saint Stephen and the Jerusalem Temple', in *Journal of Ecclesiastical History*, 2 1951, 127-142.

[9] Indeed the word *berit* appears in Ps. 89 and 132, which paraphrase Nathan's prophecy.

[10] See A. Gunneweg, 'Sinaibund und Davidsbund', in *VT*, 10 1960, 335-341; A. Caquot, 'La prophétie de Nathan . . .', l.c., 218-220; R. de Vaux, 'Le roi d'Israël, vassal de Yahvé', in *Mélanges Eugene Tisserand* 1, 1964, 125-127.

[11] Since Shilo, according to O. Eissfeldt, 'Jahwe Zebaoth', in *Miscellanea Academica Berolinensia*, 2 1950, 128-150.

[12] M. Noth, 'David und Israel in II Samuel 7' l.c. (n.3), 124-125.

[13] A.S. Kapelrud, *Orientalia*, 32 1963, 56-62.

[14] A. Caquot, 'Ahiyya de Silo et Jéroboam Ier', in *Semitica*, 11 1961, 17-27.

[15] M. Noth, 'Jerusalem und die israelitische Tradition', in *Oudtestamentische Studiën*, 8 1950, 28-46 = *Gesammelte Studien* . . ., 172-187.

[16] M. Noth, *ibid.*, 181-182.

[17] Ps. 78:68-69 compares the

election of Jerusalem and the building of the Sanctuary with the founding of the earth.

[18] M. Haran, 'The Disappearance of the Ark', in *IEJ*, 13 1963, 46-58: under the reign of Manasse who would have replaced the ark by an idol of Ashera, cf. 2 Kgs. 21:7.

[19] So, among others, J. Bright, *A History of Israel*, 1959, 283.

[20] J. H. Hayes, 'The Tradition of Zion's Inviolability', in *JBL*, 82 1963, 419-426.

[21] Besides Hayes, l.c., see G. von Rad, *Theologie des Alten Testaments*, II, 1960, 168. All the paragraph "Der Zion", pp. 166-179, should be read for our purpose.

[22] So, M. Noth, *The History of Israel²*, engl. tr. 1960, 268, n. 3.

[23] So, J. Bright, *A History of Israel*, 270-271; W. F. Albright, *The Biblical Period from Abraham to Ezra*, reed. 1963, 78-79.

[24] See Th. C. Vriezen, 'Essentials in the Theology of Isaiah', in *Israel's Prophetic Heritage. Essays in honor of James Muilenburg*, 1962, 128-146, esp. 138ff.

[25] J. H. Hayes, 'The Tradition of Zion's Inviolability', l.c., 425-426.

[26] On this aspect of Isaiah's personality, see G. von Rad, *Theologie des Alten Testaments*, II, 172ff.

[27] B. Albrektson, *Studies in the Text and Theology of the Book of Lamentations*, 1963, 219-230.

[28] See N.K. Gottwald, *Studies in the Book of Lamentations*, 1954; N. W. Porteous, 'Jerusalem-Zion. The Growth of a Symbol', in *Verbannung und Heimkehr. Festschrift W. Rudolph*, 1961, 235-252.

[29] A. Causse, 'La vision de la nouvelle Jérusalem . . . ', in *Mélanges R. Dussaud*, II, 1939, 739-750.

[30] See recently J. Lindblom, *Prophecy in Ancient Israel*, 1963, 383f., 390, 402; O. Eissfeldt, *Einleitung im Alten Testament³*, 1964, 427-428.

[31] H. Wildberger, 'Die Völkerfahrt zum Zion', in *VT*, 7 1957, 62-81; G. von Rad, 'Die Stadt auf dem Berge', in *Evangelische Theologie*, 8 1948/49, 439-447, esp. 440f.

[32] See H. Schmid, 'Jahwe und die Kulttraditionen von Jerusalem', in *ZAW*, 67 1955, esp. 190 ff.; H. J. Kraus, *Psalmen*, exc. 5 on Ps. 46.

[33] K. L. Schmidt, 'Jerusalem als Urbild und Abbild', in *Eranos-Jahrbuch*, 18 1950, 207-248.

NIHIL OBSTAT: Rt. Rev. Matthew P. Stapleton
                Diocesan Censor

IMPRIMATUR: +Richard Cardinal Cushing
                Archbishop of Boston

DATE: May 5, 1965

THE CHANGING IMAGE
OF THE PROPHET
IN JEWISH THOUGHT

Dr. Bernard J. Bamberger
Rabbi, Temple Shaaray Tefila
New York, New York

THE GOLDENSON LECTURE OF 1966

I SHALL TRY TO PRESENT SOME VIEWS REGARDING
prophets and prophecy held by Jewish thinkers through the
centuries, to project—if I may use the current lingo—a series
of varied images of the prophet. Such a survey, though it
cannot be inclusive or thorough, may be instructive, or at
least suggestive.

The earliest post-prophetic image of the prophet is that
of something precious that has been lost. One of the few
Psalm-passages bearing on our subject laments the disappearance of prophecy. In a time of national calamity, the singer
yearns for an authoritative voice, to tell how long the disaster
will last and when the day of redemption will come.[1] Perhaps, too, it was an awareness that the prophetic movement
was in decline which led to the promise at the end of the
Book of Malachi—the promise, namely, that at some future
date Elijah will reappear on earth. In true prophetic fashion
he will bring about a spiritual revival, uniting parents and
children in God's service, in advance of the final judgment.[2]

Later tradition modified this understanding of the mission
of the returning Elijah. He was indeed to herald the advent
of the Messiah, but in addition he would settle all moot
questions of Jewish law.[3] This is no mere fancy of scholars
playing idly with texts. When the Temple was rededicated
by Judah Maccabee, the priests did not know what disposal
to make of the desecrated stones of the old altar. So they put
them aside until a prophet should come to give them sure
guidance. Similarly, the people and priests designated Simon
to be leader and high priest "until a faithful prophet should
arise."[4]

And these incidents remind us of an earlier case involving certain men who claimed to be priests, but had no documentary proof of their status; they were therefore told not to eat of the most holy sacrifices until a priest should arise with Urim and Thummim.[5] From the days of Ezra onward, men felt the need, not merely for visions, predictions, admonitions or even words of comfort, but especially for clear answers to specific problems of law and observance. And when the usual methods of study did not supply such answers, they yearned for guidance from on high.

One reason why the living prophetic word was not so urgently needed was, no doubt, that the written word of the classical prophets was becoming more generally available. During the Second Commonwealth, the prophetic writings were assembled, edited, and accepted as sacred scripture. Moreover, the custom of reading publicly from the prophetic books must be quite old.[6] It is probable that, long before regular haphtaroth were appointed, there was a general preference for passages containing words of hope and redemption.

But though prophecy may have been officially ended, the impulse to prophetic activity did not entirely vanish. I do not refer only to the apocalyptic writings, composed in the last pre-Christian centuries and thereafter. For while these works imitate the literary style of Biblical prophecy (often with indifferent success), it can be argued that in essence apocalyptic and prophecy had little in common. However this may be, there were other manifestations of the prophetic impulse in the same period. The Talmud tells us that men sometimes heard the *bath qol,* the echo of a divine voice, intervening in human affairs. Of certain rabbis it was declared that they were qualified to receive the holy spirit, but their contemporaries did not merit the privilege of having prophets among them. We read further of saints who spoke up boldly to God on behalf of their people, a kind of intercession characteristic of the Biblical prophets.[7]

These rabbinic memories are confirmed in a general way by Josephus. He mentions several men who, during the Second Commonwealth, were hailed as prophets or claimed to be such. Most prominent among them was King John Hyrcan; he was a prophet, Josephus reports, and could foretell the future.[8] Several others are characterized as charlatans and false prophets for stirring up insurrections against Rome.[9] We are told also about a peasant named Joshua son of Hanania, who went about Jerusalem uttering cries of doom for seven years prior to the fall of the city. Josephus seems to believe that the unfortunate man was driven by a divine compulsion, though the Roman governor adjudged him deranged and harmless.[10] This episode reminds one of the rabbinic saying, "Since the fall of the Temple, prophecy has been taken away from the prophets and given to children and madmen."[11] Josephus also claimed that he himself possessed the power to interpret dreams and to predict the future;[12] but it is hard to tell how much of this was said to impress others and how much of it he really believed. Incidentally, he never speaks of himself as a *prophetes*.

In the course of his writings, Josephus often mentions Moses and other Biblical prophets. Since the time of Artaxerxes, he notes, there has not been an exact succession of prophets; hence the histories·of more recent centuries do not have the same authority as the old inspired writings.[13] He is dealing here with the reliabiliy and canonicity of the Biblical books up to and including Esther, rather than with the phenomenon of prophecy as such. Yet as regards date, he is in agreement with rabbinic sources. According to the Talmud, the last prophets were Haggai, Zechariah, and Malachi;[14] and frequently Malachi is identified with Ezra.[15] I do not know of any parallel to the statement in Seder Olam that prophecy continued till the time of Alexander the Great.[16]

But despite minor disagreements over chronology, the rabbinic sources all agree that the age of prophecy is long since past. The Biblical words "It is not in heaven" (Deut. 30.12) were understood to mean: The entire Torah has already been given to men; no new revelation is needed, nor should it be expected. In this sense the verse was quoted by Rabbi Joshua when a *bath qol* intervened in a dispute over a point of law; and we are told that God admitted with a chuckle that the protest was a proper one.[17] The scholar had replaced the prophet; as R. Abdimi of Haifa put it, "prophecy has been taken from the prophets and given to the sages." A Babylonian comment on this remark declares that the scholar is more important (*'adif*) than the prophet.[18]

These statements, and many others that could be adduced, are so extreme and vehement that modern students have seen in them a marked polemical intent. The rising Christian community claimed that it had been newly inspired by God, and it promulgated a revelation that was said to supplement, or even to supplant, "the old covenant." In reaction, the rabbis insisted that the process of revelation was complete at Sinai. The existing documents, as interpreted by the guardians of tradition, are fully adequate to guide the life of the individual and of the community. There is no room for new prophecies.[19]

This interpretation of the facts seems to be entirely correct if we understand it as follows: Anti-Christian polemic accounts for the emphatic, almost violent expression of a viewpoint which in essence was not new. The tendency to confine the role of prophecy to the past was implicit in the closing of the prophetic canon; the fact that so popular a book as Daniel was not included in the collection of prophetic writings indicates the finality with which that collection had been fixed.

All this follows logically from the acceptance of the Pentateuch, together with its official interpretations, as the rule of Jewish life. On the closing words of Leviticus, the Sifra remarks: "No prophet may add anything new." But this probably post-Christian statement is little more than a reaffirmation of Deuteronomy 13, which sets up a norm of orthodoxy for the prophet to follow. And that passage was composed when prophecy was still a living reality.[20]

In consonance with this approach, one of the rabbis declared: "If Israel had not sinned, they would have received only the Pentateuch and the Book of Joshua"—the latter being necessary to round out the story with the settlement in the land of promise.[21] A sinless Israel would have been one of those happy nations that have no history. The prophets were sent to warn the people against disobedience and to threaten them with disastrous consequences if they did not amend their ways, and then to comfort them after the disaster had struck. But they did no more than apply eloquently to the conditions of their own time the truths and injunctions already revealed through Moses.

The development we have been describing used to be characterized by some Christian scholars as the suppression of the free prophetic spirit by rigid legalism. According to this view, prophecy was forced to "go underground" as apocalyptic, to emerge again in full efflorescence as the Christian gospel.[22] It is therefore instructive to note that Paul—who was largely responsible for the distorted notion of Jewish legalism—did not call himself a prophet. He preferred the title of apostle, which he evidently deemed even more honorable.

Paul distinguished sharply between the prophet, who delivers an intelligible and edifying message, and the person who "speaks with tongues." The latter is indeed endowed with "the spirit," but Paul finds little benefit in his ecstatic babblings.[23]. This distinction is not always so clear in other New Testament sources. The later books of the Christian scripture, moreover, contain warnings against false prophets.[24] Order and discipline were replacing unlimited freedom of the spirit long before the Roman Church condemned Montanism for its explicit claim to prophetic inspiration.

As for the development of Judaism, it would be truer to say that the adoption of the Torah as the subject of study and the guide of life meant not the suppression of prophecy, but rather the achievement of much of the prophetic purpose. The time for mere exhortation was past; the great ideals of justice and compassion were to be translated into specific duties and into communal institutions.

The aggadists offer many penetrating remarks about various prophetic personalities and their writings, which need not be reviewed here. But particularly relevant to our theme of the prophetic "image" are the stories regarding Elijah's reappearance on earth and his association with some of the sages.[25]

Of course, Elijah had long been awaited as the precursor of the Messiah. This remained his public function, to be performed at some future date. But during the second Christian century, he came to earth "incognito" and began to manifest himself privately and discreetly to a chosen few. The rabbis seem to have discerned a change in Elijah from what he had been in the days of Ahab. They felt that the Biblical Elijah, zealous for the Lord of Hosts, was lacking in concern for God's children, the Israelites. When at Horeb he reported that Israel had overthrown God's altars and

slain His prophets, God reproached him for being an in-
former and asked, "Did they overthrow *your* altars and slay
your prophets?"[26] By the time he returned to earth, Elijah
seems to have mellowed. He was now the friend of the
humble and pious, the recognizer of obscure and unpreten-
tious virtue, the doer of kindly miracles. Occasionally there
might be a flash of the old temper; it is hard to sublimate
one's aggressive impulses completely. But for the most part
Elijah directed his indignation against scholars who did not
measure up to his exacting ethical standards. He expected
men of learning to rise above minimal requirements. One
who was insufficiently sensitive to the lot of the unfortunate,
one who surrendered a Jewish malefactor to the Gentile
authorities, even with some reason—such were now the tar-
gets of Elijah's rebuke.[27] Though the picture of Elijah in
these fascinating legends is not wholly consistent, it still
gives us a good notion of what the rabbis thought a prophet
ought to be.

As we turn now to the philosophers of the Middle Ages,
we find one aspect of their treatment of prophecy to be
familiar: they stress the uniqueness and superiority of Moses,
as regards both his prophetic experience and the content of
his message. This point is, of course clearly expressed in
the Pentateuch, and it was elaborated by Philo and the Talmudic rabbis.[28] But the medieval thinkers, especially Maimonides, put even greater emphasis upon it. This was a
reaction both to the Christian claim that the Torah had
been abrogated and to the Moslem claim that Mohammed
was the greatest of the prophets. Yet the presentation even
of this old and familiar theme was modified by the need
of dealing with another problem—the problem of harmonizing Biblical religion with the scientific world view derived

from Greece. If the world is governed by changeless impersonal laws which can be formulated mathematically, how can we find room in it for a revelation from a righteous and loving God?

In the Middle Ages there were few who solved that problem by rejecting revelation. Maimonides dismisses such unbelievers in one short sentence, as not worth arguing with.[29] More numerous were those who rejected philosophy as manifestly untrue because it contradicted Scripture; keeping their eyes fixed on the sacred books, they refused even to examine the teaching of the rationalists. But those who were willing to face the new intellectual challenge had to seek some method of accommodating reason and revelation to each other.

Even so conservative a personality as Judah HaLevi, who regarded the Greek wisdom as a plant that bears flowers but no fruit, was too enlightened to disregard the new cultural influences. He based his theological position, not on speculative theory, but on what he regarded as empirical evidence—the to him incontrovertible fact of the public revelation at Sinai.[30] Presumably, then, he did not need to account for prophecy or explain it: it is a datum of experience. And yet HaLevi did offer a kind of rationale of prophecy.

The prophet, for HaLevi, is not merely an ordinary person whom God in His grace has selected to be His messenger. Just as animal life is superior to vegetable existence, just as man is superior to the animals, so the prophet is superior to other men not in degree, but in essential nature. He is a kind of superman, a new type of created being. The prophet is the instrument through whom the divine presence and the divine will are mediated to Israel, and thereby to mankind. But this process of transmission can be fully effective only if certain preconditions are satisfied: the Jewish people must be resident in the Holy Land, the Temple must be built and the sacrificial cult maintained, the Hebrew language must be in use. HaLevi, then, indicates something of the sequence of causes and effects leading to prophecy. Sin and consequent exile have disrupted this process, and caused our present plight; prophecy no longer functions, and Israel, the heart of the world, is sick.[31]

Maimonides, of course, represents a much more advanced type of rationalism. His position is based on the teaching of Arab Aristoteleans, who had dealt with the question of prophecy as follows:

They asserted the existence of a being known as the Active Intellect, an emanation coming ultimately from God, through whom the influence of the First Cause is transmitted to the sublunar world, especially to man. Man may prepare himself by intellectual and moral discipline to receive in ever fuller measure the influence radiated by the Active Intellect—to tune in more clearly, so to speak. If one possesses exceptional intellectual gifts and highly sensitive imagination, if he develops these powers to their fullest extent while cultivating the loftiest traits of character and devotion, he will attain the level of prophecy. That is to say, he will receive through the Active Intellect an extraordinary insight into divine truth, plus the ability to visualize and communicate these sublime abstractions in vivid symbolic forms.[32] The prophetic state, in short, was regarded as a human attainment, not a gift from on high; like all human attainments, it comes about through the combination of natural endowment, proper training, and diligent effort.

This naturalistic, psychological approach to the phenomenon of prophecy was adopted by Maimonides, with two important qualifications which we shall shortly state. On the basis of this approach he could argue that prophecy always occurs through a dream or vision; the miraculous experiences which the prophets report and the grotesque actions some of them performed are to be understood as subjective occurrences, not outward events.[33] Maimuni was able likewise to enumerate various gradations and levels of prophetic achievement, exemplified in the case of different men, and also in varying moments in the life of the same individual. The lowest of these levels are in fact sub-prophetic; they account for instances where a person plainly not of prophetic caliber received some kind of vision or divine communication.[34] Maimonides does not deny the possibility of divination and second sight. Such phenomena may result when the Active Intellect influences the imaginative faculty, but not the intelligence.[35] Such pseudo-prophecy is unreliable; the proof of the genuine prophet is that his favorable predictions are fulfilled to the letter.[36]

Not only did different prophets attain different levels of insight; they also experienced the revelation with differing degrees of intensity. One prophet received just enough inspiration for his own enlightenment; another was driven also to communicate his vision to others; in the case of a Jeremiah, the prophetic drive was so strong that he could not keep silent even when he wished to do so.[37]

Now to this elaborate theory of prophecy as accomplishment, Maimuni adds two big provisos, for which he offers little logical justification. First, one who is fully qualified to become a prophet may still be denied the prophetic experience by the will of God. The supernatural act is the withholding of the prophetic vision, not the granting of it.[38] Second, the entire account of prophecy that has been given does not apply to Moses. The Lawgiver was literally in a class by himself. When we call him a prophet, the term means something utterly different from what it means in any other case. The revelation given through Moses was absolute; the process by which he received it was unique. Discussion of this subject is virtually impossible.[39]

Orthodox critics of the *Guide* were quick to point out some of the awkward consequences of these theories.[40] In more recent years, scholars have examined from the historical viewpoint the elements of strain and contradiction that seem to exist.[41] Our present concern, however, is not to determine whether the alleged inconsistencies in the Maimonidean doctrine of prophecy are real or only apparent. It is sufficient now for us to note that Maimuni made his own task supremely difficult because he would neither attenuate his devotion to Jewish tradition, nor compromise his commitment to reason.

A present day scholar has suggested, on the basis of certain allusions in the writings of Maimonides, that the latter hoped to attain the level of prophecy, or perhaps even believed that he had already done so.[42] That he cherished such a hope is not impossible; for he believed that the messianic advent was not far off, and it was generally agreed that prophecy will be restored when the Messiah comes.[43] But however this may be, it is ironic that Abraham Abulafia, the exponent of so-called "prophetic Cabala," should have regarded his mystic procedure as the explicit working out of Maimuni's thought.[44]

For Abulafia, prophecy was a beatific experience, wholly personal, which could be induced by intense concentration on the letters of the Biblical text, and on their combinations and permutations. This technique is compared by Professor Scholem to the methods of Yoga.[45] Abulafia did not think of prophecy as a message to the people; he sought rather to conceal the whole matter from those not qualified to receive it. This despite the fact that he claimed to have written twenty-two books of prophecies.[46] Abulafia held that prophecy is always esoteric, whereas Maimonides distinguished between those prophets who received only personal enlightenment and those charged with a mission to other men. But perhaps the clearest distinction between mystic and prophet had been made (though not in so many words) by our earliest philosopher, Philo. He discusses the theme of prophecy in more or less rationalistic terms, chiefly with reference to Moses.[47] But he does not connect this normative prophecy with the moments of mystical vision which were so important in his own spiritual life. Philo says that his soul "is often God-possessed and divines where it does not know," and he offers one of the religious insights that came to him in an hour of such bliss. [48] But he does not call such an experience prophecy.

Abulafia and his successors were careful to avoid publicizing their prophetic raptures, mindful no doubt of the dangers that may follow when undisciplined persons experiment with ecstatic practices. Such dangers were made fully manifest during the messianic movement of Sabbetai Zevi. Perhaps the most powerful figure in that strange series of events was Nathan of Gaza, who without apology or reservation styled himself a prophet. Nathan seems to have had but one major visionary experience. For the most part, he vindicated the messianic claims of Sabbetai, not by new revelations, but by the tortured methods of Scriptural interpretation employed by all the Cabalists of his time. Despite his bizarre notions, Nathan was a man of intellectual attainments; but many of those who were caught up during those years in outbursts of "prophesying" were untutored folk, including women and children. In the fashion of so-called pentecostal Christians before and since, of Moslem dervishes, and of the earliest Israelite and no doubt pre-

Israelite ecstatics, these people whipped themselves into frenzy or caught the contagion from others, "spoke with
tongues," and fell into convulsion and trances.[49]

But all this was soon repudiated and discarded. The Hasi-
dic movement was in part a reaction against Sabbatianism.
This may explain why the mystical ecstasy cultivated by the
Hasidim led only to rapturous union with God (*devekuth*)
but not as a rule to revelation, and why the leaders of the
Hasidim never, to my knowledge, claimed to be prophets.
Although great emphasis was laid on the personality of the
Zaddik, whose most casual words and most trivial actions
were treated as Torah; although the son of the Great Mag-
gid was called Rabbi Abraham the Angel, and R. Jacob
Isaac of Lublin was known as the Seer, none of the rebbes
was called a *navi*.

The full greatness of the later prophets was recognized
only in modern times. This may have been due in part to
growing interest in the Bible as literature, with resulting attention to the beauty of the prophetic utterances. Another
factor was the rise of Biblical criticism; those who argued
that the Pentateuch was largely, if not wholly, post-Mosaic
ascribed much more originality to the prophets. And in the
century of liberalism, the passages which assert the primacy
of morality, in contrast to ritual, evoked an enthusiastic response.

We cannot now examine at length the views of modern
Jewish thinkers on the subject of the prophets.[50] Yet even a
hasty inspection shows that in this period as in former periods, men's understanding of the ancient seers was colored
by their own concerns and their own standards of value.
Abraham Geiger, for example, believed that the Jewish people had an inherent genius for things religious, and he refers

to the prophets as striking examples of this genius.[51] For Ahad HaAm, the prophet was rather the embodiment of the national Jewish ideal—the ideal of justice, of truth in action. The prophet is distinguished by his extreme and unyielding commitment to this principle. In contrast, the priest, who is willing to compromise with the realities of his time, succeeds in gaining at least partial adoption of the ideal in practice.[52].

Salomon Formstecher expounded a view of history derived from post-Kantian German thought. He depicts the prophets as visionaries standing on the threshold of a new era, an era during which political tyranny and religious absolutism would slowly and painfully be overcome by the forces of outer and inner liberty. It was the function of the prophets, at the very outset of this period, to proclaim the glorious future to their own and to subsequent generations.[53] Formstecher hardly mentions the prophetic attack on the social evils of their own time. But that fact is central to Hermann Cohen's understanding of the prophets; it was the mark of their genius, he declares, to recognize that the advancement of their ethical concerns required their involvement in politics.[54] Cohen constantly refers to the prophets as the men who first identified religion with the pursuit of exacting and universalistic moral standards. One of his admirers remarks that whereas Maimuni had examined the prophetic process without discussing the content of the prophetic message, Cohen did just the opposite.[55]

The thinkers just mentioned, despite their differences, all represent modernist trends.[56] Actually, some devotees of Reform Judaism have equated it with "prophetic Judaism"— an identification that seems to me somewhat presumptuous. More legitimate is the position of those who, in the name of Judaism, are presently laboring for social justice, racial equality, and world peace, when they claim to be following in the footsteps of the prophets. That is the kind of prophetic Judaism which Samuel H. Goldenson nobly preached and practiced. But one distinction may be noted. The ancient prophets were often quite specific in enumerating social evils and in naming those whom they held responsible; but the only cure they offered for such evils was repentance, return to God, and obedience to His laws. The modern exponents of prophetic Judaism, however, advocate specific legislation or administrative policies to correct certain abuses, and they engage in organized efforts to attain social ends. Such a practical and activist approach can only be applauded; but as a matter of history, this method appears more Deuteronomic, or even rabbinic, than prophetic.

But the moderns I have mentioned were philosophers, theologians, preachers, not primarily exegetes. Have not the professional Bible scholars of recent years, armed with so many new, glittering instruments, been able to present to us the image of the prophets as they really were?

I am not lacking in appreciation or in gratitude for what modern Biblical scholarship has accomplished. Among its distinguished practitioners are beloved teachers and friends, from whom I have learned much. Modern Biblical science has greatly advanced our understanding of Scripture, and has permanently disposed of many old misunderstandings. But fascinated as I am by the various reconstructions of Israel's past, I am troubled not only because these reconstructions are widely divergent, but because all of them are built in large measure on conjectures we are unable either to refute or to confirm by objective evidence.

The modern Bible scholar has great resources not previously available. He operates in an atmosphere of historical awareness which should protect him against reading contemporary attitudes back into the past. He has highly disciplined and refined methods of philological and historical criticism. Above all, he has access to the vast body of knowledge, made available through archaeology, concerning the languages, literatures, and cultures of the Biblical world.

Yet even with all these tools, we have not arrived at certainty, above all in respect to the prophets. The newly discovered texts supply striking parallels to the laws, chronicles, sagas, religious and secular lyrics, and wisdom literature of the Bible. Even in these cases, critical caution is necessary. A sentence in Egyptian, Akkadian, or Ugaritic may shed light on a somewhat similar Biblical passage; it does not necessarily determine the meaning of that Biblical passage.

But for the writings of the great prophets, no real parallels have been published. Divination texts or documents containing *post eventum* forecasts hardly advance our understanding of Amos. Our chief source for the interpretation of the prophets remains the Bible itself; and here many problems remain for which no certain solution has been found.

To cite just one instance: prophecies of utter doom are often followed abruptly by assurances of redemption and restoration. A generation ago, critics were sure that the encouraging words were latter additions; today many competent scholars are convinced that one and the same prophet followed his predictions of catastrophe with words of hope. In this and many other instances, it seems inevitable that the scholar, however hard he tries to be scientifically impartial, will be influenced by his general outlook on life, on history, and on Judaism.

Our survey, fragmentary as it was, has shown how often —perhaps invariably—men have approached the prophetic text with their own concerns and preconceptions, and so have arrived at colored or distorted notions about the prophets, their activity, and their message. Yet few of the interpreters we have mentioned failed to note and to stress some aspect of the prophetic experience or message which is important and worthy of attention. Such a survey should not make us supercilious toward our forebears. It should make us ready to learn from all, and humbly skeptical about all the conclusions, ancient, medieval, and modern—including our own.

Having said this, I hardly dare conclude without sketching my own image of the prophets, acknowledging freely that it is a personal impression, and leaving it to others to uncover my subconscious motivations. The prophets, then, appear to me in superb grandeur. Their greatness does not depend on the question of their originality. Whether they proclaimed a revolutionary new doctrine, or whether they developed their teaching out of old Israelite tradition, it was a great teaching. They proclaimed the holiness of God and the special grace and heavy responsibility implicit in His choice of Israel. They upheld sublime principles of personal and social morality. They affirmed a universalism that did not negate the national existence of Israel, and they first gave mankind the vision of a warless world. But not only what they taught is important; equally important is how they taught. They were not quiet sages, observing the world and reflecting soberly on life. They were passionate participants in the concerns of their time. Theirs was a burning indignation at present wrong and an incandescent faith in the ultimate triumph of right. Thousands of years after their time, one who reads their words—even in translation—feels how they throb and flame.

This intensity is the cause rather than the effect of their literary beauty. It derives in great measure from the belief of the prophet that he was not just voicing his opinions, not just speaking the truth as he saw it, but acting literally as the spokesman of God. This conviction, which imparts grandeur to the prophet, also makes him remote and unapproachable. We revere the prophets, and for such a man as Jeremiah we feel a deep compassion; but the prophets are too austere to be treated as familiar friends. Even a saint can afford to smile at himself, and to view his faults and virtues alike with a disarming sense of humor. But the prophet dare not do so; he is the bearer of God's word, and to take his own career lightly would be frivolity before the divine.

The prophets appear to me as an unrepeatable phenomenon. Men of great intellectual and literary gifts, who attained profound moral and religious insights, they were not yet sicklied o'er with the pale cast either of theological speculation or of psychological introspection. In their day prophecy was still a legitimate and unchallenged part of the culture. A sacred book had not yet taken the place of spontaneous and intuitive experience. The time had not come for analytical self-questioning. In an earlier age, the prophet might be little more than a tribal leader rousing his people to courage in battle. Later on, only the mentally deranged was likely to believe that he had been made the vehicle of divine revelation. But at this one time, great men could unselfconsciously regard the word blazing within themselves as God's word; and because of its truth and its might, we can still accept it as such. It seems unlikely that such a phenomenon will occur again, unless Father Elijah should reappear to usher in that outpouring of the spirit foretold by Joel. Till then, we can only praise Him "who chose excellent prophets and was pleased with their words."

NOTES

[1]Ps. 74.9. The interpretation of this verse is not absolutely certain; see commentaries. Surprisingly, the word *navi* occurs in Psalms only here, in Ps. 105.15 with reference to the patriarchs, and in the heading of 51.

[2]Malachi 3.23f.

[3]L. Ginzberg, *Legends of the Jews*, IV p. 233 and VI p. 339, nn.106ff.

[4]I Maccabees 4.42ff, 14.41.

[5]Ezra 2.61ff.

[6]Elbogen, *Der Jüdische Gottesdienst*, pp. 174ff., argues that public reading of prophetic selections must have antedated the canonization of the prophetic books. Writers on the canon all point out that the tripartite division of Scripture was certainly known to Ben Sira's grandson, about 130 B. C. E., and perhaps to Ben Sira himself.

[7]See Sotah 48b; an example of intercession, Mishnah Ta'anith 3.8, Babli *ibid.* 23a, and cf. Jer. 7.16, Amos 7.2ff.

[8]*Antiquities* 13.300.

[9]*War* 2.258-263 (=*Ant.* 20. 167ff.) and 6.288ff.

[10]*War* 6.300ff.

[11]Bava Bathra 12b.

[12]*War* 3.351ff., 399ff.

[13]*Against Apion* 41.

[14]Sotah 48b.

[15]Megillah 15a; cf. Ginzberg, *Legends,* VI p. 432.

[16]Seder Olam Rabba ch. 30.

[17]Deut. R. 8.6; Bava Mezi 'a 59b; Bamberger, "Revelations of Torah After Sinai," *HUCA* XVI, p.111f.

[18]Bava Bathra 12a.

[19]N. N. Glatzer, "Torath Ha-Nevuah BaTalmud" (reprint from *Sefer HaShanah liYehude America,* 1942) and "A Study of the Talmudic Interpretation of Prophecy," *Review of Religion,* January 1946, pp. 115ff.

[20]Sifra, end; Deut. 13.1ff. and cf. 18.9-22.

[21]Nedarim 22b; on the authorship of this statement see Bacher, *Agada der palästinensischen Amoräer* III p. 655f.

[22]See, e.g., R. H. Charles, *Eschatology,* p. 200ff. This notion is corrected effectively by I. Abrahams, "The Cessation of Prophecy," *Studies in Pharisaism and the Gospels, Second Series,* pp. 120ff.

[23]I Corinthians 12.28 and ch. 14.

[24]Acts 19.6, 21.9f. On false prophets, I John 4.1, II Peter 2.1.

[25]The material is given *in extenso* in Ginzberg's *Legends* IV pp. 202ff., and the corresponding notes; Friedmann's introduction to Seder Eliahu Rabba, and Samuel M. Segal's *Elijah.* But

there is still ample room for
critical study.

[26]Mekhilta Pisha I (Lauterbach
I p. 9); Cant. R. 1.6.

[27]Examples of Elijah's kindliness,
Gen.R.33.3, Ta'anith 22a; of
his temper, Berakhoth 6b, Sanhedrin end; of his exacting demands on scholars, Kethuboth
106a, Yerushalmi Terumoth 8,
46b.

[28]Num. 12.6ff., Deut. 34.10ff.,
Philo *Moses* I beginning, II 187,
Lev. R.1.14.

[29]Moreh Nevukhim II 32.

[30]Cf. also Maimonides, Hilkhoth
Yesode HaTorah 8.1.

[31]Kuzari I 32-43, 95; II 8-14,
36ff., 68. See Neumark, "Jehudah Hallevi's Philosophy in its
Principles," *Essays in Jewish
Philosophy,* especially pp.247ff.,
251-253, 259. Neumark shows
how the philosophic element in
HaLevi's thought has been
minimized by some interpreters,
but perhaps goes too far in the
opposite direction.

[32]Moreh II 32, 36.

[33]*Ibid,* 36, 41-44, 46.

[34]*Ibid,* 45.

[35]*Ibid,* 37.

[36]Yesode HaTorah 10.1ff.

[37]Moreh II 37.

[38]*Ibid,* 32.

[39]*Ibid,* 33, 35, 37, 39, 45 end;
and cf. Mishnah Commentary,
Sanhedrin 10.1; Hilkhoth Yesode HaTorah 7.6.

[40]Nahmanides on Gen. 18.1,
Crescas, Commentary to Moreh
Nevukhim.

[41]See, in addition to the standard
histories of Husik and Gutt-
man, A. Lewkowitz, "Mai-
muni's Theorie der Prophetie,"
*Judaica: Festschrift zu Hermann
Cohens 70en Geburtstag, pp.*
167ff., Z. Diesendruck, "Maimonides' Lehre von der Prophetie," *Jewish Studies in Memory of Israel Abraham;* H. A.
Wolfson, "Hallevi and Maimonides on Prophecy," *JQR,*
April and June 1945; A. Reines,
"Abrabanel on Prophecy in the
Moreh Nebhukhim," *HUCA,*
vols. 31, 33-36. Leo Strauss
(in S. Pines' translations of the
Guide, pp. xv, xxiv) states that
Maimonides deliberately inserted contradictions into his treatise.

[42]A. J. Heschel, "HaHe'emin Ha-
Rambam She-zakhah liNe-
vuah?", *Louis Ginzberg Jubilee
Volume,* Hebrew Section, pp.
159ff. The title means: "Did
Maimonides Believe that He
Had Attained to Prophecy?"
But oddly, in the English Table
of Contents the essay is called
"Did Maimonides Strive for
Prophetic Inspiration?"

[43]Joel 3.1ff., and see Moreh II
36 end, and especially *Moses
Maimonides' Epistle to Yemen,*
ed. A. S. Halkin, pp. xv, xix.

[44]G. G. Scholem, *Major Trends
in Jewish Mysticism,* p. 124.

[45]*Ibid,* p. 136. But at least sometimes there was a comprehensible content to the prophetic experience; Abulafia claimed that

in a vision he had received the secret date of the end of the exile. See Jellinek, *Auswahl kabbalistischer Mystik*, Hebrew section, p. 18.

[46]Jellinek, *Philosophie und Kabbala*, pp. 3ff., 21-23. In this document, p. 21, Abulafia laments that circumstances have interfered with his solitary meditations, and that in consequence the holy spirit has departed from him. Despite the use of this terminology, and of the adjective "prophetic" (*nevu'i*) he seems to avoid calling himself a *navi;* but there is no doubt that he considered himself such.

[47]H. A. Wolfson, *Philo* II, pp. 11ff.

[48]De Cherubim 27f.

[49]Scholem, *Shabbethai Zevi, passim*. On the prophetic call of Nathan, see esp. pp. 166f., on the ecstatic prophesiers, pp. 340ff., 505-506.

[50]A valuable contribution on this subject is Dr. Jacob Agus' lecture, "The Prophet in Modern Hebrew Literature," *HUCA* vol. 28.

[51]A. Geiger, *Judaism and Its History*, trans. Charles Newburgh (NY 1911), pp. 39-48.

[52]*Selected Essays by Ahad Ha-Am*, trans. Leon Simon, p. 311ff. ("Moses"), 125ff. ("Priest and Prophet.")

[53]Formstecher, *Religion des Geistes*, pp. 234ff.

[54]Hermann Cohen, *Religion der Vernunft*, pp. 26, 29; and note the index s. v. *Propheten*.

[55]A. Lewkowitz (see n. 41 *supra*) p. 168.

[56]A defense of traditional viewpoints which reflects an awareness of the new trends is the learned volume of Z. H. Chajes, *Torath Neviim*.

INDEX

as enemy of Samuel, 164
residence of, 164
Schelling, Friedrich Wilhelm Joseph
von, 48
Scholem, Gershom, on Hasidism, 156
Schopenhauer, Arthur
disciples of, 143
pessimistic outlook of, 134
Scientific American (periodical), 188
Scientific inquiry, subjugation of human conduct to, 26
Scott, R. B. Y., 128, 211
Scripture
legitimacy of, 18
theme of, 75
See also New Testament; Old Testament; Torah; *and specific prophets*
Second Temple, 167
Sefer Hahezyonoth (Vital), 53
Sefireh treaties, 164
Sennacherib (King of Assyria)
attack on Jerusalem by, 290-91
blasphemy of, 235
Shechinah, 52, 53, 55, 57, 71
Shem, Children of, 85
Shiloh, 282
destruction of, 164, 165-66, 170, 173, 174
Jeremiah on, 164
Samuel on, 166
Tabernacle of, 164
Shim'iot, 86
Shimoni, David, nationalism of, 74
Shlonsky, Abraham, 75
Shoham, Matithyahu, on Elijah, 77
Shulhan Aruch, Ahad Ha'am on, 67
Signs
Moses' use of, 8
prophetic use of, 8
Silberman, Lou H. ("Prophets and Philosophers: The Scandal of Prophecy"), 81-99
Silver, Abba Hillel, 185
Sinai, Mt.
covenant at, 211, 281
golden calf and, 247
revelation at, 129, 306, 310
Skehan, Patrick W., 171, 173
Skepticism, Jewish, divine retribution

in, 26
Slavs, literature of, 170-71
Snow, C. P., 197
"So-Called 'Suffering Servant' in Isaiah, The" (Orlinsky), 225-73
Social justice
prophets on, 37, 48, 49, 111, 128, 132, 180-82
real religion and, 114
Socialism
Halutz as forerunner of, 73
Jewish youth and, 72
J. H. Brenner on, 72-73
labor and, 73
Society of Biblical Literature, 211
Socrates
argument for legitimacy of, 12
death of, 13
inability to invoke belief, 13
Jeremiah's similarity to, 12, 13
Sodom (Biblical city), 247
Solomon (King of Israel), 138, 163
banishment of Abiathar by, 284
building of temple by, 281-82
dream of, 282
empire of, 277
hostility to temple of, 279, 280
Song of Moses, 170
Songs of Wrath (Bialik), 70
"Sons of Moses" founded by Ahad Ha'am, 66
Sophocles, 138
Soul
as progenitor of values, 46
as recipient of values, 46
salvation based on, 120-21
yearning of, 75
South Africa, Apartheid in, 109
Spencer, Herbert, 38
Spengler, Oswald, 138
Spinoza, Benedict, 29
on revelation, 90
Spirit of Holiness, *see Ruah Hakodesh*
Spiritual life, three coordinates of, 46
Stahl, Frederick, 59
Steinheim, Solomon Ludwig, on revelation, 91
Stellung der vorexilischen Schriftpropheten zum Kultus, Die (Hentsch-